NEW APPROACHES
TO EFFECTIVE LEADERSHIP

NEW APPROACHES TO EFFECTIVE LEADERSHIP

Cognitive Resources
and Organizational Performance

Fred E. Fiedler
Joseph E. Garcia

JOHN WILEY & SONS

New York   Chichester   Brisbane   Toronto   Singapore

Library of Congress Cataloging in Publication Data:

Fiedler, Fred Edward.
New approaches to effective leadership

   Bibliography: p.
   Includes index.
   1. Leadership.   I. Garcia, Joseph E.   II. Title.

HM141.F475   1987   303.3′4   86-24528
ISBN 0-471-87456-6

Printed in the United States of America

10 9 8 7 6 5 4 3 2 1

Preface

It is now more than twenty years since the introduction of the contingency model (Fiedler, 1964), and it has aged well in the face of controversy and criticism. It has been the basis for more than 400 articles and papers and is cited at this time in more management texts than any other theory (Kerr, 1984). But it is now time to move on.

While self-congratulations may be tempting, critics of the model have pointed to major gaps in our understanding and problems in our methodology. Several of the model's critics have charged that the contingency model is a "black box," that we do not know why and how the interaction of the personality attribute, reflected by the LPC score, affects leadership performance. The development of cognitive resource theory was spurred in large part by the need to understand what's in that black box. What, exactly, do various types of leaders do that enables their groups to perform their assigned tasks successfully? We clearly do not have all the answers, but if this book stimulates as much research as the contingency model has over the years, it will more than live up to my expectations. After all, theory building is a process, not a product.

This book is not intended as light reading for a rainy evening. If leadership seems complex, let us remember that Plato, Machiavelli, Carlyle, Freud, and Weber, to mention but a few of the early giants, have also tried their hand in this area. If leadership were easy to understand we would know all about it by now. I hope that this book takes us a few steps farther in understanding this problem that has fascinated me throughout my professional life.

I am delighted to acknowledge the many suggestions and criticisms offered by my colleagues, not only because their kind interest demonstrated that my work was taken seriously, but because they devoted time and effort to pointing out what the theory lacked and how it could overcome these shortcomings. My colleagues and I have tried to heed these recommendations and we have attempted to come to grips with the various theoretical and methodological problems. The extent to which we have succeeded remains to be seen.

Finally, as senior author, I wish to express my sincere thanks to the many colleagues who have worked with me over the years, and to the many who conducted serious independent research on the contingency model and contributed to the theory their new insights and their carefully conducted research. And if I speak of "our" conclusions, and what "we" think of the data, it reflects the fact that more than 100 colleagues and graduate students with whom I have had the privilege of working over the years and who have shared with me the pleasure of the chase.

My colleague and coauthor, Joseph Garcia, took primary responsibility for the chapters which review the literature on history, stress, intelligence, and task requirements, and he has collaborated with me on all other aspects of the book. Jon Blades' (1976) major contributions are noted in Part 3. Patrick Bettin collaborated with us in writing the chapter on leadership experience, and the chapter on leader intelligence has borrowed heavily from an unpublished paper by Dennis Dossett. I have taken the primary responsibility for the chapters in Parts 2 and 3 of the book, which deal with the contingency model and cognitive resource theory. Some of this material has been described in less detail in previous papers and presentations.

Particular thanks go to Lee R. Beach, Martin M. Chemers, and Terence R. Mitchell, whose close cooperation has helped me for many years, and whose unsparing criticisms have kept me from getting into theoretical quagmires. I am especially indebted to Robert A. Baron, Martin M. Chemers, William Erdly, Robert W. Rice, and Cynthia K. Stevens for carefully reading parts of the manuscript, and above all, to Judith Fiedler, who critically read, reread, and read once more the various versions of the book until it almost said what I had in mind.

Research on leadership is an expensive sport. It could not have been done without financial assistance as well as a great deal of encouragement. I would like to express my thanks for extended support to the Office of Naval Research and Bert T. King of the Group Psychology Program, and to the Army Institute of Research for the Behavioral Sciences and its former Technical Director, J. E. Uhlaner, as well as to Robert Sasmor and Milton Katz of the Office of Basic Research. Support was also provided by the Advanced Research Projects Agency, and most recently, the Naval Personnel Research and Development Center. We are indebted to Maxine Nelson and Sarah Cooper Lehman for their assistance with the preparation of the manuscript.

With permission of my coauthor I should like to dedicate this book to the many students, associates, and colleagues, past and present, who have at various times in my professional career worked with me on leadership research. Many will find their ideas reflected in this book and if I failed to acknowledge them it is because their contributions have long since become an integral part of our thinking. I am more indebted to them than they will ever know and would like to express my thanks to each and every one of them. If someone's name has been omitted from this long list it has been by oversight rather than intent.

Colleagues and Students Associated with the Group Effectiveness Laboratory at the University of Illinois, 1951–1969: Sheldon Alexander, James Alsobrook, Lynn R. Anderson, Judith Goodrich Ayer, Duangduen Lekhiananda Banthumnavin, Nancy Barron, Alan R. Bass, Peter Bates, Annie Beckers, Anthony J. Biglan, Doyle W. Bishop, Milton R. Blood, Martin M. Chemers, Walter A. Cleven, Lee J. Cronbach, H. Peter Dachler, David DeVries, Joan Dodge, Elizabeth Ehart, Nathaniel Eisen, Jack Feldman, Martin Fishbein, Uriel Foa, Nico Frijda, Ilene Gochman, Eleanor P. Godfrey, J. Richard Hackman, Walter Hartmann, Thomas T. Hewett, William Higgs, Franz E. Hohn, John Hornik, Charles L. Hulin, G. J. Hunt, Edwin B. Hutchins, Jr., Daniel R. Ilgen, Lawrence Jones, Robert E. Jones, James W. Julian, Dorothy McBride Kipnis, Robert Kohn, Ping Koo, Irving Lazar, George Leavitt, Perry London, Vivian McCraven, Joseph E. McGrath, Melvin Manis, Bilha Mannheim, Eleanor H. Mikesell, Terence R. Mitchell, Willem A. T. Meuwese, Charles Morris III, Albert F. Myers, Josephine Naidoo, A. S. K. Nayar, Stanley M. Nealey, Robert Nemo, Paul Ninane, Jozef M. Nuttin, Jr., Gordon O'Brien, Gerald R. Oncken, Sophie Oonk, Charles E. Osgood, Edward Ostrander, Terry Owen, Stanley Peters, Eileen Golb Potter, George Potter, James Purdy, Stanley M. Rudin, Suthita Santhai, Steven Schwartz, M. Peter Scontrino, Samuel C. Shiflett, Ivan D. Steiner, Lawrence M. Stolurow, David Summers, John Symonds, Lorand Szalay, James S. Terwilliger, Erich Thomanek, Hubert Touzard, Harry C. Triandis, Walter Uhlman, John Vannoy, Mary Vidmar, Willard Warrington, Alexander Wearing, Nuanpen Wichiarajote, W. Wichiarajote, Michael Wood, and Charles Wrigley.

Colleagues and Students Associated with the Organizational Research Group at the University of Washington, 1969–1985: David Allen, Jeffrey W. Anderson, Valery Barnes, Patrick J. Bettin, Jon W. Blades, Dewey W. Blyth, Alan Boni, Paul M. Bons, Donald F. Borden, Cheryl Clark, Louis S. Csoka, Dennis R. Dossett, William Erdly, David Flake, Raymond Frey, Dean R. Frost, Joseph E. Garcia, Martin M. Gillo, Ilene R. Gochman, Steven Green, Norman Groner, Robert O. Hansson, Sarah M. Jobs, John K. Kennedy, William H. Knowlton, Jr., James R. Larson, James Larson, Jr., Gary P. Latham, Albert F. Leister, Jr., Mark McGuire, Mary McGuire, Linda Hastings Mahar, Renate Mai-Dalton, Scott Marcy, Susan E. Murphy, Delbert K. Nebeker, Dennis Patrick, William Pollard, Alan Posthuma, Earl H. Potter III, Joyce Prothero, Linda Rice, Mary Richardson, Donald

E. Schmidt, M. Peter Scontrino, Sanshiro Shirakashi, Richard Smith, Cynthia K. Stevens, Cynthia Stobough, Eric Strom, David W. Taylor, Maryanne Vandervelde, William A. Wheeler, and Mitchell M. Zais.

FRED E. FIEDLER

Seattle, Washington
January 1987

Contents

CHAPTER ONE

Introduction

The quality of leadership is one of the most important factors in determining the success and survival of groups and organizations. And although technology plays an overriding part under some conditions, effective leadership has oftentimes compensated for lack of equipment and resources. It enabled Henry the Fifth and his disease-ridden, hungry army of 15,000 to win a stunning victory over the French army of 45,000 men at Agincourt. It enabled George Washington to defeat the well-trained and better equipped English forces, and it enabled Robert E. Lee's troops to stand off the superior forces of the Union for over four years. Among the more recent examples is the dramatic turnaround of the Chrysler Corporation under Lee Iacocca. The leader's power is equally impressive in a macabre sense when we consider Hitler's impact on Germany or the Reverend Jim Jones' ability to induce over 800 of his followers to commit suicide.

It would be difficult to imagine a world without leaders. They include not only the statesmen, national leaders, and presidents of large organizations, but also the service station managers and building managers who supervise four or five employees as well as the dentist who employs a secretary and two or three dental technicians. The need for effective leadership is ubiquitous and so highly valued that some top executives earn more than 100 times the salary of their rank and file subordinates, and they get the credit as well as the blame for the success or failure of their organization. The continued existence of groups, corporations, and nations depends largely on the leader's ability to get others to work toward mutual goals. And in the economic sphere, where the difference between profit and financial disaster may amount to less than 1 percent on gross sales, proper management of personnel and resources is essential.

It is not too surprising, then, that the topic of leadership has fascinated scholars throughout history. Plato's *Republic* and Niccolò Machiavelli's

1

The Prince are only two of many attempts to account for this phenomenon. *Stogdill's Handbook of Leadership* (Bass, 1981) reviews over 5000 articles on the topic. Although the significance of a scientific problem cannot always be assessed by the poundage of journal pages, it is certainly one indication. By this measure, leadership is very high on the list of important topics.

This book presents a new theory of leadership. (Yes, still another!) Our focus is primarily on the leader and on the effectiveness with which the group performs its assigned task. This approach admittedly neglects such other important factors in group behavior as member satisfaction and personal growth. Nor do we dispute the value of job satisfaction, the quality of work life, and the need to provide for the personal growth of individuals who make up the work force, but these are questions which others are more qualified to address.

A FEW DEFINITIONS

As with most commonly used words, the specific meaning of well-known terms is not always clear even though "everybody knows" what they mean. Without implying that other uses of these words are incorrect, this section briefly defines key terms we propose to use in this book.

Cognitive Resources

This term refers to the intellectual abilities, technical competence, and job-relevant knowledge obtained by formal training or experience in the organization.

The Leader

This term refers to the person who is elected or appointed or who has emerged from the group to direct and coordinate the group members' efforts toward some given goal. The leader generally plans, organizes, directs, and supervises the activities of group members and develops and maintains sufficient cohesiveness and motivation among group members to keep them together as a functioning unit.

The leader typically determines when to begin and end a meeting, who will speak, and when to change the topic. The leader may assign tasks, set goals, and determine procedures. Very rarely is the chair of a meeting overruled by the group on a point of order or on a decision. Most groups support the authority of the leader as long as he or she does not grossly overstep the bounds of expected behavior (Hollander, 1958).

Individuals in leadership positions are given such titles as boss, supervisor, chief, president, team leader, chairperson, director, manager—

the differences among them are minor. It is the function rather than the title that counts. As a matter of convenience, therefore, we use the term *leader* for the person in charge of the group or organization and the term *boss* for the superior to whom the leader reports.

There have been various proposals (e.g., Gibb, 1969) to reserve the term leader for those who lead by virtue of their personal charisma and the esteem in which their subordinates hold them. The term *head* supposedly designates the administrator or manager who holds the position by virtue of administrative appointment. Our research thus far does not demonstrate the need for this distinction. Leadership, as we use the term, refers to that part of organizational management that deals with the direction and supervision of subordinates rather than, for example, inventory control, fiscal management, or customer relations.

The Group

This term defines a set of individuals who are interdependent; they perceive themselves as "belonging together" and they interact in achieving a particular purpose. They share a common fate so that an event that affects one individual also affects other group members (i.e., they may jointly share rewards or suffer punishment).

We further differentiate in this book between *interacting* groups, which are our primary concern, and *coacting* or *counteracting* groups (Fiedler, 1967). Groups are interacting if the members have a common goal and collaborate on the task in such a way that it is difficult or impossible to distinguish the contribution of one member from those of the others. Examples include a basketball team where each member contributes to the success of the group or a research team or committee in which every member contributes and builds on the ideas of others. In a coacting group each member's performance is relatively independent of the efforts of other members of the group (e.g., a bowling team where the team score is the sum of the team members' scores).

A counteracting group, about which we have very little to say in this book, typically operates as a bargaining unit or a negotiating team. Its purpose is to derive an agreement or a solution acceptable to two or more parties who have conflicting aims or values. An example is a team working on a labor contract or on an agreement with another organization or another country.

We must further distinguish between groups that have as their primary goal the accomplishment of a task and groups that are designed to benefit the individual group member. The groups we consider usually are subunits of a larger organization that staffs the group and sets its goals. These goals are typically designed to contribute to the success of the organization, and a group may well be disbanded if it fails to succeed. We do not deal with groups that exist primarily for the benefit of the individual group members. Examples are therapy groups, students in a classroom, and social clubs for the enjoyment of members.

The Organization

By organization we mean a set of interrelated and interdependent groups under one administration which share common goals and cooperate in achieving these goals. Groups within the same organization typically are assigned to perform different but interrelated subtasks (sales, production, research departments, etc.). At a more fundamental level, the group can be regarded as the basic unit of the organization in the same way that the individual is a basic unit of a group. As each member in a group has a prescribed task (e.g., ordering supplies), so does each group within the organization have its prescribed function.

With relatively few exceptions, groups are subunits of a larger organization. The organization is the natural habitat of the group, although we may not always be strongly aware of this point. Thus the classroom is a subunit of a school, a professional basketball team is the operative unit of a league, and a research group typically is a unit in a university or larger institute.

One further point critical to the relationship between the group and the organization is the leader's consciousness of the often threatening presence of the boss, or the "Big Boss." The importance of the leader's superior has been almost completely ignored by laboratory researchers. As we shall have occasion to see, the boss is a very important factor in understanding the leader's behavior and the group's performance and is best considered and examined in the organizational context.

Leadership Effectiveness

We define leadership effectiveness conceptually as the degree of success with which a group performs the primary assigned task. If a reliable objective measure of group performance is not available, then we must make do with the boss's rating of the leader's or the group's performance on the task. Such other types of leadership outcome measures as morale and job satisfaction are useful and desirable, but we have chosen to limit our definition to task performance for several reasons.

First, with few exceptions, the primary goal of work groups and organizations is the accomplishment of a task assigned by the parent organization or by the group members themselves. Second, the success or failure of a group or organization is generally defined by its progress toward achieving these primary goals. To stay in business, a restaurant must provide its customers with good food and service, but restaurants have survived and even flourished despite dissatisfied employees. The study of morale and job satisfaction is certainly a worthy and desirable goal. It is, however, secondary to the functions of most organizations.

Single Versus Multiple Criteria. A number of distinguished theorists (e.g., Stogdill, 1974; Yukl, 1981) have argued that researchers should rely on multiple criteria, that is, such additional measures as morale, job satisfaction, and absenteeism, as well as productivity, to assess the leader's effectiveness. We have no quarrel with this notion. The basic purpose of this book, however, is the understanding of task groups, and we take the more limited, bottom-line position that a task group's main reason for existing is to perform the assigned tasks. If several different tasks are to be performed, the group must be evaluated separately on each of these tasks. The development of high morale and discipline, or job satisfaction, is a primary task only if leaders are specifically given the particular assignment to, for example, "improve the morale of this unit!" Morale, job satisfaction, absenteeism, and safety are clearly important in helping the group do its job. Moreover, morale and job satisfaction may well improve the overall performance of the organization because they affect costs. But they are not, in themselves, direct measures of task performance. Bonuses go to the managers whose units are most productive rather than to those who have the happiest employees.

As a rule, definitions of group performance are easier to generate than to operationalize. We usually determine what constitutes efficient performance by comparing the efficiency of similar groups within an organization. Thus the effective football coach wins more games than he loses; the effective manager generates profits rather than losses.

There are relatively few settings in which many groups perform identical tasks under comparable conditions. And even where comparable groups do exist, direct comparisons may not be possible. In mining, for instance, crews of identical composition and size may encounter totally different geological conditions in successive weeks. Mine crews working in relatively close proximity, therefore, cannot be evaluated on the basis of the tonnage of ore they produce unless the geological conditions and the quality of the rock are nearly identical. Objective measures are frequently less valid than they seem and comparability of groups within an organization looks better from a distance than from up close.

In fact, someone may be an outstanding leader even though the organization fails to perform its task. Robert E. Lee was an outstanding military leader even though he was defeated at Appomattox; Napoleon was a brilliant general even though he lost the battle of Waterloo. We must preface judgments of leadership performance by saying "given the circumstances. . . . " This is essentially what the superior does in evaluating a subordinate leader. The judgment of a knowledgeable manager takes into consideration the specific conditions that facilitate or handicap performance. For this reason, supervisory ratings are valid performance measures when based on extensive observation.

WHY DO WE NEED ANOTHER "NEW THEORY"?

In a field crowded with books and theories, there should be some justification for demanding a reader's time and attention (especially since monographs rarely make for titillating reading). The field of leadership is awash with theories, hypotheses, reviews, books, articles, and polemics. So why one more?

Our current conceptualization of leadership contains some serious oversights that need to be redressed. The theory we propose will surely not settle all remaining questions, but we hope to tackle some of the important problems that have not been addressed in a satisfactory manner up to now. Several of these are here discussed.

The Absence of Leaders' Cognitive Resources in Current Theoretical Formulations

By and large, most of the popular theories of leadership have ignored such variables as the leader's intelligence, technical competence, and experience. There is often a diagram that refers to these cognitive resources, but the major theories have not dealt with them empirically or in a coherent, theoretical manner (Campbell, 1973). McGregor (1960), for example, is concerned principally with management philosophies; House (1971, 1972), with conditions under which structuring and considerate behavior are to be used; Vroom and Yetton (1973), with strategies to determine when the leader should behave in an autocratic or participative manner; Fiedler (1967), with task-motivated and relationship-motivated style; McClelland (1961, 1975, 1985) and Miner (1978), with leader motivation; and Bass (1985) and Burns (1978) with leader behavior which transforms the individual's goals. Among the few research programs that deal with this problem are Uhlaner's (1972) "test measurement bed," which includes cognitive abilities, and Streufert and his associates' (Streufert, Streufert, & Castore, 1968; Streufert & Swezey, 1986), which investigated the role of cognitive complexity and decision making in leadership.

In stark contrast to theoreticians' lack of concern with cognitive abilities, practitioners place a strong emphasis on intelligence, competence, and experience in decisions related to managerial recruitment, selection, and promotion. Assessment procedures generally include extensive testing and interviewing of managerial candidates to evaluate their abilities and competence. Even informal hiring procedures typically include inquiries about the candidate's intellectual ability, technical competence, and prior work experience. As if this disparity between practice and research were not puzzling in and of itself, there is also the rather counterintuitive finding that measures of leader intelligence show only a low positive correlation with performance of their groups or organizations (e.g., Ghiselli, 1963; Mann, 1959; Stogdill, 1948).

How can we explain these findings? We could decide that researchers are justified in devoting little theoretical attention to the role of leader abilities. But trying to persuade executives that they are as well off with managers who are dull and inexperienced as with those who are bright and experienced, might get us laughed out of court! On the other hand, there remains the possibility that the leader's cognitive resources make a difference in performance under certain limited conditions. Cognitive resource theory explores this hypothesis.

The Absence of a Relationship Between Leader Behavior and Performance

Unless we believe in telepathy, we must assume that the verbal or gestural behavior of leaders affects the way group members behave and perform their tasks. The underlying assumption has been that certain leader behaviors are more effective than others. The prevailing theories in the 1950s told us that participative management behavior is better than autocratic or directive behavior, that considerate leaders perform better than inconsiderate leaders. The results of the many studies relating behavior to organizational performance were mixed and difficult to interpret (e.g., Bass, 1981; Korman, 1966). Blades conducted a study which questioned whether leader behavior by itself really does make a difference in group performance (Blades & Fiedler, 1973). His study suggested that the leader needs to be directive as well as competent if the group is to be effective. Being stupid as well as directive is not a very promising combination.

COGNITIVE RESOURCE THEORY: A PREVIEW

The contingency model has been justly criticized because it predicts leadership effectiveness but fails to explain the underlying processes that result in effective performance. Cognitive resource theory (Fiedler, 1984) attempts to fill this gap. And since this is a scientific monograph rather than a mystery story, it may be appropriate to give the ending away in the first chapter. This procedure will, of course, lessen the suspense that keeps the passionate reader of treatises awake until the small hours of the night. But on the other hand, it also may make the book more understandable. The new theory is briefly summarized here and will be discussed in greater detail in Part 3 of this book.

The theory is based on the following assumptions and hypotheses:

Assumption 1. Intelligent and competent leaders make more effective plans, decisions, and action strategies than do leaders with less intelligence or competence.

Assumption 2. Leaders of task groups communicate their plans, decisions, and action strategies primarily in the form of directive behavior.

Hypothesis 1. If the leader is under stress, the leader's intellectual abilities will be diverted from the task, and the leader will focus on problems not directly related, or counter to the performance of the group task. Hence, under stress, and especially interpersonal stress, measures of leader intelligence and competence will not correlate with group performance.

Hypothesis 2. The intellectual abilities of directive leaders correlate more highly with group performance than do intellectual abilities of nondirective leaders (Blades & Fiedler, 1973).

Hypothesis 3. Unless the group complies with the leader's directions, the leader's plans and decisions will not be implemented. Hence the correlation between leader intelligence and performance is higher when the group supports the leader than when the group does not support the leader (Blades & Fiedler, 1973).

Hypothesis 4. If the leader is nondirective and the group is supportive, the intellectual abilities of group members correlate with performance (Blades & Fiedler, 1973).

Hypothesis 5. The leader's intellectual abilities will contribute to group performance to the degree to which the task requires these particular abilities (i.e., is intellectually demanding).

Hypothesis 6. Under conditions of high stress, and especially interpersonal stress, the leader's job-relevant experience (rather than his or her intellectual abilities) will correlate with task performance.

Hypothesis 7. Directive behavior of the leader is in part determined by the contingency model elements, the leader's task-motivation or relationship-motivation (determined by the Least Preferred Coworker scale), and situational control.

Figure 1.1 presents a schematic description of the theory for giving the reader a general orientation for approaching the data and reasoning in this book. This diagram and its elements are discussed in detail in Part 3 of this book. As can be seen, the theory predicts the leader's directive behavior from the personality variable (the Least Preferred Coworker score, LPC), and the leadership situation. In the absence of stress, the leader focuses his or her cognitive resources on the group task. If the leader is under stress or nondirective, the leader's experience and the abilities of supportive group members will contribute to task per-

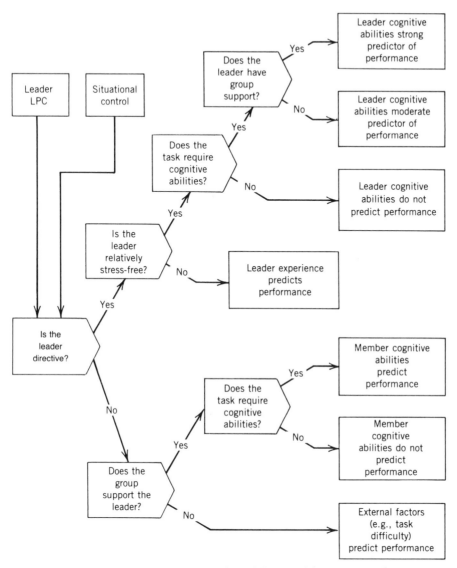

Figure 1.1. Schematic representation of the cognitive resource theory.

formance. Although the contingency model provides the starting point, our major objective in this book is to identify the links between the leader's personality and situational control with group and organizational performance. We now attempt to formulate a more inclusive theory that also explains the role of such variables as intellectual abilities, competence, and job-relevant experience—variables that previous theories have largely ignored or relegated to conceptual attics.

A note on the statistical treatment of data. Although tests of statistical significance are presented where they seem appropriate and informative, we avoid high-powered statistical analyses. There are several reasons for this decision. First, many of the analyses are based on existing data, and statistical probability tests are not strictly applicable for data of this kind. This does not mean that we cannot have confidence in results which appear over and over again in various studies. But in these cases, tests of significance are often redundant.

Second, the object of this book is to build a theory. For that purpose it is sometimes more valuable to talk about a nonsignificant correlation of .60 based on 10 cases than a significant correlation of .20 based on 200 cases. For similar reasons we have used simple and straightforward statistical methods, which are excellent tools for identifying effects that can be easily seen, understood, and reproduced, rather than effects so subtle that they emerge only in very powerful statistical tests. Such tests are more appropriate for testing hypotheses than for developing them.

ORGANIZATION OF THE BOOK

Part 1 of this book briefly traces the roots of cognitive resource theory. It considers the historical antecedents of the problem and current conceptions of stress and previous work on leadership experience and intelligence.

Part 2 briefly reviews the contingency model elements, situational control, and the Least Preferred Coworker score (LPC). Chapter 9 briefly describes the contingency model and the role of experience in leadership.

Part 3, which constitutes the heart of this book, presents cognitive resource theory and available empirical support for the hypotheses of the theory. Chapter 14 links cognitive resource theory and the contingency model and Chapter 15 discusses the effects of the task on the effective use of intellectual ability and creativity in leadership. The final chapter considers the application of cognitive resource theory to selection, training, and manpower utilization and presents hypotheses for future research.

PART ONE

ANTECEDENTS
AND BASIC ISSUES

The first part of this book considers the antecedents of cognitive resource theory as well as some basic issues that enable us to understand the complex role of cognitive abilities in determining leadership behavior and performance. These are the role of stress and its effect on cognitive processes and the meaning of experience in the context of leadership. These chapters are not intended to be exhaustive reviews of the literature. Rather, we have here concentrated on those aspects of stress, experience and intelligence which seem most relevant to understanding the role of cognitive resources in leadership.

CHAPTER TWO

Some History—Where We're Coming From

Before we wander off in new directions, it seems wise to take stock of where we have been. This is particularly true in the jungle of leadership research. Since the process of developing a new theory involves much painful labor and since cognitive resource theory, unlike Athena, did not spring full-grown from Zeus' brow, we begin with a short account of its antecedents. This chapter does not purport to be a general history of leadership, but only a brief account of where cognitive resource theory came from rather than where other theories might have come from.

FEUDALISM AND LEADERSHIP

Leadership, as we see it, has its roots in two antagonistic traditions, the feudal and the bureaucratic. The tensions created by these two opposing conceptions of leadership present a continuing challenge in the management of people and of organizations.

The historically older feudal tradition regards leadership as a highly personal relationship between the leader and the led. First, the system had strong religious sanctions. Leadership positions were ordained by "God's will"—by virtue of birth and blood. In the same way, biblical interpretations held that a wife and children are subservient to the husband as are servants to the master.

Insofar as other justification was needed, such outward signs as physical features and education provided it. Because those in the ruling classes were better fed, they were also generally taller, stronger, and healthier than the lower classes and did not have to work in the fields. Thus the ruling Castilians of Spain were the "bluebloods" because their blue veins showed through their white skin, in contrast to the Moors and tanned field hands whose dark skin masked their veins. Moreover, only members of the upper classes were likely to receive much formal education, and they therefore seemed to be "smarter" than the lower classes. At least on the surface it was not hard to believe that those who ruled were somehow destined by divine providence to their respective stations in life.

A critical element of the feudal tradition, however, was the religiously reinforced bond of personal loyalty between leader and follower. These were emotional rather than rational ties. To oppose one's prince, one's master, one's husband, was a sin if not rank heresy.

The feudal tradition is still very much alive. It is less than 150 years since only those born into the aristocracy could, under ordinary circumstances, become officers or enter the higher ranks of government services in most European countries. And still in most places today, the chances for a young man or woman from the lower class to obtain a high government post or an army commission are virtually nil.

The feudal tradition is also alive and well in the United States. Many family businesses are still run by the family patriarch, who staffs the business with his relatives at arbitrary wages and work schedules. Job specifications, fixed salaries, systematic promotions, and retirement schedules are rare or unknown as far as family members are concerned, but so are layoffs and dismissals. Political bosses typically run their empires in this fashion, and many managers in the most rigid bureaucracies demand personal loyalty from their subordinates.

It is not surprising that the early leadership research concentrated on finding the personality traits or identifying the charisma (the special "gift") that would distinguish leaders from followers. The search for leadership traits, which spawned several hundred studies, may be seen as a natural outgrowth of the belief that leaders are a different breed. Reviews by Stogdill in 1948, Mann in 1959, and Ghiselli in 1963 (see also Bass, 1981) demonstrated without much doubt that the search for leadership traits was unlikely to be fruitful. The bulk of the research found little evidence to support the notion that good leadership resided in a personality trait. The reason is readily seen if we examine the "leadership trait" idea more closely. First, everyone in our society is a leader on some occasions (e.g., chairing committees, heading work crews, organizing picnics, etc.) and a follower in innumerable other groups. If almost everyone is both a leader and a follower, it is difficult to separate the two roles on the basis of personality attributes.

Second, leadership research indicates that a person might be an effective leader in some groups and ineffective in others. Indeed, the first study ever published in the field of leadership by Lewis Terman, in 1904, made this point. Despite all the evidence to the contrary, however, most successful business executives or high-ranking military officers are convinced that they can recognize outstanding leaders at a glance. After all, don't they see one in the mirror every morning?

At the same time, assessment center studies have provided consistent evidence that more intelligent, socially adept, and highly motivated individuals tend to be more successful *over extended periods of time* (Bray, Campbell, & Grant, 1974). This is to be expected. A highly motivated, socially adept, and intelligent person is more likely to be successful in any walk of life than one who is unmotivated, dull, and socially inept. Despite the findings of the assessment center studies, it is questionable whether this is evidence for the existence of leadership traits.

Effective Leader Behaviors

But even if there are no leadership traits, should we not expect successful leaders to act differently from those who are unsuccessful? This reasonable question led to intensive content analyses of verbal behavior in small groups (e.g., Bales and Strodtbeck, 1951). These studies identified two major types of leader behavior: socioemotional and task-relevant behaviors. Similar behavior clusters were also identified by others (e.g., Cattell, 1951; Likert, 1961). Leaders tended to talk more, orient the group, keep the group on the topic, and summarize, but successful and less successful leaders could not be identified on the basis of their behaviors.

Shartle and his colleagues at Ohio State University (Shartle, 1961; Stogdill, 1974) followed a somewhat different route in their investigations. They obtained group members' descriptions of leader behaviors and identified two important factors. One, called "considerate behavior" (or consideration), identified leader behaviors concerned with the well-being and esteem of group members. This included such behaviors as listening to group members' opinions, being friendly and approachable, and being concerned about the group's welfare. The other set of behaviors, called "initiation of structure in interaction" (or structuring), consisted of assigning tasks and roles to group members, directing their work, setting and maintaining standards, and focusing on the task.

These studies, based on group member reports of leader behavior, brought about a new understanding of the role of the leader in the group. Considerate behavior was related to the group's cohesiveness and member satisfaction, but not to effective performance (Korman, 1966).

By the late 1930s, and more specifically, with the Wagner Fair Labor Relations Act and similar New Deal legislation, employers had begun to deal with strikes by adopting good management practices rather than by employing strike breakers. These practices began the first stirrings of the era of human relations approaches to leadership.

Among the most influential and widely accepted theories of this era was McGregor's (1944, 1960) Theory X and Theory Y. McGregor proposed that managers and leaders must adopt a management philosophy (Theory Y) based on the assumption that employees are inherently motivated to work, they want to contribute to the organization's success, and therefore they do not need to be driven or closely supervised. The contrasting and orthodox Theory X, which McGregor described as the prevailing managerial attitude of the time, assumed that workers were motivated only by a desire for economic gain and security.

McGregor's teaching was widely accepted by business and industry, though perhaps more in spirit than in deed. Theory Y received some empirical support, but it also suffered some disappointing failures in empirical studies. While this theory was an important milestone in the history of leadership, the present verdict must be that Theory Y works at some times but not at others (e.g., Bennis, 1961).

Closely related to McGregor's approach was Likert's (1967) System 1–4 theory which classified leadership approaches on the basis of subordinate participation. While Likert held that there were times for autocratic behavior, the participative approach was clearly the method of choice. The ground-breaking study by Lewin, Lippitt, and White (1939) suggested that democratic, participative behavior engaged subordinates and increased the performance of the group or organization. This view was supported by some studies (e.g., Coch & French, 1948) and not supported by other leadership researchers at the University of Michigan (Morse & Reimer, 1956; French, Israel, & Ås, 1960).

Before we leave the trait and behavior approaches, it is important to point out that they are based on certain common assumptions. The proponents of these approaches shared the belief that there was one best method of leadership, that there was one particular way of leading that was more effective than others: effective leaders were expected to be more considerate and more structuring. This belief was incorporated in a large number of leadership training programs which taught managers how to be more decisive, or more participative and human relations oriented (Blake & Mouton, 1964). Perhaps most importantly, these approaches shared the unspoken belief that effective leadership was a matter of one's ability to relate. Leadership was generally viewed as an affective and emotional, rather than a cognitive and rational, process. These assumptions were related to the implicit feudal conception that the relationship between leader and led is the paramount problem of management.

BUREAUCRATIC LEADERSHIP

In sharp contrast to the feudal tradition, which is based on personal ties, the bureaucratic system rejects the personal relationship between leader and follower as a basis for building an organization. The bureaucratic conception of leadership is best expressed by Max Weber's (1947) systematic writings on the topic. People in the bureaucratic organization are part of an interchangeable network of position holders. The role of the leader is clearly specified, and so are duties, responsibilities, and privileges. Moreover, the loyalty of leaders and their subordinates belongs to the organization and its goals, and this principle is often reinforced by frequent transfers and rotation policies, which discourage strong and lasting ties between leader and led.

The bureaucratic system of organizing large bodies of people was, of course, well known in antiquity. The Roman and Chinese government systems were, in many respects, bureaucracies. By and large, promotion was by merit, jobs were standardized, and loyalty was to the organization, for example, to a Roman legion and its subunits, rather than to the centurion as a person.

The advent of the Industrial Revolution in Western Europe renewed the need for bureaucratic organizations. The mechanization of work eventually led to the development of the assembly line. This necessitated rationally designed organizations that emphasized the importance of task demands and deemphasized the attributes of the individual worker and the workers' personal relationships with the supervisor.

The bureaucratic system is thus almost the exact antithesis of the personal and feudal relationship between superior and subordinate. Its ideal is an organization in which jobs and working conditions are spelled out in writing and employees can be moved from one "position," "berth," "slot," or "billet" into another. Promotion is by merit and not dependent on personal favor. Because personality differences are ignored, the bureaucratic system's main concern is with the structure of the organization, its communication system, and the design of jobs and tasks. The leader has limited power, wielding authority within narrow limits. Jobs, working conditions, standards of performance and grievance procedures are explicitly described, and performance is evaluated on the basis of objective statements of goals.

Current bureaucratic theory is perhaps best represented by structuralism. Structuralists see performance as dependent on the characteristics of the organization rather than on those of the leader. Among the best known researchers in this area are Woodward (1958, 1965), Pugh and Hickson (e.g., Pugh, Hickson, Hinings & Turner, 1968), and Simon (1947). It is also the basis for Kerr and Jermier's notion (1978) that there are various "substitutes for leadership," that is, aspects of the task and the structure of the organization which make the leader unnecessary.

Kerr and Jermier's substitutes include, for example, a highly structured task, individuals with strong professional identification and training, and a technology that determines what the individual is required to do. Knowledge of these substitutes for leadership presumably would enable us to design a situation which permits free information flow, effective decision making, and the exercise of authority without a designated leader.

The effect of the group and the task structure on the performance of group members has also been represented by the work of Maier (1970), Maier and Hoffman (1961) and Steiner (1972) in showing how the nature of the group affects the problem-solving process. Note that Maier, Kerr and Jermier, Vroom and Yetton, and the other structuralists do not consider the personality of the leader in the decision-making or problem-solving process.

This dispassionate approach to management contributes much to organizational performance. Who would want to fly with an airline that hires only pilots who are relatives of the company president? And large organizations undoubtedly work better with clearly defined roles and jobs. But omitting the role of individual personality leaves many questions unanswered. While organizational structure is important, it cannot account for differences in the performances of two organizations with exactly the same structure. What kinds of individuals, then, are most effective, and in what kinds of organizational settings?

CONTINGENCY APPROACHES

With the publication of the contingency model in 1964 came a major shift in the field of leadership. The contingency model attempted to integrate the feudal and bureaucratic approaches to leadership theory. It described the conditions in an organization in which leaders with a specific type of personality were effective. The model addressed the question why certain individuals perform better than others in identical leadership situations. The notion that leadership theory must take account of the individual's personality and the group environment is far from new. As mentioned before, it goes back to Terman's leadership study in 1904, and it was implicit in a number of subsequent studies (e.g., Vroom, 1959). But the contingency model was the first to spell out how personality and situational variables interacted, and the first to provide substantial empirical support for this position (see Strube & Garcia, 1981).

The model, in its simplest terms, states that the effectiveness of a leader, or of the organization, depends (or is "contingent") on two major elements. These are (a) the leader's motivational structure or leadership style and (b) the degree to which the leadership situation provides the leader with control and influence over the outcome. Because it is an integral part of the more extensive theoretical position described in this book, we will present a more detailed discussion of the contingency model in Part 2.

Several other theories have been based on "contingency" approaches. For the most part, however, these describe an interaction between situations and leader behaviors rather than personality. The best known is House's path–goal theory (1971), which states in essence that the leader must guide the subordinate to paths that will be satisfying and rewarding to both the subordinate and the organization. Leaders perform best when they adapt their considerate or structuring behavior to the nature of the task and to the subordinate's needs, abilities, and personality. Ambiguous tasks require structuring; structured tasks call for considerate, supportive leader behavior. For subordinates with low self-esteem, considerate leaders are likely to be most effective, whereas directive leaders are most helpful when dealing with inexperienced subordinates. A substantial number of studies show that path–goal theory successfully predicts subordinate satisfaction (House and Mitchell, 1974), but attempts to predict task performance have been disappointing (Yukl, 1981).

Vroom and Yetton's (1973) normative decision model states that the leader's decision to include the group members in the decision-making process should depend on situational factors, such as the leader's base of knowledge, need to obtain group support, or time constraints. Hersey and Blanchard's (1969) popular situational leadership theory suggests that the leader must adopt different degrees of structuring and considerate behavior over the life cycle of the group but as yet there has been no empirical support for their theory.

The Multiple Screen Model

Several studies found that leader intelligence measures correlate more highly with performance in cohesive, relaxed groups than in stressful, divisive groups (Fiedler & Meuwese, 1963; Meuwese & Fiedler, 1965). And Blades and Fiedler (1973) pointed out that the intellectual and task-relevant abilities of leaders cannot affect group performance unless the leader is also directive. Fiedler later extended previous research by proposing a "multiple screen" model (Fiedler & Leister, 1977). Although this model is distinguished mainly by its invisibility, it did clarify some of

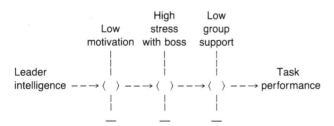

Figure 2.1. The multiple screen model. The leader's intellectual abilities affect group performance only if the product of the leader's intellectual effort can pass through various potential barriers or screens. [Adapted with permission from F. E. Fiedler & A. F. Leister (1977). Leader intelligence and task performance: A test of the multiple screen model. *Organizational Behavior and Human Performance*, *20*, 1–14.]

the conditions under which intellectual abilities contribute to leadership performance. In brief, the model hypothesized that the leader's intellectual abilities had to "pass through" a series of barriers, analogous to semi-permeable "screens," in order to affect performance. That is, if leader intelligence is to affect performance, the leader has to be motivated, supported by the group, and have a good relationship with his or her immediate supervisor. Figure 2.1 illustrates this model.

THEORETICAL GAPS AND PROBLEMS

A brief overview of the historical antecedents of current leadership history emphasizes the implicit incompatibility and the underlying tension between the feudal and bureaucratic forms of leadership. These two conceptions of leadership live in a close but uneasy marriage in the modern organization, and they give rise to incompatible demands which we must recognize and with which we must come to terms.

> The organizational leader wants the complete loyalty of subordinates, but also the concurrent right to fire them if they fail to perform.
>
> The employee deeply resents being treated like an impersonal cog of the bureaucratic wheel, but resents the favoritism and cronyism that go with the strong personal bonds of feudalistic leadership.
>
> The leader is expected to be warm and human in dealing with associates and subordinates, but also to make rational and impersonal decisions about their fate.
>
> The leader and the subordinate want mutual bonds of love and affection, but the bureaucratic organization demands impersonal fairness and justice by the leader.

Neither the trait theories nor the theories based on leader behavior have shown high predictive ability, although clearly leader behavior must in some way influence the performance of the group or organization. The structural theories explain how situations inhibit or promote effective decisions but they do not tell why two leaders working under the same conditions will often perform quite differently. Thus the exclusion of personality and individual differences from these theories significantly lowers their predictive power.

The major gap in the contingency model is the justified charge that it is a "black box." In other words, it does not provide an adequate explanation of how the interaction of personality and situation leads to differential group performance. Although its usefulness as a predictive tool has been repeatedly demonstrated (e.g., Strube & Garcia, 1981; Peters, Hartke, & Pohlman, 1985), it is unclear why this is so.

What are the general implications of this brief historical review of research for leadership theory? First, as one wit remarked, all complex problems have simple answers—which are usually wrong. We live in a pretzel-shaped universe, and a pretzel-shaped universe requires pretzel-shaped hypotheses. Most are the major findings of the research on leadership? At this point there are a few general conclusions:

1. We can say with considerable confidence that personality traits do not contribute highly to effective leadership performance.
2. Considerate leader behavior is correlated with subordinate's satisfaction. The relationship between structuring behavior and leadership effectiveness appears to be inconsistent and dependent on the situation (Korman, 1966).
3. Such "cognitive resources" as the leader's intellectual abilities, technical skill and competence, or work experience also do not by themselves contribute highly or uniformly to leadership performance.

Figure 2.2 presents one view of how the two major thrusts in leadership thinking were combined by the contingency model, and its successor, cognitive resource theory. It shows the contingency model as an integration of theories based on leadership traits and personality attributes (i.e., LPC) and situational theories (e.g., Tannenbaum & Schmidt, 1958). Later theories, for example, House (1971) and Vroom and Yetton (1973), have based their theories on the interaction of leader behavior and leadership situation.

Cognitive resource theory, in addition, involves leader behavior (directiveness) and group support, as well as cognitive resources (e.g., intelligence, technical competence, job-relevant knowledge) and the effect of stress on these cognitive functions.

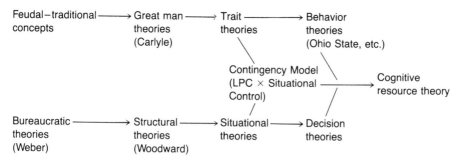

Figure 2.2. Historical antecedents of the contingency model.

SUMMARY

This brief history of leadership research reflects two traditions and two corresponding twentieth-century trends. The feudalistic approach is based on the relationship between the leader and followers. This view led to the investigation of leadership traits and leader behaviors in the twentieth century. Leadership in bureaucratic organizations is an almost exact antithesis of feudal organization in stressing the impersonal relationship between leader and subordinate. This led to concerns with organizational structure and conditions facilitating rational decision-making processes.

Contingency approaches highlight the importance of understanding the interaction between the leader's personality and the leadership situation. Cognitive resource theory, the topic of this book, integrates the contingency model and the multiple screen model by showing the conditions under which leader and group-member abilities and job-relevant knowledge contribute to effective leadership performance.

CHAPTER THREE

Stress

"Stress, like air, is everywhere!" This doggerel will not win a prize, but it does speak truth: We live in a complex environment full of uncertainty and change, the two main sources of stress (Holmes & Rahe, 1967). This is particularly true for leaders, and stress plays a large part in cognitive resource theory. It is important, therefore, that we discuss some theories about stress before applying them to leadership phenomena.

Ask managers how long they have worked on the same task under the same immediate superior and with the same key subordinates. No more than two or three in twenty can report that they have done so for more than one or two years. Their assignments changed, they have new bosses, or some of their reliable key subordinates are no longer with them. All of these changes require major readjustments: new routines, learning the idiosyncrasies of new bosses or new subordinates, and adapting to new standards. And these adjustments typically are stressful.

Aside from unstable working conditions, leadership jobs are often inherently stressful. It is rare to have adequate time and resources and most decisions have to be made on the basis of incomplete or unreliable information (Buck, 1972; Janis & Mann, 1959; Kahn, Wolfe, Quinn, Snoek, & Rosenthal, 1964). Interpersonal conflict arises in the process of coordinating agendas, schedules, and jobs. The needs of subordinates often interfere with those of superiors and those of the organization. In-fighting, jealousies, and competition for scarce resources are par for the course in many organizations, and they can substantially reduce morale and productivity. And the private lives of employees frequently compete with the needs of the organization for time and attention. Dealing effectively with these problems, so that neither the subordinate nor the business is short-changed, is often a very stressful task.

In addition, the manager wields considerable power over the fates and careers of subordinates. Giving a negative performance evaluation to an employee with whom one has been on friendly terms causes pain and stress. Making decisions on hiring, promotion, reassignment, reprimands, and firing with the knowledge that these actions affect someone's life is a responsibility which cannot be regarded lightly.

Finally, the need to delegate often creates a high degree of stress. Giving responsibility for important jobs and decisions has major psychological implications that many writers do not fully understand, blithely urging participatory management and shared decision making. There is more to delegation than meets the eye. When you delegate, you necessarily entrust your career and fate to someone else.

People can get fired for their subordinates' mistakes, and many organizations are unforgiving of the leader whose subordinate got the organization into trouble. Ship captains, for instance, are held responsible for their vessel whether or not they are on the bridge. The professional careers of leaders are often at the mercy of subordinates whose judgment they may not fully trust. And this is no less true for managers. What if the other person's decision turns out to be wrong? What if the other is careless, neglects an important aspect of the problem, or is just not competent? These questions are very real for many individuals in leadership positions.

This chapter discusses the relationship between stress and leadership effectiveness. Whether this stress stems from a feeling of generally being out of control or from being unable to cope with specific demands, the results are often the same: anxiety, unease, uncertainty, insecurity, low self-confidence, and the consequent need to cope with these feelings. Different types of people cope differently with stress and uncertainty in the leadership environment. This chapter briefly reviews several background issues related to stress that will concern us throughout the remainder of this book.

DEFINITIONS OF STRESS

Stress may be viewed in at least three different ways: as a response to some demand, as a situation, and as a relationship between a person and the environment. While some bridges between these various conceptions do exist (Baum, Fleming, & Singer, 1982), most research tends to focus on one perspective. We will, therefore, review each of these perspectives in turn.

Stress as a Response

Hans Selye, a pioneer in stress research, defined the term as "the nonspecific response of the body to any demand" (1979, p. 12). According to

Selye, the stress response proceeds in three stages known as the general adaptation syndrome (GAS). The first stage is an alarm reaction composed of an initial shock phase and then a countershock or rebound phase. This alarm reaction is followed by a stage of resistance during which the individual attempts to adjust to the demands imposed by the stressor. The final stage of exhaustion occurs when the individual's ability to adapt has reached its limit.

Selye's (1979) interpretation of stress emphasizes the role of emotional arousal in the production of the stress reaction, and ultimately in the development of diseases or psychosomatic disorders. Arousal is seen to be central to the production of stress, and "stress management" is largely construed as the lessening of arousal and anxiety. While Selye's stress theory and GAS represent important contributions to our understanding of how people respond to stress, several limitations of Selye's definition make it difficult to apply to the study of leadership.

As McGrath (1976) points out, response-based definitions of stress (such as Selye's) consider any stimulus which results in a "stress reaction" to be a stressor. Thus two people can respond differently to the same demands. Furthermore, the effects of stress are cumulative. A series of several mild stresses may, in the aggregate, produce a major reaction (Selye, 1956). The "fender-bender," ordinarily no more than an annoying mishap, may seem like a major catastrophe during a bitter divorce proceeding.

Another problem with the response-based perspective of stress concerns the stress-produced emotional arousal. The work of Schachter (1964) and Schachter and Singer (1962) shows that arousal itself is a very diffuse state and can assume a variety of emotional expressions, ranging from elation to anger, depending on the situation. Hence the presence of emotional arousal is a necessary but not sufficient description of a person's response to stress.

Finally, reactions to stress do not always correspond to the prescribed syndrome. For example, Zajonc's (1965) work on social facilitation demonstrates that performance on an overlearned task *increases* when the presumably stressful presence of an audience induces emotional arousal, but performance on new or complex tasks *decreases* under the same conditions. In sum, while Selye's theory is valuable for understanding reactions to stress, it does not provide a specific basis for predicting the effects of stress on leadership performance.

Stress as an Environmental Condition

This definition views stress as caused by environmental conditions outside a normal or comfortable range. This is exemplified in studies which explore the effects of noise (e.g., Broadbent, 1971), heat (e.g. Fine & Kobrick, 1978; Pepler, 1958), cold (e.g. Fox, 1967; Teichner & Kobrick, 1955) and crowding (Smith & Haythorn, 1972; Stokols, 1976; Stokols & Schumaker, 1982).

This perspective can be extended to managerial performance by regarding stress as caused by unusual or abnormal work conditions, such as unreasonable deadlines or nonsupportive employees. But what is meant by "abnormal" or "unusual"? Such organizations, as police departments, always live at the edge of crisis. Also, the same objective condition can produce different effects (Fiedler & Fiedler, 1975; McGrath, 1970). This is particularly likely to occur in the case of such psychosocial stressors as a carping boss.

Stress as a Relationship between Person and Situation

The third approach defines stress as a relationship between the individual and the environment (Lazarus, 1966). According to this perspective, stress results from a perceived environmental threat which requires resources beyond one's own perceived abilities and assets. This conception focuses on the individual's perceptions of self and the environment. Although circumstances are likely to differ from person to person and from situation to situation, the perception of threat and the perceived inability to meet the demands are presumed to be stable, measurable components of the stressful situation.

According to Lazarus (1966), we are stressed if we perceive a potentially threatening stimulus ("primary appraisal"). We then evaluate the likely damage of the stressor during "secondary appraisal," and do so in two distinct stages. First, we determine whether the stimulus poses a threat (i.e., "Am I in danger?"). Then, if yes, the question becomes "What can I do about this problem?" Threat (and therefore stress) does not exist if there is no attack or the attack is easily fended off. Stress occurs if a threat does exist and if it exceeds the individual's perceived abilities and resources. This perspective on stress is of particular relevance in the management of organizations.

In a recent clarification and extension of their earlier theoretical work, Folkman and Lazarus (1980) and Folkman (1984) emphasize the further importance of two distinct forms of coping. Emotion-focused coping involves attempts to control the emotional upset associated with stress; problem-focused coping is directed toward the management of the stressful circumstances. Folkman suggests that the success of problem-focused coping may, to a large extent, depend on managing the uncontrolled emotions so that they will not interfere with problem-solving capabilities. An individual who feels in control makes a different assessment of a problem from one who feels completely bewildered.

Folkman (1984) cites problem-focused coping in a study by Anderson (1977). This study described the responses of a group of businessmen to a flood that destroyed their buildings. Those who felt that they could take remedial action in coping with the problem experienced less stress than businessmen without such an orientation. This belief in the control of their own destinies presumably led to an initial perception of the situation as less threatening. Incidentally, the perception of control ("situational control") is a key element of the contingency model.

McGrath (1976) proposed an explanation of this view of stress in organizational settings. His model identifies four important components: the actual situation, the perceived situation, the individual's decision of how to respond, and the individual's behavior. McGrath argues that these elements are properly regarded in a cyclic relationship, the changes (or lack of changes) in the situation produced by the individual's behavior provide feedback that can prompt another assessment of the situation, and so on.

Within this cycle, he identifies six potential sources of stress: (1) task stress (e.g., the difficulty of the task or the sheer number of tasks assigned); (2) role stress, deriving from ambiguity or conflict in one's job specifications; (3) stress from the social and physical environment (e.g., crowding); (4) stress from the physical environment (e.g., excessive noise or heat); (5) interpersonal stress (e.g., mutual incompatibility); and, finally, (6) individual stress, based on trait anxiety or low selfconfidence. Again, while demands may arise from any one or more of these sources, the relationship between the person and the situation ultimately produces stress.

McGrath (1976) suggests that the level of stress is highest when perceived demand and personal abilities are approximately equivalent, but the anticipated outcome is both highly important and uncertain. In other words, we feel most stress when we face an important task but are not sure that we can handle it. It is important to note that stress is arousing, but not necessarily always aversive. Stress can be anxiety-provoking or challenging, depending on an individual's orientation toward the stressful demands. Betting heavily on a horse race creates stress, and this stress may be exciting but pleasant. Schuler (1980) proposed the term "opportunity stress" to refer to demanding situations with a potential for gain.

In sum, we have considered three definitions of stress. Of these, stress as a relationship between person and environment appears to be the most useful for understanding leadership performance. We now examine research on the effects of stress on performance.

STRESS AND PERFORMANCE

Perceived stress affects task-related behavior and performance in several ways (e.g., Geen, 1980; Lazarus, 1966; Spielberger & Katzenmeyer, 1959). We tend to reach premature closure (Smock, 1955), make fewer distinctions in utilizing information (Broadbent, 1971; Easterbrook, 1959; Kahneman, 1973), and behave rigidly (Staw, Sandelan, & Dutton, 1981). People under stress also are less able to perform cognitive tasks (Berkum, 1964) or make accurate observations (Siegel & Loftus, 1978). These studies all share a common thread: stress influences the ability of individuals to "use their heads."

Anxiety

Very closely related to our own research is the work on anxiety, the feeling of helplessness and of being out of control. Along with others in the field, Sarason (1980) distinguishes between trait anxiety, the level of anxiety characteristic of the individual, and state anxiety, associated with particular situations. Although state anxiety is not identical to stress, it has been defined as a response to a perceived threat and is thus a coping strategy according to Folkman's (1984) conceptualization.

Sarason's (1975) work on test anxiety (one form of state anxiety) is of particular relevance. It causes physiological arousal along with a tendency for pessimistic, self-centered thoughts or worry. Of these, worry seems to be most clearly responsible for poor performance (e.g., Deffenbacher, 1980; Tyron, 1980). In other words, the test-anxious person performs poorly on intellectually demanding tasks because irrelevant thoughts interfere with concentration on the task. As we will see later, the leader's intelligence does not contribute to performance when stress with boss is high. Further, "the wider the range of relevant cues [that is, the more intellectually demanding the task], the greater the debilitating effects of cognitive interference" (Sarason, 1984, p. 936). Put simply, the more you need to use your head to get the job done, the less you can afford to worry.

The leader's own supervisor constitutes one of the most important sources of stress and evaluation anxiety for leaders (Buck, 1972; Kahn et al., 1964). Most people spend a good deal of their time worrying about what their bosses think of them, or whether or not their boss was really trying to give them a subtle message through a joke (which wasn't very funny, anyway). How the boss evaluates one's work makes a great deal of difference; self-esteem depends to a surprisingly large degree on the approval or disapproval of one's superior. It is obvious that stress with one's boss shares important elements with the problems addressed by social facilitation theory (Zajonc, 1965) and research on test anxiety, that is, worry over one's performance.

The connection between test-anxiety and evaluation stress becomes obvious when we consider that stress with the boss is one of the most common complaints in organizations. The leader is almost constantly evaluated by the immediate superior as well as subordinates. Given a boss who is seen as ill-disposed, the leader is continually in a defensive situation in which the stakes are high, the demands are perceived as great, and there is high uncertainty as to the boss' satisfaction with one's performance.

Again, the parallel with social facilitation theory is reasonably clear. This theory examines how participants perform on a task when they are either alone or in the presence of threatening others. The typical findings of these investigations show that people tend to perform better in the presence of others if the task is simple or well-learned, and considerably worse if the task is complex or unlearned. As Zajonc (1965) and others have suggested, the mere presence of other people, and especially those perceived as threatening, implies evaluation apprehension. This increases arousal, which in turn interferes with the ability to concentrate on task demands. When the task is simple or overlearned, the task demands presumably do not require such concentration and performance is enhanced by arousal.*

A leader may also experience stress generated by subordinates. Insubordination, unreliable workmanship, personality clashes, or conflict within the group tend to create frustration and stress for the leader. But leaders usually have considerably more control over their subordinates than over their bosses. Whatever the source of stress, it is important to remember that the leader's role, almost by definition, is exceptionally visible. There is little a leader can say or do that will not soon be common knowledge and subject to comment. Success and failure are frequently a matter of public record, and what happens in the manager's office is usually known by all subordinates before the day is out. It is not surprising, therefore, that some leaders feel as if they lived in a goldfish bowl. Whatever feelings goldfish may have on this issue, this is certainly stressful for most people.

SUMMARY

Stress is a ubiquitous fact of organizational life. It profoundly affects the way in which leaders function. Our current understanding of stress derives from a growing recognition that it arises from the relationship between the individual and the environment. Early views emphasized the role of stress as a response and as an environmental condition. We now see stress as the result of a person's perceived inability to cope with environmental demands.

One major implication of stress for leadership performance is the inability to "use one's head" when worry distracts one's attention from the task. As the research on test anxiety and social facilitation demonstrates, this deleterious effect of worry is prevalent under conditions where critical evaluation is anticipated. The leader's own boss therefore is a major source of stress for many leaders. The critical evaluation by the immediate superior plays a major role in the individual's career and not only while employed by an organization. Very often, and long after leaving the or-

---

* For alternative explanations with slightly different emphasis see Cottrell & Epley, 1977; Cottrell, Wack, Sekerak, & Rettle, 1968; Sanders, 1981; or Sasfy & Okun, 1974.

ganization, the person who was then his superior will be asked to give a reference or evaluate the individual's performance. These evaluations have a profound influence on whether one is considered for promotion or hired for a job. Perhaps even more important, the evaluation by the immediate superior tends to have a strong effect on the individual's feelings of adequacy and self-esteem.

CHAPTER FOUR

Job-Relevant Experience, Tenure, and Leadership Performance

"How much experience have you had?" This question is asked in the course of practically all hiring and promotion interviews, and the more experienced leaders are almost invariably preferred over those with less experience. This is especially true when it comes to important tasks or guiding organizations through critical periods. And yet, as we have said, researchers have paid almost no attention to this important topic. In fact, *Stogdill's Handbook of Leadership* (Bass, 1981) does not even list "experience" in its 5000-item index.

First, what do we mean by "experience"? Webster's dictionary lists a number of definitions, but only some of these are directly related to the working environment. One of these is "knowledge, skill, or practice derived from participation in, or direct observation of an activity . . . the period of such activity; as teaching *experience*" (Gove, 1971). In practice, managers most commonly define experience as the time served in a particular organization, position, or occupational field, that is, as tenure in an organization or a job, and this practice has been followed in most published studies (e.g., Bons & Fiedler, 1976; Brief, Aldag, & Van Sell, 1977; Cascio & Valenzi, 1977; Csoka, 1974; Fiedler, 1970; Fiedler & Leister, 1977; Fiedler, Potter, Zais, & Knowlton, 1979; Hardy & Bohren, 1975; and Potter & Fiedler, 1981).

This chapter was prepared jointly by Patrick J. Bettin and Fred E. Fiedler.

When asked to describe their job-relevant experience, a typical answer might be, "I worked at Amalgamated Bromides for two years and managed the Grand Cochon Restaurant for five years."

We must recognize, of course, that experience is a psychological rather than a physical variable. We are really interested in the job-relevant knowledge, skills, and behavior patterns an individual acquires in the course of his or her tenure in an organization or in a job. Time is necessary but not sufficient to gain the knowledge and skills that experience provides. And there are undoubtedly some people who do not learn much, no matter how long they are on a job, and others who seem to learn the wrong things. Also, some jobs may not provide relevant skills and knowledge, no matter how long an individual occupies a position of that nature. One year's internship at the Mayo Clinic is likely to be more valuable than one year at the Crossroads Clinic in East Tumbleweed.

In general, however, time spent in an organization or in a profession enables an individual to learn about the general working environment and the professional or organizational subculture. It enables the leader to observe others, to model his or her behavior after those in similar circumstances, and to gain the self-confidence and assurance that come from "knowing the ropes" and "having been through it all." Just what is learned in this manner is difficult to ascertain from the available literature considering the dearth of longitudinal studies. We can draw some inferences, however, by comparing the behavior and performance of experienced and relatively less experienced leaders.

These observations suggest that experience is likely to affect the leader by (a) providing useful and job-related knowledge, (b) enhancing the ability to cope with stressful conditions, and (c) engendering a feeling of greater self-confidence and control of the leadership situation. As we shall show in this book, the knowledge gained from experience represents a very important cognitive resource. For this reason, it seems appropriate to present a general review of what we know from previous studies about the effects of experience on leadership.

As is true of many terms in everyday use, the construct which we call experience has different meanings for different people. The operational definition of experience is in many of our studies the time the individual has spent in the service of an organization. This simple definition certainly does not capture all the necessary nuances and is, therefore, open to valid criticism. On the other hand, as we shall show, more highly sophisticated measures of experience provide results not substantially different from very simple measures. Still, some readers may feel more comfortable with the more precise term "job tenure" when we speak of the time in service measure.

This chapter reviews findings relating to the general effects of various types of experience and job tenure on behavior and performance. Chapter 9 will consider the way in which experience enhances situational control and thus indirectly affects leadership performance.

TIME IN THE ORGANIZATION OR IN A LEADERSHIP POSITION

The widespread belief that organizational tenure or experience generally contributes to effective leadership performance is not supported by either laboratory studies or field research. One well-controlled experiment on Belgian naval personnel (Fiedler, 1966) compared the performance on four different tasks by two sets of 48 three-member teams. One set was led by career petty officers (average of 9.8 years of service) and the other by inexperienced recruit leaders (less than six weeks of military service). The tasks simulated military assignments that might be given to Belgian naval personnel. They were to (a) write a recruiting letter urging high school students to join the Belgian navy, (b) find the shortest route for a ship convoy which had to touch 10 ports, (c) do the same for 12 ports, and (d) instruct group members to assemble and disassemble a military weapon without using verbal communication. The mean intercorrelation of performance scores on these four tasks was only .14 ($n = 96$).

Petty officers and recruit leaders were matched on the basis of intelligence and leadership style. No significant differences were found between the 48 groups led by petty officers and the 48 groups led by recruits on any of the four tasks. Nor did years as a petty officer correlate with their performance even though practically all of these leaders' experience must be considered relevant for leading groups. Thus neither general experience in the navy nor leadership experience contributed to good performance.

Similar results were obtained in an experiment by Fiedler and Chemers (1968) which compared officers and recruits of the Canadian military forces. The leader of each three-man group was either a commissioned officer with 5–15 years of service or a recruit with less than 8 weeks of service. The tasks were similar to those occasionally assigned to officers in the Canadian services (routing a vehicle convoy, converting maps and plans from inch to metric scales). Although the commissioned officers, as a group, were superior to the recruits in intelligence as well as in experience and military training, the recruit-led groups performed as well as the groups led by experienced officers.

The results of the Fiedler (1966) and Fiedler and Chemers (1968) studies are consistent with those obtained in several field studies. Fiedler reanalyzed data relating organizational tenure to the performance of 21 medium-sized post offices (Fiedler, Nealey, & Wood, 1968) and data from Hunt's study (1967) on 18 chemical research teams, 11 craft shops, 21 meat markets, 24 grocery departments, and 10 departments in a large heavy machinery plant. None of the correlations between organizational experience and performance were significant in these studies. The median correlation between organizational experience or job tenure and performance in 13 different samples was −.12.

Subsequent findings also indicate that time in an organization does not contribute significantly to improved organizational effectiveness. Correlations from various studies, including those obtained prior to 1970, are shown on Table 4.1. Of the 36 correlations, 4 were significantly positive, but 12 correlations were in the negative direction. The median correlations were positive but very low. To facilitate the interpretation of data obtained in studies of army units, the table of organization of a typical army battalion is shown in Figure 4.1.

There is some evidence that ratings of performance decline for managers who have very long tenure in their positions. This is shown by results from samples of post office supervisors and managers who remained at the same level for relatively short, intermediate, and long times. Here we found an increase of rated performance during the first few years,

Table 4.1. Correlations between Leaders' Job Tenure, Experience and Performance

Sample[a]	Age		Time in Organization		Time in Leadership Position		Time in Position	
	r	n	r	n	r	n	r	n
Army squad leader	.18[#]	95	.18*	123	.22*	102	.03	128
Army platoon sergeant			.01	150			−.05	146
Army first sergeant			.19	41			.02	41
Coast guard			.18*	130				
Company manager			−.28[#]	31	−.01	31	.38*	31
Fire lieutenant	.08	55	−.02	55	−.14	54	.29*	54
Fire captain	−.14	33	−.07	33	.17	33	−.11	33
Meat department manager	−.14	19	.15	21	−.12	20	.11	21
Grocery manager	.09	24	−.08	24	−.06	24	.17	24
Research chemist team leader	.15	18	.10	18	.17	18	.12	18
University department chairman or head	.06	24	.15	24	.23	24	.38	24
Medians	.08		.10		.08		.11	

Note. In all tables of this book [#], $p < .10$; *, $p < .05$; **, $p < .01$.
[a] References to studies describing the samples: 1,2: Bons & Fiedler, 1976; 3,4: Fiedler, Potter, Zais, & Knowlton, 1979; 5: Godfrey, Fiedler, & Hall, 1959; 6,7: Frost, 1981; 8,9,10: Hunt, 1967, 11: Bettin & Fiedler, 1984.

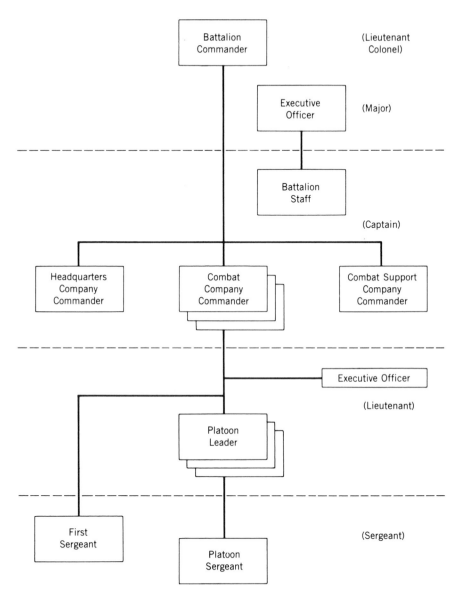

Figure 4.1. Organizational chart depicting the leadership levels of an army infantry battalion. The usual rank of each position is shown in parentheses. The dashed lines indicate jobs which have the same rank.

followed by a significant decrease for managers with most tenure. The standardized performance scores for post office managers with varying tenure as supervisors were as follows:

Less than 2 years	$-.135$	$n = 29$
2 to 5 years	$.063$	$n = 34$
5 to 10 years	$.23$	$n = 16$
Over 20 years	-1.075	$n = 8$

These findings, albeit based on very small subsamples, suggest that the managers who were not promoted after the usual time period either were not considered sufficiently competent for promotion or they were bored and no longer challenged by their jobs.

RELEVANCE AND DIVERSITY OF EXPERIENCE

The value of previous experience depends most directly on its relevance to current responsibilities. Years spent in a typing job will be less helpful for becoming a plant manager than the same time spent as the assistant plant manager. At the same time, we must recognize that many leadership jobs can be performed very effectively without the benefit of extensive relevant experience. The 17-year-old Joan of Arc did not have much military experience before defeating the English forces at Rouen, and many college professors without administrative experience have become effective department heads or deans. In the same way, many lawyers without previous management experience have become effective mayors or governors. It is important to identify, therefore, how much the relevance of prior experience contributes to the value of job tenure.

A somewhat related question concerns the value of diverse experience that presumably provides a broad perspective on how other organizations operate. This is given as the justification for the rotation programs in governmental, military, and civilian organizations. These programs periodically move executives at great expense and personal inconvenience from one job to another and from location to location. Whether or not relevant or diverse experience does in fact provide greater perspective and understanding has not been established, nor is this the point at issue. Rather, we must ask whether leaders with relevant or diverse experience perform better than those with less diverse experience. What is the evidence?

Bettin (1982) developed a sophisticated method for measuring relevant experience of army officers. This study is of particular importance since our other studies of leader experience raise questions about the adequacy of the very simple index of time in service, or time in the organization.

The performance of the officer was evaluated on a 49-item Likert scale* by the two immediate superiors, the battalion's commander and executive officer. Interrater agreement on the standardized scales was .62 ($p <$ .001), and ratings were summed (Cronbach's alpha = .94). Bettin's method for measuring the specific relevance of previously held positions was as follows: A panel of expert judges evaluated 101 different military jobs at the middle management level for their relevance to 5 leadership positions (e.g., company commander, personnel officer, battalion operations officer). Bettin then correlated the number and relevance of different positions an officer had held with his or her performance, as rated by the officer's battalion commander and battalion executive officers.

In view of the care that Bettin took to measure the relevance of previous experience to the specific job held by the subject, it is especially interesting that the correlation between relevance of previous positions to the present job and rated performance was only .26 ($n = 78$, $p < .05$) and the correlation between diversity of experience (number of different army jobs) and performance was .22 ($n = 78$, $p < .05$).†

Gordon and Fitzgibbons (1982) found that regression models failed to predict performance from seniority, that is, time in service. However, "interjob" similarity (how closely the previous jobs resembled the new position) did predict performance at a low but statistically significant level ($r = .20$, $p < .001$). Interjob similarity presumably indicates the degree to which previously acquired skills are relevant for, or identical to, those required by the new position.

While there is some evidence that relevant experience contributes slightly to performance, the data are less clear for diversity of experience. Data obtained in a study of community colleges by Fiedler and Gillo (1974) provides one of the few empirical findings related to diversity of experience. The performance of 17 community college presidents was rated by fellow presidents, the staff of the State Community College Board, and two university faculty members working with community colleges in the state. The summed performance evaluations constituted the criteria of performance. Separate ratings were made of presidents' effectiveness in providing leadership for their school's academic programs, vocational–technical programs, and college administration. Those with previous teaching and administrative experience in community colleges (i.e., in academic positions) performed better than those with experience in nonacademic professions (e.g., law, business, government) which are presumably more diverse than academic life.

---

* An attitude scaling procedure in which the respondents are asked to indicate on a five-point scale the degree of their agreement with a statement.
† Time in service correlated .72 with relevance of previous jobs, and .79 with diversity of previous jobs, and diversity and relevance ratings correlated .81 ($n = 78$, $p < .01$). Time in service is thus a good proxy for relevance as well as for diversity of previous positions.

Table 4.2. Years of Nonacademic Experience Correlated with the President's Rated Effectiveness in Guiding or Developing the College's Programs (n = 17)

Administration	$r = -.41$	$p < .10$
Academic program	$r = -.46$	$p < .10$
Vocational program	$r = -.02$	ns

Community college presidents are often chosen for their practical knowledge of business and vocational fields. However, those with diverse experience, that is, a background in business or the professions, were rated as having relatively less effective programs than those with a background limited to academic positions. The correlations between years of nonacademic experience and rated performance is shown in Table 4.2. Although the correlations are based on small samples they were certainly not positive. Along with other findings, then, there is no evidence that diversity of experience contributes to effective leadership performance although years in academic life may do so.

EFFECTS OF INTELLIGENCE ON EXPERIENCE

One possible definition of intelligence is the ability to profit from experience. It seems reasonable to assume, therefore, that more intelligent leaders learn more from their experience than those who are less intelligent. If so, we would expect higher correlations between experience and performance in organizations in which average leader intelligence tends to be high and lower correlations in which it tends to be low.

Table 4.1 included data on such diverse samples as chemical research and development teams, chairs of graduate departments, and community college presidents. The correlations between intelligence and performance for these intellectually elite samples should, therefore, have been higher than for army squad leaders and platoon sergeants whose average intelligence was demonstrably lower. However, our data do not support the hypothesis that intellectual ability substantially increases the ability to make use of experience, although the low correlations between leader experience and performance could also be caused by other factors.

In several of our own studies (e.g., Csoka, 1974), we computed correlations between time in service and performance separately for the more intelligent and the less intelligent leaders. These analyses showed slightly higher relations for the more intelligent groups, but the differences were very small and not even close to significance.

Bettin's (1982) study of army company commanders provides another interesting example. The sample was divided at the median into those with relatively high and low intelligence. Bettin found very low correlations

Table 4.3. Correlations between Experience
and Performance of Relatively Intelligent
and Less Intelligent Company Commanders

| | Intelligence | |
| | Low | High |
Experience Measures	(n = 20)	(n = 21)
Age	−.46*	.28
Time in service	−.50*	−.17
Time in position	−.15	−.05
Diversity of jobs	−.34	.10
Number of previous positions	−.39	.11

between various experience measures and the leader's performance in the relatively more intelligent group. However, the correlations are *negative*, and in two instances significantly so, in the subsample of less intelligent leaders (see Table 4.3). This suggests that the less intelligent leaders with relatively high experience may misapply previously learned knowledge in subsequent jobs. Alternatively, they may become more confident than their ability warrants, and devote less effort to the job or charge off in the wrong direction. We shall return to this problem in a later chapter.

In sum, there is very little evidence that exposure to an organizational environment, regardless of the relevance or diversity of previous jobs, benefits the more intelligent leader. There is evidence that more extended tenure tends to detract from the performance of the less intelligent leader. Relevant experience is somewhat more beneficial than irrelevant experience, but even here, the effects of experience are relatively slight and probably not of practical significance.

LEADER EXPERIENCE AND LEADER BEHAVIOR

Anecdotal evidence suggests that the more experienced leaders are more self-confident and more decisive, and feel in better control of their job than do less experienced leaders. To what extent do we see these differences in the behaviors of experienced and inexperienced leaders?

Leader behavior measures in most published studies are based on ratings by the leader's subordinates. The most widely used rating categories are the Consideration and Initiation of Structure factors (Stogdill & Coons, 1957) developed at Ohio State University. "Consideration" is defined as the extent to which a leader exhibits concern for the welfare, opinions, and feelings of the other members of the group. Considerate leaders stress the importance of job satisfaction, emphasize subordinate self-esteem, and listen to subordinates (Bass, 1981). "Initiation of Structure" refers to the extent to which a leader initiates the activity of the group, organizes it, and defines the way the work is to be done. Structuring leaders display such behaviors as maintaining standards, deciding in detail what will be done and how it will be done. Structuring leaders define and structure the leadership role as well as the roles of subordinates and actively direct the group in the performance of the task (Bass, 1981). To a considerable degree, these behavior descriptions reflect the feelings of subordinates toward their superiors, that is, a liked superior will be seen as more considerate than one who is disliked.

Bons and Fiedler (1976) conducted a longitudinal study which examined the effects of organizational change on the behavior and performance of first line supervisors. The subjects were 115 male U.S. Army infantry squad leaders of an Army division that had just been reactivated. The squad leaders were in charge of 8 to 10 soldiers and responsible for training them. Squad leader performance was evaluated by two superiors, the platoon leader and platoon sergeant.

The squad leader's time in service ranged from 1 to 22 years, with an average of 6.9 years of service (some acting squad leaders were included in the study). Since all squad leaders had served as squad members and in various related army positions, most, if not all, of their army experience can be considered relevant to their job.

Organizational change generally is perceived as disruptive when it is beyond the expectation level of its members (Grusky, 1970). Changes in military assignments are routine and expected. Highly experienced military leaders, therefore, are more accustomed to getting a new boss or new subordinates, and they should be significantly less affected by changes of this nature than inexperienced leaders.

Experience had a direct effect on behavior as rated by subordinates. Specifically, considerate behaviors decreased over the course of the training period. Second, the use of administrative, formal punishment increased, as compared to the informal punishment of reprimanding or "leaning on" a subordinate. Thus, as the leader gained on-the-job experience he was seen as more punitive and controlling and less concerned about the way subordinates would view him. Third, experienced leaders did not perceive less stress nor did subordinates rate the leader as more relaxed. In fact, the experienced leader tended to be harder and less compassionate in his dealing with subordinates.

Similar findings were supported by Landy and Lamiell-Landy (1978), who conducted a random sample survey of 544 teachers in Pennsylvania. The teachers completed a modified form of the Leadership Opinion Questionnaire (Fleishman, 1957) indicating their self-perceived consideration and structuring behavior in relating to their students. Results showed that the teachers with more than 10 years of experience saw themselves as less considerate and more structuring than did teachers with less than 5 years of teaching experience. Landy and Lamiell-Landy suggest "that the realities of teaching erode the ideals of training" (p. 525). Extensive teaching experience, in effect, seemed to result in a jaded outlook and more realistic expectations, with less emphasis on the ideals of their profession.

While experience may not increase performance under normal conditions, we know that leadership experience is especially prized in organizations which must be prepared to deal with emergencies. These organizations typically require a minimum time in rank or in a position before promotions to responsible leadership positions are considered. The time-in-rank rule applies, for example, to officers in military and fire-fighting organizations, airline pilots, and ship captains. The need for experience in these organizations is also reflected by the innumerable drills and training exercises. It is reasonable to expect, then, that experienced leaders are better able to perform under stress. Those with long experience presumably have encountered many different crisis situations and can thus respond more quickly on the basis of knowledge and skills learned in the past. We shall consider this proposition in detail in Chapter 13.

SUMMARY

We found no consistent relationship between experience or job tenure and leadership performance. This seems to be the case whether experience is measured by time in the organization, time on the job, time in a leadership position, or as relevance and diversity of previous positions. Nor did we find that the more intelligent leaders benefit from experience, but there is some evidence that less intelligent leaders may be disadvantaged by having extensive experience. This problem needs further research, and it is also discussed later in this book. Experience does seem to result in a feeling of having more control over the situation and probably increases the individual's confidence in approaching the task.

CHAPTER FIVE

Leadership
and Intelligence

Psychologists, as a tribe, have been much concerned—if not always enamored—with intelligence and intelligence testing since Binet's early attempts to measure intellectual abilities. Few human activities cannot be performed better by bright than by dull people, although bright people might become bored and careless after a period of time. It would be surprising, therefore, if intellectual abilities were irrelevant to leadership performance.

Common sense tells us that there ought to be a very high relationship between a leader's or manager's intellectual ability and his or her performance in directing a group. After all, the major functions of a leader include planning, evaluating data, decision making, developing action strategies, assessing outcomes. These are intellectual functions, and many are similar or identical to those we find on typical intelligence tests. We should, therefore, expect a strong relationship between leadership performance and intelligence.

Moreover, as noted earlier, intellectual ability is clearly one of the main criteria for selecting and promoting managers and executives. There is little call for those who are demonstrably stupid. This chapter reviews the general (i.e., main effect) contribution of leaders' and group members' intellectual abilities to performance, leaving the more complex interactions to later chapters.

We already noted that the attempt to link intelligence and leadership was, in fact, the topic of the earliest published empirical study in the field

---

We are indebted to a paper by Dennis Dossett for some of the material cited in this section.

(Terman, 1904). This study was soon followed by scores of studies that showed that the more intelligent leaders did perform slightly better than those less intellectually endowed. In 1948 Stogdill reviewed over 33 published studies which asked this question again in one way or another. Since then there have been well over 100 additional studies on this topic.

It is clear from recent work on intellectual processing that we cannot really speak of intelligence as a unitary concept, that is, as a unidimensional personality trait. There is, however, evidence that a general intelligence factor does exist and accounts for much of the variance in such intellectual tasks as performance in school and at work. Spearman called this "g," indicating a general pervasive level of intellectual functioning. To be sure, there are distinct abilities and styles of processing information beyond this general factor which were described by Thurstone (1938) and others (e.g., Cattell, 1971; Horn, 1968, 1977, 1978, 1979; Sternberg, 1977).

We are neither willing nor competent to enter the highly technical controversies that currently abound in the field of intelligence and ability testing. When we speak of intelligence in this and subsequent chapters, we simply mean a score indicative of general intellectual functioning. We grant in advance that some intelligence measures we have used are rough and approximate. Many were obtained well before the more recent controversies about intelligence erupted, and they are, in any event, the best we could get, given all the other constraints at the time of the various studies.

Very few theories of leadership have paid attention to cognitive abilities, and most of the recent work has focused on cognitive complexity (e.g., Mitchell, 1970b; Harvey, Hunt, & Schroeder, 1961; Streufert & Swezy, 1986; Streufert, Streufert & Castore, 1968). These authors found that individuals differ in their ability to handle and integrate different concepts, as well as in their approach to leadership problems. At this point, the work appears to be promising, but it needs to be carried further before we know its place in leadership theory.

The literature relating the commonly accepted measures of intelligence to leadership performance is well summarized by such authoritative works as *Stogdill's Handbook of Leadership* (Bass, 1981), and various reviews of the literature (e.g., Campbell, Dunnette, Lawler, & Weick, 1970; Ghiselli, 1963; Korman, 1968; Mann, 1959; Stogdill, 1948). The basic conclusions drawn by these reviewers are:

1. Leader intelligence correlates positively but weakly with managerial effectiveness (r's ranging between .08 and .30, accounting for between less than 1 to 9 percent of the variance in effectiveness).

2. Intellectual ability correlates positively but not highly with leadership status. Reported median correlations fall between .20 and .30 and thus account for 4.5 to 10 percent of the variance.

3. Verbal intelligence is more highly correlated with leadership performance than is nonverbal intelligence.
4. The difference between intellectual abilities of leaders and group members is probably related in a slightly curvilinear manner to leadership effectiveness. Leaders who are somewhat brighter than their members tend to perform better than those who are either substantially below or substantially above their members in intelligence.

Our own studies support these findings. We have conducted research on a wide variety of groups in which correlations were obtained between the leader's intelligence and group performance, and we have used various measures of intelligence. These included the armed services' General Qualification Test, or the Multi-Aptitude Test, as well as the Wonderlic Personnel Test. The latter is a 12-minute test consisting of 50 items covering vocabulary, numerical, and logical problems, and has been extensively utilized in business settings. It correlates well with the usual measures of intellectual ability. One study by the U.S. Office of Personnel Management (Guion, 1965) reported a correlation between the Wonderlic and the Multi-Aptitude Scale of .87 and .86 in two samples of vocational trainees and similar results have been reported elsewhere.

Table 5.1 summarizes various correlations between leader intelligence and ratings of leader performance or group performance measures in our

Table 5.1. Correlations between Leader Intelligence and Organizational Performance in Various Studies

	Intelligence × Performance	n
Review by Stogdill (1974) of 17 studies	.28	
Review by Ghiselli (1966) of studies of:		
Executives	.29	+1000
Foremen	.24	+5000
Military leaders		
Squad leaders	−.04	158
Platoon sergeants	−.02	129
First sergeants	.16	41
Platoon leaders	.23	98
Infantry company commanders	.26	39
Infantry battallion staff officers	.16	41
Executive officers	.35	28
Company commanders	.19	44
Battalion staff	−.23	45
Coast Guard officers	−.02	130
Median	.16	

own research. As can be seen, these correlations are generally positive but low and insignificant.

The leader's intelligence also affects leader behavior and the members' reactions to the leader. It is related to the leader's activity, popularity, and participation (Zeleny, 1939). Crutchfield (1955) found a negative correlation between conformity and the Concept Mastery Test of −.51, and of −.63 between conformity and rated intellectual competence. While this relationship was not obtained by Simpson (1938), Crutchfield's results support Hollander's (1960) finding that leaders with relatively high intelligence are less dependent on others.

The research shows that intelligence seems to play a relatively minor role in determining leadership performance; it certainly does not play the major role one might expect. In addition, some tasks require intellectual effort while others require interpersonal skills or psychomotor abilities. Intelligent leaders should perform better on intellectually demanding tasks, but not necessarily on tasks requiring physical coordination or interpersonal skills. Several studies speak to this point.

LEADER INTELLIGENCE AND PERFORMANCE

Anderson and Fiedler (1964) experimentally compared the effects of participatory and supervisory leadership on group creativity. U.S. Navy ROTC cadets were assigned to four-man groups with a senior as leader and freshmen and sophomores as group members. In 15 groups the leader participated in the role of committee chairman. In the other 15 groups the leader was instructed to be a supervisor, that is, to restrict himself to praise and exhortation, procedural suggestions and evaluation. The leader also had the right to reject solutions which did not meet his standards.

Pretests included various creativity measures, as well as a 15-item intelligence scale. Each group performed four tasks: inventing stories based on Thematic Apperception Test (TAT) cards, finding alternative uses for a clothes hanger and a ruler, developing arguments for and against the use of dangerous military training exercises, and listing ways in which a person who does not possess particular talents could legally gain fame and immortality.

The TAT stories and the argument construction were interactive tasks; listing alternative uses and gaining immortality were coactive tasks. The correlations between performance and leader intelligence were in the opposite direction from those between performance and member intelligence. That is, when the correlations between leader intelligence and performance were positive, the correlations between member intelligence and performance tended to be negative. This finding was difficult to interpret at the time of this study and will be discussed in Chapter 13.

In general, intellectual ability of participating leaders contributed more than the intelligence of supervisory leaders in the case on the TAT task, which required a high degree of verbal facility. The intelligence of supervisory leaders contributed more to the group's performance on the Argument task which required a structured and logical solution. In other words, whether the participative or supervisory leaders contributed to the group product seemed to depend on the task. The more intelligent leaders contributed more ideas to the participative sessions, but they expressed more criticism in the supervisory condition.

MEMBERS' INTELLECTUAL ABILITIES AND PERFORMANCE

Most people assume that groups composed of intelligent and able group members will outperform groups composed of less intelligent and able members. After all, business, industry, and government agencies spend millions of dollars each year recruiting and selecting people on the basis of their abilities. We should expect, therefore, that member intelligence and other relevant abilities would correlate highly with group performance. However, the average correlations between member intelligence and ability scores and group performance have been quite low (e.g., McGrath & Altman, 1966). This suggests that group-member intelligence and ability do not play a major part in determining group performance or that many groups fail to utilize members' abilities.

The problem is of particular importance in light of the stress on participative management in recent years. Participative management makes sense only if group members' abilities contribute to group performance. If the intelligent and able members cannot use their abilities, we would not need to select people on the basis of their ability. And if the intellectually able group members are to be effectively utilized, we must try to identify the conditions under which this occurs.

Some writers have questioned whether leaders are at all necessary under certain conditions. Kerr and Jermier (1978) proposed, for example, that member abilities, professional commitment, and a structured task could substitute for leadership. While we would agree that member abilities as well as other factors mentioned by Kerr and Jermier are important, we find it difficult to believe that they could compensate or overshadow the leader's role. For example, a symphony orchestra meets all of Kerr and Jermier's conditions. The members of these orchestras perform a highly structured task with instructions provided by the score; the players are highly professional, and usually motivated and committed to their work. And yet the results of having an orchestra play without a competent conductor are proverbially bad if not disastrous. We know of no major orchestra that has managed to do without a conductor. This does not mean that substitutes for leadership do not exist but it suggests that these substitutes are likely to play a very limited role.

Other theorists (e.g., McGregor, 1960; Likert, 1961; Argyris, 1964) have taken the position that a participative type of leadership will improve performance by utilizing the talents and abilities of group members. Studies by Coch and French (1948), Lawrence and Smith (1955) and Misumi (1974) have generally supported this hypothesis. Others (e.g., Morse & Reimer, 1956; Vroom, 1959, 1960) have failed to find participative management to be universally beneficial.

Campbell, Dunnette, Lawler, and Weick (1970, p. 422) commented on this state of affairs: "In view of the far-reaching implications prescribed for these variables by many writers (e.g., Likert, 1967), it is surprising that the body of empirical research is so small and that practically no attention has been devoted to interactional affects." This statement is very appropriate. There is, indeed, no doubt of the presence of interactive effects and contingent relations among leader abilities, member abilities, and performance.

SUMMARY

There is evidence of a positive but very low relationship between leader intelligence and performance. This relationship is well documented in the literature and appears in our own studies.

The empirical literature contains very little research on the contribution of member abilities to performance. However, we should expect that interaction effects exist which could explain the abiding faith of managers and executives that the more intellectually able leaders and group members perform better than those who are less able. Since it is generally unwise to ignore institutional wisdom of long standing, we must look further for the role which intellectual abilities of leaders and members play in organizational performance.

PART TWO

THE CONTINGENCY MODEL AND DIRECTIVE LEADER BEHAVIOR

The second part of this book deals with the contingency model and its components, situational control and the personality attribute measured by the least preferred coworker (LPC) scale. As we shall see later, these form an important basis for understanding the role of directive behavior in cognitive resource theory.

Most of the material in Chapters 6 to 9 has been presented in previous papers and the reader who is well acquainted with the contingency model literature may wish to skim these chapters.

CHAPTER SIX

Situational Control

The concepts of power and influence are intimately related to the concept of leadership, and for many writers in the field, the exercise of power is at the very heart of the leadership process (see the review by Hollander and Julian, 1970). In effect, the leader's power and influence determine the degree to which the leader can implement plans, decisions, and action strategies. It is also clear that power, influence, and control derive from the leadership situation. This chapter discusses the major components of the leader's "situational control" and their measurement.

Situational control, as we shall see later, is a major determinant of the leader's behavior. Although psychologists' approach to predicting behavior has concentrated on personality rather than environment, how we behave is determined more by the environment than by personality. This is most fortunate since it makes people's behavior in everyday life reasonably predictable: we ski in winter and swim in summer, we enter houses through doors rather than windows, and in most countries we drive on the right side of the street if we want to survive the day. It is not surprising, therefore, that the leadership environment should play a major part in determining how leaders behave.

One important aspect of the environment is its effect on our feeling of security. When the effects of the environment are unpredictable, we feel anxious and out of control. Accounts of being caught in a dense fog, of solo trips across the ocean or the desert, or of experiences in sensory deprivation studies frequently report disorientation and anxiety. And while it is true that a highly structured environment does not guarantee low anxiety, an environment which lacks structure (e.g., dense fog, complete darkness) generally creates feelings of insecurity, unease, and lack of control.

In trying to define the leadership situation, we are therefore concerned with the leader's "situational control." High control provides the feeling that we can get what we want. If this happens to be to accomplish the task, then there is no need to worry about successfully completing the job. Insecurity is likely to occur when the task outcome is uncertain. What makes the leader certain that the job will be done? The leader must answer three important questions. First, "Will the group members do what I tell them, are they reliable and do they support me?" Second, "Do I know what I am supposed to do, and how the job is to be done?" Finally, "Do I have the support and backing of the "big boss" and the organization in dealing with subordinates?"

LEADER–MEMBER RELATIONS

The most important element in situational control is the group members' support. We feel a lot more comfortable and relaxed when we know that we can depend on our subordinates. It is difficult to feel relaxed if we cannot be sure that our orders and directions are carried out. If the subordinates are unreliable, the leader is likely to worry about subordinates' activities and to supervise their work closely.

A number of studies have demonstrated that the leader–member relations (LMR) dimension is the single most important factor in determining situational control. Beach and Beach (1978) gave subjects a set of hypothetical tasks which were to be conducted when leader–member relations were good or poor, the task was structured or unstructured, and position power was high or low. Subjects felt most confident in completing a task when the group members were supportive. Nebeker (1975) showed that supervisors had high confidence in their work-related decisions when they rated their subordinates as supportive, and Mitchell (1970a) found the leader–member relations dimension to be the most important factor in a study of group decision making.

The importance of the leader–member relationship is dramatically demonstrated by charismatic leadership. Weber (1946) proposed that the "personal magnetism" of these leaders makes others follow them blindly even to the point of self-destruction. This is somewhat mindboggling, since we usually think of self-preservation to be the most basic instinct in human existence. And yet numerous instances throughout history have supported this assertion.

House (1977) listed three elements of charismatic leadership: (a) a clear set of goals and a sense of their value, (b) an unshakable faith in the necessity of achieving these goals, and (c) the ability to communicate the goals and the certainty of attaining them. These are not the only factors, however. While we usually think of charismatic leadership as a personal attribute, this was not Weber's (1946) intent. Weber saw charisma, the

Greek word for gift, at least in part as generated by the trappings of office, the apparent ominscience derived from having prior information, and the aura of infallibility which comes from being able to select one's battleground, and hence seeming to take chances and winning against overwhelming odds. Hitler's defiance of the world in his successful invasions of the Saar, of Austria, and of Czechoslovakia are instances of this type.

The pomp and ceremony of such institutions as monarchies, the church, and the military are examples of environmental props for enhancing charismatic leadership. The charismatic leader knows how to make effective use of these dramatic symbols of power to build a strong following. Leaders who enjoy good relations with group members, even though they may not have much charisma, need little else to make the group bend to their will. If subordinates are already eager to comply, they will accept the leader's definition of the task and methods for accomplishing it.

Measurement of Leader–Member Relations

Several scales have been developed in the past 20 years for measuring leader–member relations in a convenient and reliable way. The scale most frequently used in our earlier studies asked the subjects to complete a group atmosphere (GA) rating. The GA scale usually consists of 10 bipolar items (e.g., enthusiastic–unenthusiastic, lots of fun–serious, helpful–unhelpful, productive–nonproductive, close–distant, cooperative–uncooperative, supportive–hostile, boring–interesting, and successful–unsuccessful). The GA score is the sum of the 10 items. Split-half reliabilities range from .92 to .95 (e.g., Meuwese, 1964; Posthuma, 1970).

A briefer leader–member relations scale (LMR) was developed in conjunction with a leadership training program. This scale is shown in Figure 6.1. The split-half reliability of this scale is moderately high (.64) from a sample of 66 military leaders ($p < .01$; Fiedler & Mahar, 1979). A sample of average leader–member relations scores are shown in Table 6.1, to indicate their range. The average score is approximately 32 and, although the means may seem to differ from organization to organization, the variances are large, and differences between samples are not significant.

A third method for measuring leader–member relations is based on sociometric indices indicating the members' acceptance of the leader. These preference ratings ask group members to identify, for example, a member of the group whom they would most like to have as their leader, or who is most influential.

Sociometric methods for identifying whether the leader is the most accepted member of the group provide reasonably satisfactory results even though the correlations between the leader's GA ratings and the members' sociometric preference choices or LMR scores tend to be low. Whether the group members' or the leader's estimate of leader–member relations is a better index of situational control seems to depend on the

Circle the number which best represents your response to each item.	Strongly Agree	Agree	Neither Agree Nor Disagree	Disagree	Strongly Disagree
1. The people I supervise have trouble getting along with each other.	1	2	3	4	5
2. My subordinates are reliable and trustworthy.	5	4	3	2	1
3. There seems to be a friendly atmosphere among the people I supervise.	5	4	3	2	1
4. My subordinates always cooperate with me in getting the job done.	5	4	3	2	1
5. There is friction between my subordinates and myself.	1	2	3	4	5
6. My subordinates give me a good deal of help and support in getting the job done.	5	4	3	2	1
7. The people I supervise work well together in getting the job done.	5	4	3	2	1
8. I have good relations with the people I supervise.	5	4	3	2	1
Total Score					

Figure 6.1. Leader–member relations scale. [Reprinted with permission from F. E. Fiedler & M. M. Chemers (1984). *Improving leadership effectiveness: The leader match concept*, 2nd ed. New York: Wiley.]

degree to which the group can cause the leader anxiety and stress. Leader–member relations scores are typically unrelated to the other elements of situational control or to such personality measures as intelligence (Fiedler, 1967).

Changes in Group Atmosphere Scores. As we would expect, relations between leaders and group members change over time. This has been shown by a study of 138 army squad leaders who were subjects in a longitudinal study (Bons & Fiedler, 1976). GA scores were obtained at the beginning and again at the end of a six to eight month training cycle. The test–retest correlation for this sample was only .29, indicating that the climate of these small task groups changed considerably over the relatively short time these men were together. The stability of GA scores will, of course, depend on the nature of the group.

Interpretation of Leader–Member Relations

Several studies have considered the relationship between leader–member relations and group atmosphere scales. In some of our studies, the correlations between the group atmosphere ratings as perceived by the leader and as perceived by their followers have been fairly high; in others they have been relatively low. In the squad leader study (Fiedler & Leister, 1977), for example, the correlation, while highly significant, was only .23 ($n = 158$, $p < .01$). Further research is obviously needed to determine why the perception of group climate by leaders and followers is similar in some groups but not others.

Table 6.1. Average Leader–Member Relations Scores in Various Population Samples

Job Title	LMR Score
Battalion chiefs Urban fire department	29.87
National Guard Senior Officers	32.45
Administrators City Treasurer's Office	29.50
Principals Public Schools	32.94
Head nurses United States and Canada	21.04
Nurse supervisors United States	31.36
Hotel managers	32.57
Second level managers Mexico	34.55
State executives reporting to the Governor	34.18
Assistant State Executives	32.00
Company commanders U.S. Army	32.16
Battalion staff officers U.S. Army	33.61
Captains Urban fire department	29.90
Lieutenants Urban fire department	30.98
Fire Fighters Urban fire department	31.27

Source: Reprinted with permission from F. E. Fiedler & M. M. Chemers (1984). *Improving leadership effectiveness: The leader match concept,* 2nd ed. New York: Wiley.

Summary

Leader–member relations constitute the most important element in determining the leader's control and influence in the group. Different measures of leader–member relations scales have high internal consistency but not very high intercorrelation. There is some question, then, about the construct validity of group climate. Nonetheless, these measures appear to be important and useful indices for identifying the conditions under which different types of leaders tend to perform effectively.

THE TASK

The second important component of situational control is the structure of the task. By "task structure" we mean the degree to which the task is clearly spelled out as to goals, methods, and standards of performance. A vaguely defined, ambiguous task creates uncertainty and thus decreases the leader's situational control. If you aren't told what to do, it's difficult to know whether you'll be successful in getting it done. Task structure, therefore, has considerable importance for the leader's ability to control the group.

If a construction foreman is told to "put up a shed of some sort somewhere near the construction site," it is up to the foreman to decide where to place the shed, how big it is to be, and how it is to be constructed. Unless the foreman knows what the boss really has in mind, he is likely to agonize over these questions. What will the boss say if the shed is erected on Site A rather than B? Is this too far or too close to the construction site, should it have a window, and so on? No matter what the foreman decides, the boss might well say, "Why ever did you do *that?* Why didn't you make it bigger (or smaller)? Do I have to spell out everything?" If the foreman has a blueprint in hand, and a set of specifications, there is no problem. He knows exactly what to do and how to do it, and the blueprint will detail what the shed should look like when it is done. The foreman will certainly get no argument from subordinates if there is a blueprint, and the boss will not be able to complain if the foreman follows all the instructions. In other words, the blueprint and specification sheet give the foreman considerable control over the eventual outcome of the job.

Many jobs do not provide much structure. Committees, panels, boards, and other policy- and decision-making groups usually perform highly unstructured tasks that have no clearly specifiable outcome, no "best" method, and no way in which the ultimate success of the group's deliberations can be judged with any confidence. How can you tell, for example, that a particular school policy will result in better education five or ten years later? In the contingency model we have adopted Shaw's (1963, 1973) taxonomy to measure four dimensions of task structure. These are goal clarity, goal–path multiplicity, solution specificity, and decision verifiability. Each of these dimensions is described in turn.

Goal Clarity. The first requirement of task structure is a clearly defined assignment. It is difficult to succeed if you don't know what you are supposed to do. Surprisingly, many tasks are assigned without specified goals or standards that the completed task has to meet. Among the many examples of this type are tasks given to hotel, restaurant, or repair shop managers ("We want you to improve service") or to school administrators ("See to it that our children learn something"), or to policy- and decision-making groups ("Decide what's best to do").

In some cases, of course, it is not possible to state what the exact goals are or what standards will be used to judge performance. In many other cases, however, defining goals requires time and effort that the managers at higher organizational levels are not always willing to give (e.g., to determine specifically how "good service" is to be defined, and by what particular criteria it will be judged).

Goal–Path Multiplicity. A second aspect of task structure concerns the methods to be employed. For many jobs (e.g., assembling an engine) there is only one accepted method. Other jobs can be performed in innumerable ways: the creation of a video program, the development of a new process for manufacturing a product, devising a new sales campaign, or developing a new policy. If the job can be performed in only one way, and if the prescribed method is followed, a successful outcome is virtually assured. If there is no prescribed method, time may be wasted, and the group will run into blind alleys. In fact, the job may never get done.

Solution Specificity. A third element of task structure is the specification of how many different outcomes are acceptable. There is only one successful outcome to an appendicitis operation: the infected appendix is removed and the patient recovers. There are numerous possible outcomes to writing a good television script: should it be a comedy, a farce, or a documentary? Should a picnic have organized games, a potluck dinner, a band, and dancing? If the outcome is not specified, there is considerable uncertainty about how to define the task, and how it will be judged.

Decision Verifiability. While working on an important task, we often want to know if we are on the right track. A job that permits periodic checks to assure that everything is going according to plan creates less anxiety than one without these milestones. Having to go back to the drawing board may be annoying or boring, but it is not anxiety-arousing. The task of assembling an engine or a piece of electrical equipment ordinarily provides intermediate tests to determine the progress of the work. These intermediate tests give the leader control over the task as well as over the group. In contrast, running a social work agency or developing a new five-year plan provides few checks that would allow course corrections along the way.

Measurement of Task Structure

A scale for measuring task structure is shown in Figure 6.2. The four subscales spell out each of Shaw's (1973, 1963) four dimensions of task structure. These subscales are not intended to be independent: A task

Circle the number in the appropriate column	Usually True	Sometimes True	Seldom True
Is the goal clearly stated or known?			
1. Is there a blueprint, picture, model or detailed description available of the finished product or service?	2	1	0
2. Is there a person available to advise and give a description of the finished product or service, or how the job should be done?	2	1	0
Is there only one way to accomplish the task?			
3. Is there a step-by-step procedure, or a standard operating procedure which indicates in detail the process which is to be followed?	2	1	0
4. Is there a specific way to subdivide the task into separate parts or steps?	2	1	0
5. Are there some ways which are clearly recognized as better than others for performing this task?	2	1	0
Is there only one correct answer or solution?			
6. Is it obvious when the task is finished and the correct solution has been found?	2	1	0
7. Is there a book, manual, or job description which indicates the best solution or the best outcome for the task?	2	1	0
Is it easy to check whether the job was done right?			
8. Is there a generally agreed upon understanding about the standards the particular product or service has to meet to be considered acceptable?	2	1	0
9. Is the evaluation of this task generally made on some quantitative basis?	2	1	0
10. Can the leader and the goup find out how well the task has been accomplished in enough time to improve future performance?	2	1	0

Figure 6.2. Task structure rating scale. [Reprinted with permission from F. E. Fiedler & M. M. Chemers (1984). *Improving leadership effectiveness: The Leader Match Concept*, 2nd ed. New York: Wiley.]

Table 6.2. Means of Task Structure Ratings for Various Population Samples

Job Title	Task Structure[a]
Hotel managers	15.88
Head nurses United States and Canada	14.61
Second level managers Mexican conglomerate	13.98
Company commanders U.S. Army	12.46
Battalion staff officers U.S. Army	12.38
Fire fighters Urban fire department	11.54
Principals Public school	10.86
National Guard senior officers Headquarters staff	9.50
Lieutenants Urban fire department	9.37
Captains Urban fire department	8.25
Battalion chief Urban fire department	8.13
Administrators City treasurer's office	7.75
State executives Second level	6.36
State executives Reporting to the Governor	6.35
Nurse Supervisors Third level managers, United States	6.15

Source: Reprinted with permission from F. E. Fiedler & M. M. Chemers (1984). *Improving leadership effectiveness: The leader match concept*, 2nd ed. New York: Wiley.
[a] High scores indicate high task structure.

which can be performed by a multiplicity of methods also tends to have a variety of possible outcomes and few milestones by which to measure progress. The split-half reliability of this scale, which has been used extensively in leadership training, was .77 (Fiedler & Mahar, 1979a). While there are other methods for categorizing tasks, our main concern here is with the uncertainty and anxiety the task is likely to engender in the leader. A job assignment in which there is a clear goal, only one approved method for performing it, and one right solution that can be objectively verified obviously gives the leader assurance that the task can be accomplished by simply following instructions. In these terms, the structured task gives the leader control over the outcome.* Table 6.2 lists

* For an equal-appearing interval scale for measuring task structure by J. G. Hunt, see Appendix D in Fiedler (1967).

the task structure scores for various populations samples with which we have had experience. We do not know the generalizability of these data, but list them here only to provide some reference points for the range of task structure scores which can be expected in various organizations.

POSITION POWER

The third major dimension of situational control is the power the organization confers on the leader for the purpose of getting the job done. This is the most obvious component for giving a leader control over the members of the group. However, the actual power of a leader is, in most cases, rather limited. Regardless of how much power the leader might have in theory, in practice it is difficult to maintain absolute control over recalcitrant subordinates. This is only too clear to anyone in charge of a prison. In addition, subordinates have a certain amount of "counterpower" over leaders. There are innumerable ways in which subordinates can frustrate a leader, from playing dumb (being "passive-aggressive") to getting the leader into trouble. President Nixon's resignation was forced at the final stage by the refusal of his staff to support him further.

We must also note that the leader's own boss plays an important part in determining the degree of the leader's power. A boss who backs subordinate leaders provides them with a considerable number of options in dealing with their groups. The ability to reward and punish must frequently be legitimized by the leader's immediate superior. If this boss does not back the subordinate leader, the group soon knows that it has a paper tiger at its head, and that the real authority lies with the person at the next higher level.

It is also true that many jobs simply do not allow the leader to have high position power. This is the case even in such authoritarian organizations as the military service. A court-martial might have a general as the presiding officer and a sergeant as its lowest ranking member. But military regulations explicitly prohibit the presiding officer from suggesting or telling the lower ranking members how to vote or to interfere with their attempts to get at the facts. (That these rules may be broken on occasion is not the point.) Similar rules apply to legislative bodies, to committees, and to most decision- and policy-making groups. Again, the power of the presiding officer is explicitly limited by various bylaws of the organization and such manuals as *Robert's Rules of Parliamentary Law and Order* (1979).

Position power generally implies the ability to reward and to punish. This is difficult to do unless the leader understands how the task should be done and when it has been done correctly. Moreover, traditions, customs, and precedent govern to a great extent how the leader can discipline subordinates. It is simply not acceptable in certain organizations to fire an old employee. Union rules or custom may prohibit the supervisor from docking employees for being less than 10 minutes late, and in some organizations certain infractions are routinely overlooked.

Despite all the constraints, most leaders have high position power. Even the chairman of a volunteer committee has considerable power over group members. True, group members could walk out at any time, or simply refuse to cooperate, but a group rarely overturns a ruling by the chair or rebels against the leader. Nor do we often see the refusal of group members to go along with a chair's legitimate request (e.g., for approving an agenda, for silence, for remaining in session or adjourning).

The degree to which even an appointed leader is accepted by members of the group is easily illustrated. In three different organizations, we asked group members to indicate whom, in the group, they would most like to have as a leader if they were to be transferred and whom they considered most qualified to lead. The appointed, formal leaders were most chosen by 52 percent of the members in airforce bomber crews, in 74 percent of tank crews, and by 72 percent of the senior staff in consumer sales cooperatives (Fiedler, 1958).

Measuring Position Power

What are the indices of position power? Leaders with power usually have a special title to indicate their rank, such as president, chairman, foreman, superintendent, or captain. The title provides social recognition that the particular person has a special leadership function and role.

A second and more important characteristic of position power is the leader's right to recommend or dispense reward and punishment. A reward is not necessarily limited to a pay raise or a promotion, nor is punishment limited to firing, demotion, or lower pay. We need to think of a potential reward as anything a subordinate would like. This could include a desk near the window, a new wastepaper basket, or lunch with the boss. A penalty consists of anything a person does not like: a desk in a dark corner of the office, an unpleasant assignment, or just being ignored.

The leader's position power is also related to the group's physical distance to the next higher boss. A branch manager in the wilds of the Rocky Mountains has more position power than the manager of a branch office in the company headquarters building. It is important to keep these distinctions in mind. We cannot reduce research findings to a neat formula or a scale without doing some violence to reality.

Figure 6.3 shows the scale used in a number of our studies and Table 6.3 shows the position power ratings given by members of various samples with which we have worked. Again, these ratings, for example, of fire department officers or of nurses, are not necessarily representative of all fire departments, or all nurses.

Circle the number which best represents your answer.

1. Can the leader directly or by recommendation administer rewards and punishments to subordinates?

2	1	0
Can act directly or can recommend with high effectiveness	Can recommend but with mixed results	No

2. Can the leader directly or by recommendation affect the promotion, demotion, hiring or firing of subordinates?

2	1	0
Can act directly or can recommend with high effectiveness	Can recommend but with mixed results	No

3. Does the leader have the knowledge necessary to assign tasks to subordinates and instruct them in task completion?

2	1	0
Yes	Sometimes or in some aspects	No

4. Is it the leader's job to evaluate the performance of subordinates?

2	1	0
Yes	Sometimes or in some aspects	No

5. Has the leader been given some official title of authority by the organization (e.g., foreman, department head, platoon leader)?

2	0
Yes	No

Total

Figure 6.3. Position power rating scale. [Reprinted with permission from F. E. Fiedler & M. M. Chemers (1984). *Improving leadership effectiveness: The leader match concept*, 2nd ed. New York: Wiley.]

**Table 6.3. Position Power Scores Obtained
from Various Occupational Group Samples**

Job Title	Position Power Score
Head nurses	9.48
United States and Canada	
Second level managers	9.46
Mexico	
National Guard senior officers	9.2
Hotel managers	9.03
Company commanders	8.83
U.S. Army	
State executives reporting to	
the Governor	8.79
Assistant state executives	8.38
Battalion chiefs	8.25
Urban fire department	
Principals	8.08
Public school	
Captains	8.05
Urban fire department	
Lieutenants	8.0
Urban fire department	
Battalion staff officers	7.92
U.S. Army	
Fire fighters	6.6
Urban fire department	

Source: Reprinted with permission from F. E. Fiedler &
M. M. Chemers (1984). *Improving leadership effectiveness:
The leader match concept,* 2nd ed. New York: Wiley.

THE MEASUREMENT OF SITUATIONAL CONTROL

Early research on the contingency model scaled situational control by
dividing the groups in a particular study at the median into an upper
and lower half on the basis of leader–member relations (GA or LMR),
task structure (TS), and position power (PP). Dividing the sample of
groups at the median on each of the three measures yielded eight cells,
or "octants" for determining degrees of situational control (see Figure
6.4).

Very high situational control (Octant 1) means, for example, that the
leader has good relations with the group, a highly structured task, and
high position power. Low situational control (Octant 7) indicates that the
leader has low LMR, low TS, and high PP. Figure 6.4 in effect weights
the three components in a 4:2:1 ratio, and this weighting is, of course,
open to question. In fact, this weighting scheme was proposed before a
sufficient number of groups were available to base the weights on empirical

evidence. It was, therefore, a considerable surprise that a number of studies have found these weights to be reasonably close to the mark. This type of scaling has the obvious disadvantage however of not allowing for intermediate degrees of leader–member relations, task structure, or position power.

Nebeker (1975) developed a continuous measure of situational control. He showed that high situational control can be interpreted as high confidence in what one proposes to do (low decision uncertainty). Nebeker had subjects estimate the probability that certain behaviors, such as criticizing poor work, supervising, and instructing, would have the desired results when dealing with subordinates in a given situation. Using 43 naval aviation shop foremen, Nebeker (1975) found a correlation of $-.56$ ($n = 43, p < .01$) between situational control scales and decision uncertainty, and a correlation of $-.30$ ($p < .05$) between perceived control and decision uncertainty. (The greater the certainty, the higher the situational control.)

In a second study of 49 public works managers, the correlation between situational control and decision uncertainty was $-.25$ ($p < .05$) and between situational control and perceived control and influence $.55$ ($p < .01$). Most importantly, Nebeker's (1975) study showed that the 4:2:1 ratio was as good as the empirical weights obtained from a multiple regression study of foremen and middle managers. Nebeker computed multiple regressions in which LMR, TS, and PP were used to predict decision uncertainty. He compared these with the zero-order coefficients obtained by the theoretical combination. In both studies, the actual coefficients obtained were equivalent for either method ($r = .56$ vs. $R = .58$ in one study and $r = .40$ vs. $R = .39$ in the other).

He concluded on the basis of these findings that the zero-order coefficients account for as much of the variance as do the multiple regression coefficients, and that

> Such a comparison actually favors the theoretical combination, since the multiple regression solution can capitalize on error variance. Fiedler's theoretical combination of the component variables of situational favorability is about as close to optimal in predicting uncertainty as could possibly be expected.*

Nebeker suggested, therefore, measuring that situational control by using the formula

$$\text{situational control} = (4 \times \text{LMR}) + (2 \times \text{TS}) + \text{PP}$$

where LMR, TS and PP are standardized scores of these measures.

* Reprinted with permission from D. Nebeker (1975). Situation favorability and perceived environmental uncertainty: An integrative study. *Administrative Science Quarterly*, 20, 281–294. Copyright Administrative Science Quarterly.

LMR	High				Low			
TS	High		Low		High		Low	
PP	High	Low	High	Low	High	Low	High	Low
	1	2	3	4	5	6	7	8
	High control		Moderate control				Low control	

Figure 6.4. Situational control scale determined by high or low leader–member relations, task structure, and position power.

A further study by Mai-Dalton (1975) found an almost identical relationship between uncertainty and situational control. She investigated the effect of changing situational control on leader behavior under different conditions. The leaders had either high or low position power, and either did or did not receive training on how to approach an in-basket test (a test of managerial skills in which the subject is required to sort through and respond to a set of tasks and requests in a simulated managerial job). There were thus four levels of situational control—training-high position power; training-low position power; no training-high position power; no training-low position power. Subjects also completed a group atmosphere scale and rated the degree of uncertainty they felt about being able to complete the task. Their uncertainty rating was correlated with situational control components. The correlations between uncertainty and each of the three components were $-.32$ for group atmosphere, $-.35$ for task structure, and $-.41$ for position power. The multiple regression of these variables on uncertainty was $R = .54$ ($p < .01$), almost identical to the results reported by Nebeker (1975).

It should be clear, of course, that the ratio 4:2:1 for leader–member relations, task structure, and position power will not be obtained in all situations. Under some conditions, position power or task structure will outweigh leader–member relations. It is unlikely, for example, that Ghengis Khan needed good leader–member relations to have high situational control.

One example in our research is the cross-cultural group in which members are not fluent in each other's language or knowledgeable about each other's culture. A group of this type tends to seem threatening to the leader and to its members since it is easy to say the wrong thing without intending to do so. Moreover, it is also often possible that members do not understand the leader's instructions or do not wish to understand the leader's orders.

A group of this type is very difficult to control, especially when the members of one faction are antagonistic toward those of another faction. We also found in several studies (e.g., Fiedler, O'Brien, & Ilgen, 1969; Meuwese & Fiedler, 1965) that stressful conditions, and especially job stress, have similar effects to those of situational control. This is understandable when we recall that the stressful situation typically implies uncertainty and lack of control.

SITUATIONAL CONTROL AND PERFORMANCE

One would expect that leadership performance would be directly affected by situational control, that leaders with high control would perform substantially better than those with poor situational control. This is not so in most cases. A number of studies (e.g., Chemers, Rice, Sundstrom, & Butler, 1975; Csoka & Fiedler, 1972; Fiedler, 1972) have shown that groups in which the leader has high or low situational control are about equally effective. This is a very important point since it shows that the effect of decreasing situational control is not tantamount to decreasing leadership performance or organizational effectiveness.

An illustration of this point comes from a laboratory experiment (Fiedler, Meuwese, & Donk, 1961) on Dutch college students assigned to 32 groups. Half of these groups were homogeneous and half were heterogeneous in religious composition, that is, all Catholic members, all Calvinist members, or half the members from each denomination. (Denomination is an important social factor in the Netherlands.) The group climate in the heterogeneous groups was substantially less harmonious than in homogeneous groups. Furthermore, in half the groups the leader had relatively higher position power than in the other half of the groups, that is, one half had appointed leaders while the other worked in an emergent leadership situation. Table 6.4 shows the groups in order of their situational control. The results demonstrate that the groups in which leaders had low situational control were on the average no less effective than the groups in which situational control was high. (Mean differences are not significant.)

Although there have been isolated studies in which the performance of groups in the low-control situations was poorer than those in the high-control situation, the results of the Dutch study are quite representative of other findings. Chapter 12 describes five different studies with groups rated as having high, moderate, or low situational control. In none of these studies did we find significant differences between mean performance in the relatively higher and lower situational control conditions.

A number of critics (e.g., Ashour, 1973a,b; Graen, Alvares, Orris, & Martella, 1970) have taken the contingency model to task for being too flexible in the operational definitions of the situational control dimensions. They are, of course, correct in contending that the operational definitions of situational control have differed, depending on the measures which could be obtained, and on the type of group which had been studied. Without doubt, we need a measure of situational control which is absolute in the sense of being applicable to any group under any conditions (see Rice & Kastenbaum, 1983). Whether the flexible definition of situational

**Table 6.4. Effectiveness of Dutch Groups Operating
under Different Conditions of Situational Control**

Compositon	Leadership	Situational Control	Mean Performance
Homogeneous	Formal	High	105.28
Homogeneous	Informal	Moderate	87.50
Heterogeneous	Formal	Moderate	116.62
Heterogeneous	Informal	Low	105.75

control is necessarily bad is another question. The well-known philosopher of science Abraham Kaplan (1964) (cited by Landman & Manis in Berkowitz, 1983, p. 107) states,

> The demand for exactness of meaning and for precise definition of terms can have a pernicious effect, as I believe it often has had in behavior science. . . . Tolerance of ambiguity is as important for creativity in science as it is anywhere else. (pp. 70–71)

SUMMARY

In conclusion, this chapter discussed the concept of situational control. It presented methods for measuring leader–member relations, task structure, and position power, and for combining these measures into a single situational control score. The theoretical weighting of the components of situational control is appropriate for typical groups, but it is clear that these weights have to be modified for special conditions. Alternative methods for measuring situational control have been used and give predicted results.

CHAPTER SEVEN

The Leader's Personality and the Least Preferred Coworker Score

Most psychological theories see the leader as influencing the team's performance by behaving in two sets of ways (e.g., House, 1971; Vroom and Yetton, 1973). Principally, the leader can concentrate on the task, emphasize group performance, and assign members their role in the group and their jobs; and he or she can focus on maintaining the group's morale, making the group attractive, and motivating the group members to work with one another in the accomplishment of the task. The focus has thus been on leader behavior rather than on leader personality. The personality measure of the Contingency Model is measured with the Least Preferred Coworker (LPC) Score, which has been the object of considerable controversy. This chapter briefly describes the scale, its psychometric properties, and its meaning.

THE LEAST PREFERRED COWORKER SCORE (LPC)

The LPC score is obtained by first asking an individual to think of all the people with whom he or she has ever worked—these may be members of the present work group or those with whom he or she worked many years ago. The least preferred coworker need not be someone who is personally disliked, but it must be the one person with whom it was most difficult to work, and with whom the respondent, therefore, would least like to work again. Note that there can be only one person who qualifies for this dubious honor.

The Least Preferred Coworker is described on a bipolar eight-point scale bounded by descriptive personality adjectives. The instructions and the complete scale are shown in Figure 7.1.

The LPC score is the sum of the 18 items. By convention, the more positive, "good" end of the scale is always given a score of 8. Although scales of varying lengths have been used in the early research, during

Instructions for completing the LPC scale:

Throughout your life you have worked in many groups with a wide variety of different people—on your job, in social clubs, in church organizations, in volunteer groups, on athletic teams, and in many others. You probably found working with most of your coworkers quite easy, but working with others may have been very difficult or all but impossible.

Now, think of *all the people* with whom you have ever worked. Next, think of the *one person in your life* with whom you could work least well. This individual may or may not be the person you also disliked most. It must be the one person with whom you had the most difficulty getting a job done, the one single individual with whom you would least want to work. This person is called your "Least Preferred Coworker" (LPC).

On the scale below, describe this person by placing an "X" in the appropriate space. The scale consists of pairs of words which are opposite in meaning, such as Very Neat and Very Untidy. Between each pair of words are eight spaces which form the following scale:

Very									Very
Neat	__ :	__ :	__ :	__ :	__ :	__ :	__ :	__	Untidy
	8	7	6	5	4	3	2	1	

Think of those eight spaces as steps which range from one extreme to the other. Thus, if you ordinarily think that this least preferred coworker is quite neat you would write an "X" in the space marked 7, like this:

Very									Very
Neat	__ :	__ :	__ :	__ :	__ :	__ :	__ :	__	Untidy
	8	7	6	5	4	3	2	1	
	Very Neat	Quite Neat	Some-what Neat	Slightly Neat	Slightly Untidy	Some-what Untidy	Quite Untidy	Very Untidy	

However, if you ordinarily think of this person as being only slightly neat, you would put your "X" in space 5. If you think of this person as very untidy (not neat), you would put your "X" in space 1.

Sometimes the scale will run in the other direction, as shown below:

Frustrating									Helpful
	__ :	__ :	__ :	__ :	__ :	__ :	__ :	__	
	1	2	3	4	5	6	7	8	

Before you mark your "X," look at the words at both ends of the line. There are no right or wrong answers. Work rapidly; your first answer is likely to be the best. Do not omit any items, and mark each item only once. Think of a real person in your experience, not an imaginary character. Remember, it is not necessarily the person whom you liked least, but the person with whom it is (or was) most difficult to work. Ignore the scoring column on the right margin of the page for now.

Now use the scale to describe the person with whom you can work least well.

Figure 7.1. LPC scale and instructions for completing the scale. [Reprinted with permission from F. E. Fiedler, & M. M. Chemers (1984). *Improving leadership effectiveness: The leader match concept.* 2nd ed. New York: Wiley.]

Least Preferred Coworker (LPC) Scale

Pleasant	__ : __ : __ : __ : __ : __ : __ : __	Unpleasant	__
	8 7 6 5 4 3 2 1		

Pleasant __:__:__:__:__:__:__:__ Unpleasant __
       8 7 6 5 4 3 2 1

Friendly __:__:__:__:__:__:__:__ Unfriendly __
      8 7 6 5 4 3 2 1

Rejecting __:__:__:__:__:__:__:__ Accepting __
      1 2 3 4 5 6 7 8

Tense __:__:__:__:__:__:__:__ Relaxed __
      1 2 3 4 5 6 7 8

Distant __:__:__:__:__:__:__:__ Close __
      1 2 3 4 5 6 7 8

Cold __:__:__:__:__:__:__:__ Warm __
      1 2 3 4 5 6 7 8

Supportive __:__:__:__:__:__:__:__ Hostile __
      8 7 6 5 4 3 2 1

Boring __:__:__:__:__:__:__:__ Interesting __
      1 2 3 4 5 6 7 8

Quarrelsome __:__:__:__:__:__:__:__ Harmonious __
      1 2 3 4 5 6 7 8

Gloomy __:__:__:__:__:__:__:__ Cheerful __
      1 2 3 4 5 6 7 8

Open __:__:__:__:__:__:__:__ Guarded __
      8 7 6 5 4 3 2 1

Backbiting __:__:__:__:__:__:__:__ Loyal __
      1 2 3 4 5 6 7 8

Untrustworthy __:__:__:__:__:__:__:__ Trustworthy __
      1 2 3 4 5 6 7 8

Considerate __:__:__:__:__:__:__:__ Inconsiderate __
      8 7 6 5 4 3 2 1

Nasty __:__:__:__:__:__:__:__ Nice __
      1 2 3 4 5 6 7 8

Agreeable __:__:__:__:__:__:__:__ Disagreeable __
      8 7 6 5 4 3 2 1

Insincere __:__:__:__:__:__:__:__ Sincere __
      1 2 3 4 5 6 7 8

Kind __:__:__:__:__:__:__:__ Unkind __
      8 7 6 5 4 3 2 1

SUM __

Figure 7.1 (*continued*)

the past 10 years we have used the 18-item scale, shown in Figure 7.1. The average item mean of the scale is 3.71, with a standard deviation of 1.05 (Posthuma, 1970) and based on 2014 cases from a wide variety of population samples. In an analysis of the most recent scale, Fiedler established norms based on 898 cases with a mean and standard deviation of 68.75 and 21.8. Using these most recent norms, a score of 73 or above is defined as high; a score of 63 or less is defined as low. Not surprisingly, we know a good deal more about the high and the low LPC persons than about those in the middle category (Fiedler & Chemers, 1984).

History of the Score

The LPC score had its serendipitous origin in an attempt to develop a measure of diagnostic and therapeutic competence of clinical psychologists, using Stephenson's (1953) Q-technique (Fiedler, 1951). It seemed reasonable to assume that a competent clinical psychologist would be able to predict the self-concept of a patient on the basis of various tests and interviews.

The patient was given a set of cards that listed various personality adjectives and characteristics. The patient then made a self-description by sorting these cards into categories ranging from most to least characteristic of himself or herself. The clinician then attempted to sort the same adjectives in order to predict the patient's self-concept. Unfortunately, most clinicians were not able to do so reliably. They did, however, reliably rate patients as similar or as dissimilar to themselves; this measure was called the "Assumed Similarity." Moreover, the degree to which clinicians assumed similarity between themselves and their patients correlated significantly (.58) with their own reputed competence as therapists (Fiedler, 1951).

A subsequent study asked fraternity members to rate themselves, and then to predict the self-ratings of their most and least liked fraternity brother (Fiedler, Warrington, & Blaisdell, 1952). As expected, members rated the most liked person as more similar than the least liked person. The assumed similarity score was, therefore, interpreted as reflecting psychological warmth or closeness. Subsequent studies conducted on leadership in small groups showed that there was very little variation in the similarity assumed to best liked or preferred others. Rather, the variation and the concomitant reliability of the scale resided in the description of the least preferred person or least preferred coworker that, as a result, has been most used in our research.

Internal Consistency of LPC

The LPC score has very high internal consistency. The results from several different studies are shown in Table 7.1. A comprehensive review of studies

Table 7.1. Representative Split-Half
Correlations of the LPC Score

Author and Scale	Reliability	*n*
Godfrey, Fiedler, and Hall (1959)		
23-item scale	.92	482
Arbuthnot (1968)		
17-item scale	.86	106
Meuwese (1964)	.91	178

(Rice, 1978a) has reported a median split-half reliability of between .89 and .90 for the scale.

Several factor analyses of various LPC scales also have been reported. These analyses generally yielded one major item factor describing personality attributes, and a small factor describing task-relevant behavior (e.g., efficient–inefficient, hardworking–lazy). Earlier LPC scales have reported a major personality attribute factor and a two or three item task factor (e.g., Foa, Mitchell, & Fiedler, 1971; Fox, Hill, & Guertin, 1973; Rice & Seaman, 1981).

A recent revision of the scale consists of items which contribute variance only to the personality description factor. We must consider, in this connection, that the LPC scale asks that you describe your least preferred coworker. This instruction in effect defines the least preferred coworker as ineffective and incompetent on the job. The major portion of the variance will, therefore, reside in personality items which are not logically relevant to being a poor coworker and, for this reason, reflect varying degrees of aversive feeling toward the person with whom one cannot work. Above all, there is as yet little if any empirical evidence that the task item factor contributes much to the prediction of leadership effectiveness, although some investigators (e.g., Rice & Seaman, 1981) have urged that the task factor deserves further attention.

Stability of LPC Scores

Aside from questioning its meaning, most attacks on the scale have focused on its test–retest reliability, that is, whether LPC measures a stable personality attribute. This is a critical question for the contingency model as well as for leadership selection and training: unless LPC is stable over time it cannot predict future performance. Moreover, the basic premise of the contingency model is that the leader's effectiveness depends on the interaction between personality and situational control. These criticisms notwithstanding, there is probably more evidence about the stability of LPC than on any other social-psychological measure (see, e.g., Robinson & Shaver's (1973) compendium of social-psychological tests and measures).

Rice (1978a) reviewed 23 studies which reported a test–retest reliability for LPC. Time intervening between the first and the second test ranged from two to three days to two and one-half years. Rice found a median correlation of .67, and a mean correlation of .64, with a standard deviation of .36. Table 7.2 presents the various studies reported by Rice, as well as several not included in Rice's analysis. Management training workshops have been listed separately since it is difficult to determine how much trainees learned in the intervening period about the meaning of the LPC score. It would be surprising, indeed, if most trainees who took an LPC scale did not ask what the scale measures, and it would be equally surprising if the instructor or someone else did not give them some information. This probably did not happen in the Siefert study which retested within two or three days, but it may well account for the low retest correlations in the Arbuthnot and the Stinson and Tracy studies.

In his own review of test–retest correlations, Rice (1978a) points out,

> There is often an impressive level of stability in LPC scores, especially when there are no dramatic changes or incidents in the respondent's life during the test–retest interval. For example, in adult populations not experiencing unusual intervening events, stability coefficients of .81, .75, .73, and .67 have been reported over test–retest intervals ranging from three weeks to 18 months. Similarly, college students engaged in their routine coursework have yielded stability coefficients of .85, .70, .66 and .46 over test–retest intervals ranging from three weeks to five months.

Rice goes on to say,

> Other data are just as clear in showing that the score is *not* always stable. Experiences such as executive development workshops, management games, and military training sometimes can reduce drastically the stability of LPC. Several studies have shown stability coefficients below .50 among respondents with such intervening experiences.*

Some changes in the LPC score will, of course, take place over time when traumatic conditions intervene. One study compared the stability of LPC scores of army officers who saw combat in Vietnam with that of officers who remained in the United States (Bons, Bass, & Komorita, 1970). The authors found a higher retest correlation for those who performed peacetime duties than for those who saw combat.

In fact, the stability of the LPC score is as high as that of the best personality tests. By way of comparison, the stability of the California Personality Inventory was reported as .65 for males and .68 for females over a one-year period for 13,000 subjects (Mehrens & Lehman, 1969).

* Reprinted with permission from R. W. Rice (1978a). Psychometric properties of the esteem for least preferred coworker (LPC scale). *Academy of Management Review, 3,* 106–118.

Table 7.2. Test–Retest Reliability Coefficients from Different Studies, and as Part of Management Training Workshops

Author and Scale	Time Interval Between Tests	Retest Correlation	n
Bons (cited in Fiedler, 1974)			
Army squad leaders	8 months	.72	45
Bons, Bass, and Komarita (1970)			
Army officers in Vietnam	2.5 years	.45	350
Drucker (cited in Fiedler, 1967)			
Army recruits with ROTC training I	8 weeks	.57	54
Army recruits with ROTC training II	8 weeks	.47	32
Army recruits without ROTC training I	8 weeks	.41	133
Army recruits without ROTC training II	8 weeks	.31	62
Fiedler (1958)			
Airforce officers	8 weeks	.68	562
Fiedler (unpublished, 1985)			
Police sergeants	8 years	.51	11
Fox (1976)			
Tax examiners	4 weeks	.75	114
Undergraduates	9 weeks	.68	61
Undergraduates	8 weeks	.66	80
Gruenfeld, Rance, and Wissenberg (1969)			
Undergraduates	4 weeks	.85	126
Prothero and Fiedler (1974)			
Faculty, nursing	15–18 months	.67	18
Reilley (cited in Fox, 1976)			
Student nurses	5 months	.70	14
Rice and Seaman (1981)			
Undergraduates	10 weeks	.71	21
Undergraduates	9 weeks	.63	33
Stinson and Tracy (1974)			
Industrial supervisors	3 weeks	.81	13
Undergraduates	3 weeks	.80	42
Industrial supervisors	6 months	.73	24
Undergraduates	8 weeks	.46	47
Management Training Workshops			
Arbuthnot (1968)			
Executive development workshop	1 year	.01	48
Siefert (cited in Fiedler, 1973)			
Management trainees	2–3 days	.92	18
Management trainees	4 weeks	.75	2 classes
Stinson and Tracy (1974)			
Business game participants 1	8 weeks	.23	30
Business game participants 2	8 weeks	.49	104

The retest reliability of the Minnesota Multiphasic Personality Inventory over one week is listed as .60, and the Hartshorne and May honesty scale over six months as .50 (Sax, 1974). One unpublished two-year retest of LPC scores of 18 nurses yielded a correlation of .67 ($p < .01$).

THE MEANING OF LPC

We interpret the LPC score as an individual's attitude or emotional reaction to a person who impedes or frustrates the accomplishment of the task (Fishbein, Landy, & Hatch, 1969). A "low LPC person" is someone who gets a very low LPC score because he or she describes the least preferred coworker in very negative and rejecting terms. The "low LPC" leader says, in effect, "Accomplishing a task is so important that you must be totally worthless or despicable if you keep me from getting the job done, and I reject everything about you." The reaction to the coworker is so strong that it blinds the leader to any good personality characteristics this poor coworker might have. After all, the mere fact that someone is ineffective or incompetent does not necessarily mean that he or she has to be dishonest, gloomy, or unkind. The low LPC score (63 or lower) reflects a strong emotional reaction to the poor coworker rather than a rational assessment of that other person and indicates a high need to accomplish the task (high task-motivation).

The individual who attributes relatively good personality traits even to the least preferred coworker is much less emotionally involved with task accomplishment. The person says, in effect, "You may be a very poor coworker, you may be frustrating, inefficient, or lazy. But the coworker role is just one of many, and that doesn't mean that you might not be quite pleasant or worthwhile in other respects." The least preferred coworker might be seen as stupid but calm, clumsy but honest, unpleasant but trustworthy. He or she is viewed more as an individual with differentiated personality traits rather than only as a coworker. A person with a high LPC score (73 or higher) is therefore called relationship-motivated.

The Middle-LPC Group

We have also identified a middle category (64–72) of people who differ from both the low- and the high-LPC people. These middle-LPC people, whom we call "socio-independent," tend to be less concerned with the attitudes and opinions of others and less involved with either their superiors or their subordinates or the way in which their personality impinges on others (Bass, Fiedler, & Krueger, 1964; Fiedler, 1967).

A major study by Kennedy (1982) suggests that middle-LPC persons are flexible and generally effective. Research also suggests that these middle-LPC persons are less involved with both the task and others in their work setting. As a result, they tend to be less emotional about the job, enabling them to gain more from training and experience than those with either high or low LPC scores.

Mai-Dalton (1975) conducted a study in which 122 undergraduate women took an in-basket test requiring them to respond to hypothetical letters and memos they supposedly found upon returning from a trip. Each subject played the role of a graduate student who needed to conduct a laboratory experiment with the assistance of three other students. In one experimental condition the assistants played students who were highly motivated as well as dependent on the good will of the graduate student. In the other condition these assistants were supposedly uninterested in the project, while the graduate student urgently required their cooperation. Half the subjects in each condition were given general training in how to approach an in-basket test while the other half received no training. This training served to make the in-basket task seem substantially more structured. The subjects' responses to the material in their in-baskets were categorized and formed the basis of the analysis.

Mai-Dalton (1975, pp. 17–30) found that task-motivated individuals were courteous, ingratiating, and nondirective when they felt they needed to solicit the cooperation of their assistants. Relationship-motivated individuals were courteous and friendly in all situations, whether or not they needed help from their assistants, but they were directive and structuring in the condition in which they had received training and therefore felt in control. Socio-independent subjects were considerably less friendly and courteous than either relationship-motivated or task-motivated subjects, even when they felt they needed help. What most determined their behavior was whether they clearly understood the task. If they understood the in-basket problem they were directive and structuring, and they apparently did not show concern with being courteous. According to Mai-Dalton, these individuals benefited more from the training program that improved task structure than either the task-motivated or the relationship-motivated persons.

Thus task-motivated individuals were considerate in order to get the job done. Relationship-motivated persons were considerate whether or not it promoted job accomplishment, but they were directive when they felt in control. Socio-independent persons appeared less concerned with relating to others and most concerned with meeting the demands of the task. Mai-Dalton's study provided support for a study of high school principals by McNamara (1968) which showed that principals in the middle LPC group had significantly lower group atmosphere scores than either task- or relationship-motivated principals.

While few personality measures correlate with the LPC score, high-LPC persons tend to be cognitively somewhat more complex (Mitchell, 1970b), more likely to be later-born rather than first-born children (Chemers, 1970), and exhibit the type B rather than type A, time urgent, competitive, achievement striving personality (Chemers, personal communication). In addition, Nebeker and Hansson (1972) found that high-LPC persons were more optimistic about human nature than their low-LPC counterparts and more attached to their work group (Hanssen & Fiedler, 1973).

Current Interpretation

We currently interpret the LPC score as measuring a motivational hierarchy, indicating the degree to which the individual sets a higher priority or value on task accomplishment (task-motivated, low-LPC) or on maintaining good interpersonal relations (relationship-motivated, high-LPC). This implies that each person has these two goals but that they have different value for the high- and for the low-LPC person. The low-LPC person lives by the principle of "business before pleasure"; the high-LPC person feels that the close relationship with coworkers is the prerequisite to team success. This does not mean, however, that high- or low-LPC persons will always behave in accordance with these primary goals. Extensive reviews of the literature by Rice (1978b) support this interpretation although Rice prefers to think of LPC as a measure of task vs. relationship value orientation.

As Maslow (1954) pointed out in the context of his need-hierarchy theory, satisfied needs no longer motivate. Consequently, task-motivated individuals are likely to behave in a task-relevant manner only as long as that particular need or goal has not been satisfied. Once they know that the accomplishment of the task is certain or highly probable they will turn to the less important goal of developing or maintaining good relations with coworkers. In the same manner, relationship-motivated leaders will not strive after good interpersonal relations when they already have good interpersonal relations. Under these conditions they will turn their attention to the demands of the task.

To illustrate this point in the area of leadership let us consider the case of a low-LPC manager. (a) We have a person who is highly motivated to accomplish a task. (b) He is assured that the task is getting done because he has a supportive and motivated work group, the task is structured and presents no problem, and like most managers, he has high position power. (c) For these reasons, this manager no longer has to worry about the task. He knows it will get done. He, therefore, spends more time socializing and having coffee with his subordinates.

Does this mean that this leader no longer cares whether the task gets done? Obviously not, but it is unnecessary to be directive when everything is under control. The task-motivated leader is concerned with the task only when its accomplishment is in doubt. For the same reason, the high-LPC leader is more concerned with interpersonal relations when situational control is moderate or low. But high-LPC leaders become directive as they turn their attention to the task when they have high control, that is, good interpersonal relations, high structure, and high position power. Because behavior differs with high, moderate, and low situational control, LPC cannot, and does not, correlate with the usual measures of leader behavior. These changes in behavior and in attitudes have been described previously (e.g., Fiedler, 1967, 1970), and as we shall see, they have important consequences for task performance in different situations.

In summary, the least preferred coworker or LPC score is a highly reliable and surprisingly stable measure of personality. It appears to indicate the degree to which an individual is primarily motivated by the goal of accomplishing assigned tasks or by the goal of developing and maintaining close relations with others in the work group. However, in high-control situations in which these goals are, by definition, satisfied or secure, these individuals turn their attention to their secondary goals. For this reason, directive and considerate behaviors cannot correlate with LPC unless we also take account of the conditions in which the behavior is observed.

Although it seems customary in texts and articles to refer to the LPC score as controversial by citing criticisms which go back more than 15 years, it is difficult to see what is so controversial about the score at this time. There are very few social-psychological measures with higher internal consistency and test−retest reliability, and few for which there are more validity data available. Thus there is some disagreement about the interpretation of the scale, but the same can be said of practically any other personality measure including the venerable intelligence score or of anything else for that matter, including Darwin's theory of natural selection, the Bible, dissonance theory, meta-analysis, and the value of higher education.

CHAPTER EIGHT

The Contingency Model— Warts and Beauty Spots

The previous chapters described the two major elements of the contingency model, situational control and LPC. This chapter briefly describes the contingency model and its basic propositions, shortcomings, and validity. Since the contingency model has generated well over 400 articles and papers it will be familiar to many readers. For those not so singularly blessed, we present a brief description of the model, although we shall refrain from rehashing past controversies.*

DESCRIPTION OF THE CONTINGENCY MODEL

The contingency model states that the effectiveness of a leader or a group depends (or is contingent) on:

1. The leader's need structure, specifically, whether the leader is primarily motivated to seek task accomplishment or to seek satisfaction of interpersonal needs.
2. The leader's situational control, that is, the leader's confidence that the task will be accomplished.
3. The interaction between the leader's need structure and situational controls. Task-motivated (low-LPC) leaders tend to perform best in situations in which they have high control as well as in those in

---

* For these see, for instance, Ashour, 1973a,b; Fiedler, 1971a,b, 1973, 1977, 1978a; Graen, Alvarez, Orris, and Martella, 1970; Graen, Orris and Alvarez, 1971; McMahon, 1972; Mitchell, Biglan, Oncken, and Fiedler, 1970; Schriesheim and Kerr, 1977a,b.

which their control is low. Relationship-motivated (high-LPC) leaders perform best in moderate-control situations.

The hypothesis is usually tested by assigning groups in a particular study to one of the eight situational control octants. As already described in Chapter 6, the octants categorize groups into those with high or low leader–member relations (LMR), high or low task structure (TS), and high or low position power (PP) (see Figure 6.4). Alternatively, groups (octants) can be assigned to high, moderate, and low levels or zones of situational control. The leader's LPC score is then correlated with group performance in the set of groups within a particular octant or level of situational control.

This analysis led to a bow-shaped pattern of correlations. Negative correlations between the leader's LPC scores and group performance tend to occur in the high- and low-control situations; positive correlations tend to occur in the moderate-control situation. Figure 8.1 shows the correlations obtained in the original 13 studies (broken) and for subsequent validation studies (see Fiedler, 1978a). The vertical axis on this graph indicates the magnitude of the correlation coefficients; the horizontal axis describes the degree of the leader's situational control. The graph shows that task-motivated leaders tended to perform best in situations in which they had high control (Octants 1–3) and those in which their control was relatively low (Octant 8); relationship-motivated (high-LPC) leaders tended to perform best in moderate-control situations (Octants 4–6).

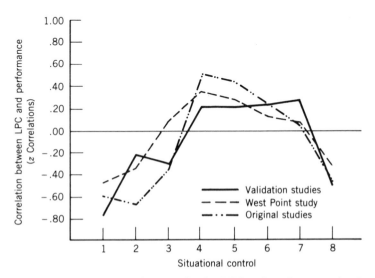

Figure 8.1. Median correlations between leader LPC and performance for the original studies, validation studies (to 1982), and the Chemers and Skrzypck (1972) study.

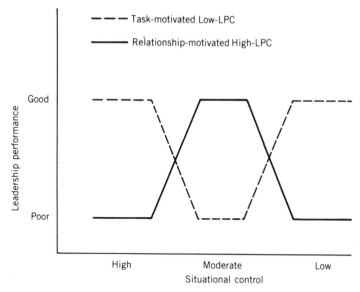

Figure 8.2. Graphic representation of the contingency model, indicating the inter-action of the leader's motivational structure, measured by the least preferred coworker (LPC) scale, and situational control and leadership performance. [Adapted with permission from F. E. Fiedler (1978b). A dynamic theory of leadership. In B. King, S. Streufert, & F. E. Fiedler (Eds.), *Managerial control and organizational democracy*. Silver Spring, MD: V. H. Winston & Sons.]

Another way of showing the contingency model relationship is seen in Figure 8.2. This graph indicates the leader's or the group's performance on the vertical axis and high, moderate, and low situational control on the horizontal axis. The performance of the high-LPC leader is indicated by the solid line, that of the low-LPC leader by the broken line. This figure points to several important implications. First, most individuals are effective in some situations and not effective in others. For this reason we cannot réally speak of a "good leader" or a "poor leader"; effective leadership depends on the leader's personality as well as situational control. While this point of view was not held by most leadership researchers and management theorists at the time the contingency model was first published in 1964, it is now widely accepted (Kerr, 1984). The graph further implies that a leader's performance is likely to improve as this person moves into a situation that matches the leader's LPC score. Performance will decrease as the leader moves into a zone of situational control that does not match his or her LPC score. A change in situational control will, therefore, cause a change in leadership performance.

Increases in situational control may occur for several reasons besides changes in leader–member relations, task structure, or position power. They may result from training, job-related experience, or greater stability in the leader's working environment. Situational control may decrease if the leader gets a new or difficult boss, new or difficult subordinates, more complex task assignments, and so on, or is placed in a more stressful environment. The leader's task-motivation or relationship-motivation may also change, but this, as discussed in the chapter on leadership style, is unlikely to happen in the short run.

WARTS ON THE CONTINGENCY MODEL

The contingency model has provided many critics with a rich source of publications. Three of the areas in which the contingency model is vulnerable are briefly discussed here. These are the specificity of the LPC score, the generality of situational control, and the model's failure to explain the process by which a leader obtains good performance (the "black box").

The Specificity of the LPC Score

One criticism of the contingency model has been that it is method-bound. This is certainly the case for the LPC score. It has been difficult, thus far, to develop an acceptable substitute for LPC, although this has not been for want of trying. The measure does not correlate highly with the usual personality trait scores, and it does not correlate with various leader behavior ratings. Several investigators correlated these measures with LPC and then found to their own surprise (though not to ours) that LPC and the Ohio State dimensions discussed earlier were not related. Only when situational factors are taken into account do we find correlations between LPC and various interpersonal behaviors.

A study by Michaelson (1973) showed that leaders with considerate, socioemotional behaviors performed best in moderate-control situations while those with task-relevant behaviors performed best in the same situations in which task-motivated leaders (low LPC) performed best. Shaw and Blum (1966) found similar results by comparing leader behaviors in groups with relatively structured and nonstructured tasks. But on the whole, the criticism is justified that LPC makes the contingency model method-bound. This presents a problem requiring further effort (cf. Rice, 1978a). It seems clear at this point that any attempts to relate the LPC score to other personality attributes or to behaviors are unlikely to succeed unless a measure of situational control, anxiety, or uncertainty is used as a moderator (see Bass, Fiedler, & Krueger, 1964; Sashkin, Taylor, & Tripathi, 1974).

Questions related to the internal consistency or stability of the LPC score have already been discussed. A current thesis project by Erdly (1986) has developed scales for describing the behaviors of high- and low-LPC persons. Again, these scales correlated with the LPC score in the expected direction only when the leadership situations were divided into those arousing relatively high or low levels of anxiety or stress.

Generality of Situational Control

A second criticism, less often heard, though certainly no less important, concerns the lack of an absolute metric for the situational control dimension. There is little doubt that this would be of considerable value. In the meantime, the question is whether the situational control dimension has been interpreted too "flexibly," as some critics have claimed. The pros and cons of this issue have been discussed by Rice and Kastenbaum (1983). These writers agree with the authors that the contingency model's basic hypothesis is best represented at this time by measures which conceptualize situational control in terms of a high, moderate, or low zone (see Chapter 6).

Whether a broad interpretation of the dimension is a good or a bad thing depends, in large measure, on whether one wants a specific or general theory. As we have seen, situational control has been operationalized in different ways, for example, different religions (Fiedler, Meuwese, & Oonk, 1961), heterogeneity in language and culture (Fiedler, 1966), or stress induced by working in a foreign environment (Fiedler, O'Brien, & Ilgen, 1969). O'Brien (1969) has shown that situational control can be measured by means of digraph theory to indicate the degree to which the leader is able to have a direct influence on the task. Most of these studies have supported the contingency model predictions (Fiedler, 1971b, 1978a). For example, Strube and Garcia (1981) reviewed 27 tests of the model in which situational control was classified into zones as opposed to the traditional octants. The combined z's for these studies was 4.66 ($p = 1.58 \times 10^{-6}$) in support of the model. These results were consistent with the predictions that low-LPC leaders would perform best in the high and low situational-control zones and high-LPC leaders would perform best in moderate situational-control zones. (Probabilities for high: $n = 11, p < .01$; moderate: $n = 9, p < .005$; and low: $n = 7, p < .005$.) Apparently the use of broader operationalizations of situational control does not detract from the predictive validity of the theory.

As mentioned earlier, it would be highly desirable to find an absolute measure for situational control—a yardstick which could be identical or equally applicable in all conditions. This turns out to be very difficult, of course. One approximation was developed in conjunction with the Leader Match training program. Based only on the perceptions of the leader, this measure has its limitations and may require statistical connections since most leaders have a slight tendency to rate their own task as somewhat less structured and their position power as somewhat lower than outsiders would rate them. Task-motivated leaders also may have a tendency to see the same task as slightly more structured than relationship-motivated leaders. At this time, situational-control scales provide an approximate but convenient and usable method for assessing this important dimension of the model.

Failure to Explain the Leadership Process

The most pertinent criticism of the contingency model is its inability to explain the specific process that allows us to predict performance from the interaction of LPC and situational control. An important finding of the Peters, Hartke, and Pohlman (1985) meta-analysis of the model is that additional moderators are necessary to account for the relationship between LPC and performance. In their summary Peters and his associates (1985) agree with the general conclusions of the previous meta-analysis by Strube and Garcia (1981); however, they accurately point out that the contingency model requires further development to account more fully for leadership performance.

Dealing with the incompleteness of the contingency model is an important issue. And it is to this point that cognitive resource theory addresses itself.

A TECHNICAL NOTE ON VALIDITY OF THE CONTINGENCY MODEL

The section that follows is not directly relevant to the development of the cognitive resource theory. The brief summary of validation research is included for readers who might find it useful in their work. Those familiar with or not interested in these findings should skip to Chapter 9.

We generally validate a theory by asking three questions: First, do the empirical data support the theory's basic propositions? Second, does the theory predict and explain nonobvious and nontrivial results? Third, to what extent does it give us control? Specifically, in this case, does it enable us to improve leadership performance? This section considers each of these questions in turn.

Tests of the Basic Contingency Model Hypotheses

The basic hypothesis of the contingency model is that low-LPC leaders perform better than high-LPC leaders in high- & low-control situations (Octants 1, 2, 3, and 8); high-LPC leaders perform better in moderate-control situations (Octants 4, 5, 6). A substantial number of validation studies have tested these hypotheses of the contingency model, and most studies supported these predictions, although not always at a statistically significant level. Several important validation studies are here briefly described.

Chemers and Skrzypek's (1972) West Point Study. This carefully controlled experiment merits particular attention. It was conducted at the U.S. Military Academy, West Point, with 128 cadets who were assigned to 32 separate 3-man teams. An unavoidable weakness of many field tests of the model is that LPC scores and leader–member relations (LMR) scores were obtained concurrently with performance evaluations. It is, then, possible that these scores might have been affected by previous success. Even more important, the possibility exists that good or poor leader–member relations, which largely determine the leader's situational control, might be influenced by the effectiveness of the group (Konar-Goldband, Rice, & Monkarsh, 1979).

Chemers and Skrzypek overcame the above problems found in field studies by obtaining LPC and sociometric preference ratings three weeks prior to the study. High- and low-LPC leaders were selected from among those who fell at least one standard deviation above or below the mean of the sample. In addition, groups were assembled on the basis of previously collected sociometric ratings so that they would have either high or low LMR scores. In half the groups, the leaders and members had expressed liking for working with each other; in the other half, leader and members had previously expressed their dislike for working with each other.

In half the teams the leaders were given strong position power (i.e., members were told that the leaders would have final say on all group decisions and that their ratings would influence members' military grades). In the low position power groups, leaders were told to act as chairmen. Two tasks were administered in counterbalanced order. Half the groups began with an unstructured task requiring them to design a program increasing interest in world politics among enlisted men who are assigned overseas. The other, more structured task required the group to draw a plan for a barracks building to scale from a set of specifications. After completing the first task, each group then performed the other task in the series. The study is of particular importance for three reasons. First, the Chemers and Skrzypek study assembled groups a priori to fit all eight octants of the contingency model. This is one of the few studies in which leader–member relations were experimentally manipulated. Second, the criterion was based on the performance of the entire team. Third, correlations were obtained between leader LPC and objective performance measures, namely, accuracy of drawing the barrack, and judgments by independent raters of the quality of the written product on the unstructured task.

The correlation curve was shown in Figure 8.1. As can be seen, the results of the original studies and the Chemers and Skrzypek study are practically identical. When we compare the correlation points on the two curves, the rank–order correlation was .86 ($n = 7$, $p < .01$). Note that Octant 6 was not predicted on the basis of the first 13 studies. The study also permits an estimate of the proportion of the variance accounted for by the contingency model, at least under these experimental conditions.

Table 8.1. Significant Analyses of Variance Results in Laboratory
Studies Conducted by Hardy and His Associates

Study	Octant							
	1	2	3	4	5	6	7	8
Hardy, 1971	L > H	ns	L > H	H > L				
Hardy, 1975					H > L	H > L	H > L	L > H
Hardy et al., 1973		ns		H > L		H > L		L > H

Shiflett's (1973) analysis of variance showed that the contingency model accounted for 28 percent of the variance ($F = 6.19$, $p < .025$).

Studies by Hardy and Associates. Hardy (1971, 1975) and Hardy, Sack, and Harpine (1973) also assembled groups on the basis of LPC scores and sociometric ratings one to three weeks prior to the experiments (see Table 8.1). The Hardy (1971) study used 56 groups of four college students to test Octants 1 to 4, the Hardy et al. (1973) study used 56 groups of high school students to test cells with weak position power (Octants 2, 4, 6, and 8). The 1975 study was based on 39 groups of elementary school students from the fourth grade, testing Octants 5–8. The results are remarkable in showing how early in life the contingency model variables predict performance.

Reviews of the Validation Evidence. A number of papers have discussed the validity of the contingency model (e.g., Fiedler, 1971b, 1978a; Fiedler & Chemers, 1974; Graen, Alvarez, Orris, & Martella, 1970; Mitchell, Biglan, Oncken, & Fiedler, 1970). These will not be covered in detail since more effective methods of evaluating validity have become available with the advent of meta-analysis. This method summarizes the results of multiple tests of the same hypothesis (Glass, 1976; Hunter, Schmidt, & Jackson, 1982; Rosenthal, 1978, 1984; Schmidt & Hunter, 1977), and thus determines how well a body of results fits the predictions of a theory. Two meta-analyses have assessed the validity of the contingency model.

One meta-analysis, based on 145 validation tests of the contingency model, was published by Strube and Garcia (1981). A second meta-analysis based on 100 validation tests is by Peters, Hartke, and Pohlman (1985). Strube and Garcia's meta-analysis, using Rosenthal's (1978) approach, yielded a probability level of 2.99×10^{-28} in support of the model, which should allay most doubts as to the model's robustness. The second meta-analysis by Peters et al. also supported the contingency model, as indicated previously. Table 8.2 summarizes the results of validation studies published between 1963 and 1984.

Table 8.3 summarizes studies which assigned groups to high, moderate, or low situational control zones. As can be seen, the results are essentially identical to those obtained in studies which classified groups into eight octants.

Table 8.2. Summary of Contingency Model Tests in Laboratory and Field Studies

Study	Octant							
	1	2	3	4	5	6	7	8
Laboratory studies ($n = 13$)								
Chemers et al., 1975						.79		−.65
Chemers & Skrzypek, 1972	−.43	−.32	.10	.35	.28	.13	.08	−.33
Fiedler, 1966	−.72	.37	−.16	.08	.16	.07	.26	−.37
	−.77	.50	−.54	.13	.03	.14	−.27	.60
Fiedler, 1971b		.34		.51				
Graen, et al., 1971	.47	−.41	.46	.33	.25	−.39	.43	−.33
	−.41	.18	.02	−.08	−.52	−.43	.45	.44
Hollingsworth et al., 1977						−.21		−.46
Hovey, 1974				−.36				−.59
Mitchell, 1970b		.21		.43				
		.17		.38				
Rice et al., 1982		−.23		−.22		.55		−.28
		−.39		−.44		.67		.24
Rice & Chemers, 1973						.30		−.40
Sashkin, 1972			−.29					
			−.19					
Schneier, 1978		−.55						
Shifflet & Nealy, 1972			.16	.05				
Shima, 1968		−.26		.71				
Field studies ($n = 8$)								
Csoka, 1975	−.66		−.69	.80				−.80
Csoka & Fiedler, 1972	−.50	−.47	−.57	−.78	.67	.75		−.66
	−.71		−.66	.22				−.75
Fiedler et al., 1969		−.21		.00		.67		−.51
Hill, 1969		−.10	−.29			−.24	.62	
Hunt, 1967	−.64		−.80		.21		.30	
	−.51	.60				−.30		
O'Brien et al., 1969		−.46		.47		−.45		−.14
Sashkin et al., 1974			−.05			.34		
Turner, 1972[a]	−.47			.62				
Median correlations	−.64	−.21	−.24	.22	.21	.13	.30	−.47

[a] Turner, 1972 was incorrectly identified as Tumes in previous reviews (e.g., Fiedler, 1978a; Strube & Garcia, 1981).

Nonobvious Results

The second test of a theory's validity is its ability to predict nontrivial and nonobvious results. A theory should enable us to understand phenomena that have not been seen or understood before. The contingency model makes a number of these nonobvious predictions. For example, an increase from low to moderate control should improve the performance of the high-LPC leader but *decrease* the performance of the low LPC leader. An

Table 8.3. Summary of Contingency Model Tests from
Studies Using Alternative Measures of Situational
Control $(n = 9)^a$

	Zone		
Study	High	Moderate	Low
Anderson, 1966	−.50	−.22	.12
	.21		
Fiedler & Barron (1967) [Medians]	−.49	−.04	−.50
Geyer & Julian, 1973		.03	−.48
Hewitt et al., 1974			−.13
Kabanoff, 1981	−.28	.43	
Lawrence & Lorsch, 1967[b]	−.50	.66	
	−.10		
	−.13		
Nealy & Blood, 1968[b]	−.22	.79	
Nealy & Owen, 1970[b]	−.50		
O'Brien, 1969	−.08	.77	−.13
Median correlations	−.25	.43	−.13

^{a} A field study conducted by Hardy & Bohren, 1975 using analysis of variance
found support for the model in the moderate and low control zones.
^{b} Field study; all other studies were laboratory studies.

increase from moderate to high situational control should improve the
performance of high LPC leaders but *decrease* the performance of low
LPC leaders. And since experience and training generally tend to make
leaders more secure and knowledgeable about the task, training or experience should decrease the performance of low LPC leaders as they
move from a low to moderate control zone, and decrease the performance
of the high LPC leaders as they move from a moderate to a high control
zone (see Figure 8.3).

The validity of these nonobvious predictions is best demonstrated by
Chemers, Rice, Sundstrom, and Butler's (1975) ingenious experiment of
32 groups of Army ROTC cadets and psychology students. Three-man
teams were given the task of deciphering simple coded messages. Half of
the leaders had high LPC scores and half had low LPC scores. Half of
the leaders within each of these subgroups were given training in decoding
messages while the other half were involved in an irrelevant activity.
Task performance was measured objectively on the basis of how many
coded messages (cryptograms) were deciphered in 30 minutes. Because
of the strong antimilitary feelings in 1970 the group atmosphere scores,
obtained after the task sessions, were significantly below the normative
mean, and most group leaders reported feeling stress.

The task of deciphering coded messages is highly unstructured for those
who do not have training, but it is structured for those with training.
That is, leaders in the training condition were told, for example, that the

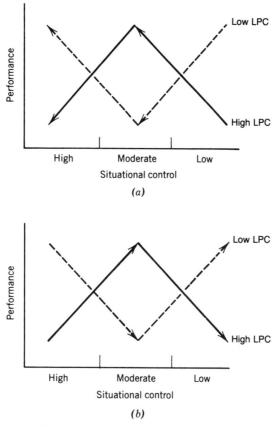

Figure 8.3. Effects of (*a*) increasing and (*b*) decreasing situational control on the performance of high and low LPC leaders.

most common English letter is an "e," the most common English word is "the," that certain combinations (e.g., "ou") occur frequently in the English language. The situational control of trained leaders, then, was greater since they had expert power as well as a relatively structured task. The position power of leaders without training is low, the group climate is poor, and the task is unstructured. In groups with untrained leaders, therefore, situational control is considerably lower.

The contingency model predicts that the task-motivated leaders without training (i.e., in the low-control situation) will perform better than re-lationship-motivated leaders in that situation. However, since training gives the leader moderate control, the relationship-motivated leaders will perform better than task-motivated leaders in the training condition. These counterintuitive predictions were borne out by the study at a highly significant level. The results are shown on Figure 8.4. Findings similar to those of the Chemers et al. (1975) study occur when we compare leaders

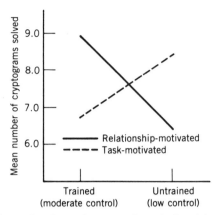

Figure 8.4. Comparison of task performance by relationship-motivated (high LPC), and task-motivated (low LPC) leaders with and without task training. [Reprinted with permission from M. M. Chemers, R. W. Rice, E. Sundstrom, & W. M. Butler (1975). Leader esteem for the least preferred co-worker score, training and effectiveness: An experimental examination. *Journal of Personality and Social Psychology*, *31*, 401–409. Copyright American Psychological Association.]

with and without extensive organizational experience (time in the organization). This point will be discussed more fully in Chapter 9.

Changing Leader Performance

Does the contingency model tell us how to improve leadership performance? A successful training program, based on a specific theory, can provide support for the theory on which it is based. Leader Match (Fiedler, Chemers, & Mahar, 1976; Fiedler & Chemers, 1984) meets these expectations. It argues that effective leadership performance depends, at least in part, on the leader's ability to remain, or get into, leadership situations that match his or her LPC score. In contrast to other leadership training programs (e.g., Blake & Mouton's Managerial Grid, Hersey & Blanchard's LEAD, and Vroom & Yetton's TELOS) leaders are *not* instructed to change their leadership style or behavior. Leader Match teaches trainees to identify whether they are task-motivated, relationship-motivated, or socio-independent and then identify or diagnose their situational control. They then learn how to modify their situational control, when necessary, so that it matches their leadership style.

For example, to improve leader–member relations the leader can increase the amount of time spent with the work group, have more social interactions with subordinates, or share more information with group members. Leader–member relations can be decreased by being more formal, or by communicating with subordinates to a greater extent by telephone and memo. Task structure can be increased by seeking clear and specific directions or by obtaining technical training. It can be decreased by seeking more challenging assignments or asking for broader task assignments.

Position power can be increased by capitalizing on the formal authority given by the organization and delegating authority, while sharing in decision making decreases position power. The program also provides guidance for improving the match between leadership style and situational control of subordinate leaders.*

Does Leader Match support the validity of the contingency model? Leader Match training has been empirically tested in 17 different samples and in a variety of different organizations (Fiedler & Chemers, 1984). These include police sergeants, middle managers of a county government, public works supervisors, volunteer public health managers, first-line supervisors of a department store chain, and fire department officers. It has also been tested in nine studies of military personnel in various units and from various ranks. A recent followup study of the training program in an underground mine showed that the effects of training had maintained themselves after five years.

In each of these studies, those assigned to the training condition and those assigned to the control group were randomly chosen from a common pool. The performance of leaders in the trained and control groups was evaluated by superiors who either had no knowledge of which leaders or managers had received Leader Match training, or who in most other cases could not even recall very clearly that there had been a training study a half-year or year earlier. To cite Wexley and Latham's book, *Developing and Training Human Resources in Human Organizations* (1981), "[Fiedler, Chemers, and Mahar] provided more empirical evidence than any other training group which satisfies the requirements for evaluating training effectiveness" (p. 156).

Although one can always take issue with a particular set of findings, an extensive meta-analytic review of management training programs by Burke and Day (1986) indicates that Leader Match is an effective method for improving leadership performance. Finally, a successful training program by itself does not validate the theory on which it was based, but given all the other evidence, Leader Match provides additional support for the validity of the contingency model.

SUMMARY

This chapter describes the contingency model, its limitations, and its strengths. Although the necessity for further development has been shown, the model has received support from three sources of evidence. Support is found in the many empirical tests that have been conducted; in the nonobvious and nontrivial hypotheses which have been generated and successfully tested; and in the application of the theory to the development of an empirically validated training program.

* The 1984 version of Leader Match also includes training material on increasing the effective use of cognitive resources.

CHAPTER NINE

The Contingency Model, Job Experience, and Tenure

It seems obvious that job-relevant experience provides knowledge and information about the task and the organization that should assist a leader in directing and supervising subordinates. Why then don't we find systematic relations between measures of leader experience and leader performance (Fiedler, 1970)? At this time the contingency model and its successor, cognitive resource theory, appear to be alone in offering an answer.

As will be recalled from Chapter 6, the contingency model defines situational control as the degree to which the leader has control, power, and influence to determine the outcome of the task. Experience enables leaders to understand and structure complex tasks and to manage difficult and stressful interpersonal relations encountered before, as in handling an irate employee. Therefore, experienced leaders tend to perceive themselves as having more situational control than do inexperienced leaders (Bons & Fiedler, 1976; Csoka & Fiedler, 1972; Fiedler, 1972; McNamara, 1968).

As leaders gain experience, and with it situational control, we would expect that the performance of relationship-motivated and task-motivated leaders would change in the direction predicted by the contingency model. That is, the performance of relationship-motivated leaders should improve as they "move" from the low control zone (in which they perform poorly) into the moderate zone (in which they perform well). The performance of task-motivated leaders should improve with experience as they "move" from the moderate to the high situational control zone, but it will decrease as they move from the low to the moderate control zone. This prediction can be traced on Figure 8.2. Several studies are here described which support these hypotheses.

BONS AND FIEDLER'S SQUAD LEADER STUDY

The effect of experience is most clearly seen in a study of 39 infantry squad leaders in charge of training recruit squads of 10 men over a period of six to eight months (Bons & Fiedler, 1976). This was a new assignment for these squad leaders since the unit training program was experimental in nature. It is reasonable to assume that squad leaders gained experience over the six to eight month period in which they worked with the same superiors and subordinates. This was in fact shown by ratings of their own situation control which increased from moderate to high.

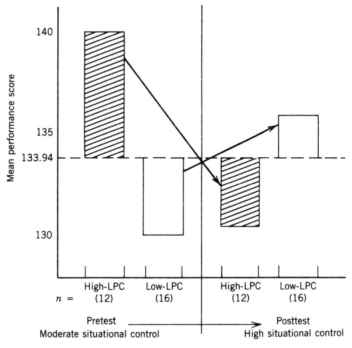

Figure 9.1. Changes in the performance of high and low LPC leaders as a function of increased experience and more structured task assignment over five months. [Adapted with permission from F. E. Fiedler (1978b). A dynamic theory of leadership. In B. King, S. Streufert, & F. E. Fiedler (Eds.), *Managerial control and organizational democracy*. Silver Spring, MD: V. H. Winston & Sons.]

The performance measure in this study was based on an extensively used rating scale developed by Bons in close collaboration with military officers of the division in which the study was conducted (Bons & Fiedler, 1976). We shall refer to the Bons scale throughout the remainder of this book. In brief, superiors used an eight-item five-point scale to indicate to what extent the subordinate exceeded (score of 5), met (3) or failed to meet (1) various job requirements on such aspects as the way he handles his job when demands are extra heavy or when he finds himself under severe pressure, "or the way he organizes his people and specifies the ways of getting the job done." Split-half reliability of this scale was .92 and the interrater agreement was .65.

The same superiors rated the squad leaders at the beginning of the training cycle and again at the end, shortly after the squad passed the combat readiness inspection. As predicted by the contingency model (see Figure 9.1), the relationship-motivated leaders were rated as more effective than task-motivated leaders at the beginning when situational control for most leaders was moderate. Task-motivated leaders were rated as more effective at the end of the training cycle, when situational control had become high.

OTHER CONTINGENCY MODEL STUDIES

Similar results were obtained in a study of 32 farm supply cooperatives (Godfrey, Fiedler, & Hall, 1959). All sales cooperatives belonged to the same federation of consumer companies but each company had its own board of directors and its own general manager. The performance criterion in this case was based on objective measures: the three-year average ratios of net income to total sales and of operating expense to total sales. The sample was divided into companies with highly experienced and relatively less experienced managers, as indicated by tenure in the organization. These managers had relatively high position power, and the highly experienced managers were rated by independent judges as having high situational control (Figure 9.2).

Findings of this nature were also reported by Hardy and Bohren (1975), who studied 53 college teachers in a large eastern U.S. university. This study used a 2 by 2 factorial design, that is, high experience = five or more years and low experience = one year of experience; and high- and low-LPC teachers. Hardy and Bohren found that low-LPC teachers with less experience were relatively more effective than those with high experience. Again, teaching experience reduced performance for task-motivated leaders as they presumably "moved" from the low-control situation in which their LPC and situational control were matched, to the moderate-control situation in which they were mismatched. Experience

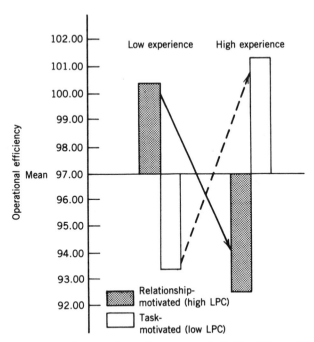

Figure 9.2. Differences in the task performance of relationship- and task-motivated company managers as a function of increased experience. [Adapted with permission from F. E. Fiedler (1972a). Predicting the effects of leadership training and experience: A contingency model interpretation. *Journal of Applied Psychology, 56,* 114–119. Copyright American Psychological Association.]

increased the performance of relationship-motivated teachers who moved from low situational control into a situation that matched their LPC score.

The contingency model hypothesis was also supported in several other investigations. These included data on post office managers and supervisors at various levels (Fiedler, 1972), Canadian elementary and secondary school principals (McNamara, 1968, also cited in Fiedler, 1972), and unpublished findings from a study of community college presidents (Fiedler & Gillo, 1974). These studies show that the advantages of job-relevant experience for the high-LPC leader are offset by the disadvantages of experience for the low-LPC leader when experience improves situational control from low to moderate. Similarly, the advantages of experience for the low-LPC leader are offset by the disadvantages of experience for the high-LPC leader when situational control changes from moderate to high. These findings explain therefore why we do not find that experience in general improves leadership performance.

	Situational Control	Leaders' Focus	Hypothesized Cognitive Resource Use
High LPC leader	High	On Task	Intelligence
	Moderate	On Interpersonal Relations	Experience
Low LPC leader	High	On Interpersonal Relations	Experience
	Moderate	On Task	Intelligence

Figure 9.3. Schematic presentation of the Bettin hypothesis on the contribution of experience to leadership performance under different situational control conditions.

BETTIN'S STUDY OF COMPANY COMMANDERS AND STAFF OFFICERS

Still another connection between the contingency model and leadership experience is suggested by Bettin's (1983) study of military officers. Bettin took as his starting point the finding that task-motivated leaders focus on interpersonal relations when their situational control is high, whereas relationship-motivated leaders focus on the relationship when control is moderate or low. As we shall see in Chapter 15, experience tends to be especially useful in the performance of tasks that depend on the ability to manage interpersonal relations. Bettin hypothesized, therefore, that experience should contribute to good performance in the leadership situation in which the leader concentrates on having good interpersonal relations: that is, low LPC leaders in high control situations and high LPC leaders in moderate or low control situations. This set of hypotheses is schematically shown in Figure 9.3.

Bettin's sample consisted of 78 company commanders and staff officers from 10 infantry battalions. These jobs are regularly held by army captains, although seven of these officers were first lieutenants at the time of this study. These officers took the LPC scale, rated their leader–member relations, and completed a 23-item stress measure based on the House and Rizzo (1972) scales of role ambiguity and uncertainty. A 24-item scale measured stress with boss.* The relevance of the officers' experience was judged by senior officers on the basis of detailed military assignment and training records.

The company commanders' jobs in this study received the same task structure ratings as those of staff officers, but company commanders were rated as having more position power, and they reported less job stress.

* The Job Stress and Boss Stress scales correlated .69 ($n = 79$, $p < .001$), indicating that the two scales thus measure related constructs.

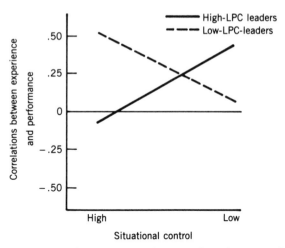

Figure 9.4. The relationship between experience and performance for high and low LPC army captains under different conditions of situational control.

Leaders reporting low job stress as well as high leader–member relations were classified as having high situational control; those above the median in job stress and below the median in leader–member relations were categorized as having moderate control. As mentioned earlier, performance was evaluated on a 49-item Likert scale by the battalion's commander and executive officer. Bettin's finding supported his hypothesis. Relevant experience correlated with rated leadership performance in situations in which the individual concentrated on interpersonal relations; task-motivated leaders made effective use of their experience in high-control situations; relationship-motivated leaders did so in moderate control situations (see Figure 9.4).

SUMMARY

One of the major effects of experience in an organization is an increase in the leader's situational control. This in turn results in differences in the performance of relationship-motivated and task-motivated leaders. Whether organizational experience will increase or decrease performance depends on the match between the leader's style and the situational control. The performance of low LPC leaders *decreases* but the performance of high LPC leaders *increases* as organizational experience changes situational control from low to moderate. The performance of low LPC leaders *increases* but that of high LPC leaders *decreases* as organizational experience changes situational control from moderate to high. These effects explain the consistent finding that experience in general does not improve leadership performance (see Chapter 4). It is also apparent from Bettin's study that task-motivated and relationship-motivated leaders make different use of their experience in performing their leadership functions.

PART THREE

COGNITIVE
RESOURCE THEORY

Part 3 describes new developments in our thinking since the contingency model. Chapter 10 describes cognitive resource theory, while the next chapters present analyses from field studies and laboratory experiments which provide empirical support for the seven propositions and related hypotheses of this theory. Chapter 14 suggests how cognitive resource theory relates to the contingency model, and Chapter 15 deals specifically with the effects of the task on the utilization of intellectual abilities and creativity. The concluding chapter points to problems and new directions raised by the research and cognitive resource theory.

CHAPTER TEN

The Cognitive Resource Model

The previous chapters discussed the role of leader intelligence, experience, stress, and the elements of the contingency model. This chapter proposes an integration of these diverse elements. For easy reference, Figure 10.1 restates the assumptions and hypotheses of cognitive resource theory, previously discussed in Chapter 1 and represented schematically in Figure 1.1.

The theory says that in the best of all best possible worlds, the leader's intellectual abilities are the major source of the plans, decisions, and strategies that guide the group's actions. These plans, decisions, and strategies are communicated to the group in the form of directive behavior, and acted upon if the group supports the leader's and the organization's goals, or if the leader is not distracted by stress. We shall here consider this best-case scenario, as well as those inimical to the utilization of the leader's intellectual abilities.

ASSUMPTIONS AND PROPOSITIONS OF COGNITIVE RESOURCE THEORY

Assumption One

We start with the assumption that leaders devote intellectual effort to developing plans and strategies and to making decisions, and that the more intelligent leaders do so more effectively than less intelligent leaders.

Assumption 1. Intelligent and competent leaders make more effective plans, decisions, and action strategies than do leaders with less intelligence or competence.

Assumption 2. Leaders communicate their plans, decisions, and action strategies in the form of directive behavior.

Hypothesis 1. The leader's intellectual abilities correlate with group performance only when the leader is not under stress.

Hypothesis 2. Under low stress conditions, the intellectual abilities of directive leaders correlate more highly with group performance than do intellectual abilities of nondirective leaders.

Hypothesis 3. The correlation between the directive leader's intelligence and performance is higher if the group is supportive than if the group does not support the leader.

Hypothesis 4. If the leader is nondirective and the group is supportive, the intellectual abilities of group members correlate with performance.

Hypothesis 5. The leader's intellectual abilities will contribute to group performance to the degree to which the task requires these particular abilities (i.e., is intellectually demanding).

Hypothesis 6. Under conditions of high stress, the leader's experience and skills (rather than his or her intellectual abilities) will correlate with task performance.

Hypothesis 7. Directive behavior of the leader is in part determined by the contingency model elements, the leader's task-motivation or relationship-motivation (LPC), and situational control.

Figure 10.1. Assumptions and hypotheses of cognitive resource theory.

The leader's cognitive resources, therefore, determine the quality of the plans, decisions, and action strategies which guide the group.*

Assumption Two

Leaders use directive behavior to communicate these decisions and strategies to the group.

The assumption as to the leader's role in the planning and decision-making process has to be qualified to some extent. In the creative or problem-solving group, that is, the typical committee, the leader usually shares the planning functions with members of the group. Nevertheless, the leader's ability to contribute to the eventual outcome of the group's work is potentially greater since the leader usually writes the final report and thus directly affects the quality of the group product. Under ordinary circumstances, however, the leader must focus on the task in order for his or her intellectual abilities to contribute to performance.

Hypothesis One

Even the brightest leaders may give clear instructions that have disastrous results. Aside from the unforeseeable effects of malevolent chance and

* This assumption received indirect support in Mai-Dalton's (1975) in-basket study, which showed that the more intelligent leaders tended to have better conceptualized plans than less intelligent leaders. The correlation was significant but low (.32, $n = 122$).

the jealous gods, how can we understand these lapses? One possible explanation is that the leader simply may not have had his or her eye on the ball. This typically occurs when stress and anxiety distract or block the leader from concentrating on the problem.

We know from a broad range of research (e.g., Lazarus, 1966; Sarason, 1980) that stress narrows an individual's focus and diverts attention to concerns about one's own adequacy and self-worth. This is especially likely if the leader cannot deal with the source of stress in a rational manner. The typical response to this kind of situation is to worry and fret about what the boss meant and what could be done to keep the boss from being unpleasant or making unreasonable demands. As a result, the leader cannot deal effectively with the demands of the task.

Stress with the boss is especially likely when a superior pressures a subordinate to produce more while at the same time withholding such resources as information, feedback, and guidance needed to perform the job. It would be difficult for most leaders to face their boss with the charge of making their work needlessly difficult. And yet it is certainly not unknown that a boss may get covert satisfaction from seeing a subordinate struggle with a difficult problem. All of these stress-generating conditions make it difficult for the leader to focus on the task and to contribute intellectually to the group's performance. These and similar findings suggest three likely consequences. First, under stress, the leader is distracted and withdraws from the problem by letting the group drift without giving directions. Second, the leader, although well-intentioned, develops poor plans and action strategies because he or she cannot focus on the task. Third, the leader guides the group's efforts into nonproductive channels (e.g., trying to look good, building defenses against such possible disasters as getting fired).

If the leader's actions are counterproductive to the organization's goals, we might expect negative correlations between leader intelligence and group performance. Leaving aside the possibility of deliberate sabotage, one suggested scenario in support of this reasoning is as follows:

1. Under stress, the leader is distracted from the task and adopts strategies which will avoid or reduce stress. These strategies might entail, for example, looking for another job, building better relations with group members in order to gain emotional support, or trying to make oneself look good.
2. The more intelligent leaders are likely to be more effective in these stress avoidance maneuvers than are less intelligent leaders, and thus divert the group further from the assigned task than would less intelligent leaders. Hence,
3. We obtain a negative correlation between leader intelligence and performance. Hence:

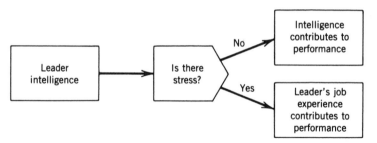

Figure 10.2. Cognitive resource theory hypotheses for tasks requiring intellectual effort. Hypothesis One.

In groups in which the leader experiences stress that distracts from the task, the leader's task-relevant abilities are uncorrelated or negatively correlated with performance. (See Figure 10.2.)

Hypothesis Two

If the task has to be performed by a group, the leader's ability can contribute to group performance only if the leader communicates the products of his or her intellectual effort. Although it may be possible to communicate plans, action strategies, and decisions by gesture, or indirectly by suggestions, the communication typically takes the form of directive behavior. Hence, intelligence scores or other measures of competence will correlate more highly with group performance if the leader is directive than if the leader is nondirective.

This hypothesis, originally proposed by Blades (1976), now seems obvious. If the leader doesn't communicate his or her plans, they cannot be implemented by the group. And unless the leader tells the group how to implement these plans they cannot be translated into action. "Telling" the group usually involves behaviors subsumed under such labels as structuring, production emphasis, and directing. In other words intelligence, technical competence, and job-relevant knowledge imply the ability to deal appropriately with given problems. Further, the best plans and most ingenious action strategies will affect group performance only if they are communicated to group members for implementation.

Given low stress conditions, the correlation between task performance and intellectual abilities will be higher if the leader is directive than if the leader is nondirective. (See Figure 10.3.)

Hypothesis Three

The leader is dependent on the group for implementation of plans and action strategies. As already shown by the contingency model, the leader's

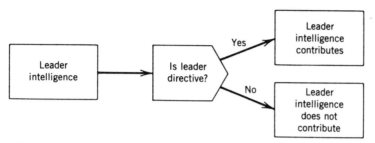

Figure 10.3. **Cognitive resource theory hypotheses for tasks requiring intellectual effort. Hypothesis Two.**

ability to rely on group member support is the most important single element in determining situational control. If the group members support the leader and the goals of the organization, they will try to comply with the leader's directions. Hence there will also be a high correlation between leader abilities and task performance. If the group members fail to comply with the leader's directions, the leader's plan and strategies will not be implemented. Outright refusal and mutiny are rare; considerably less rare are uncommitted group members who are unmotivated and give little or no support to the leader or the goals of the organization. In general, nonsupportive groups present a source of interpersonal stress and have an effect similar to other types of stress (e.g., with the immediate superior) that distract the leader from focusing on the task.

Under low stress conditions, the correlation between the directive leader's intelligence and task performance will be higher in supportive groups than in nonsupportive groups. (See Figure 10.4.)

Hypothesis Four

What can we expect from groups in which the leader fails to provide direction? On the average, groups with nondirective leaders are no less

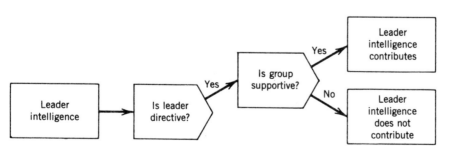

Figure 10.4. **Cognitive resource theory hypotheses for task requiring intellectual effort. Hypothesis Three.**

effective than those with directive leaders. This suggests that someone else may assume the leader's functions of planning and implementing action strategies. One obvious possibility is that the group members take charge of planning and organizing if the leader fails to do so. The group members' abilities rather than those of the leader will then correlate with group performance.

Blades (Blades & Fiedler, 1973) hypothesized that member abilities contribute to group performance only if they support the organization's task-related goals. If the group members are not supportive, they are likely to have their own agenda, and this alternative agenda (for example, having a good time or a pleasant job) may be unproductive or incompatible with the organization's goals. In the former case, we would then expect the group members' abilities to correlate positively with performance. In the latter case we would expect negative or zero correlations between group-member abilities and performance.

In groups in which leaders are nondirective (or under stress) the group-member's abilities correlate with performance if the group members support the leader or the organizational goals (see Figure 10.5).

Hypothesis Five

The leader's intellectual abilities should contribute more highly to tasks that require these intellectual abilities than to tasks which do not require intellectual abilities. While this proposition seems to belabor the obvious, our research raises some interesting questions as to the exact nature of the abilities the leadership task itself requires in different groups. To be sure, musical ability will not contribute to the effectiveness of a basketball coach, and mechanical skills will not contribute to the management of

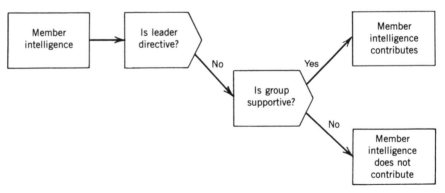

Figure 10.5. Cognitive resource theory hypotheses for task requiring intellectual effort. Hypothesis Four.

interpersonal conflict. The question is how such general abilities as intelligence or task-specific abilities contribute to the task.

The proposition points to the need for a taxonomy that tells us which particular cognitive abilities are required for a given task. Several excellent taxonomies have been proposed (e.g., Fleishman & Quaintance, 1984; Hackman, 1968; Shaw, 1963). Of these taxonomies, Fleishman and Quaintance's seems most appropriate for our purposes since it deals with the abilities required in the performance of a particular job. Also, some tasks require participative leadership and can be performed properly only if the leader shares the planning and decision-making functions with members of the group. Examples are committee assignments, jury decisions, and the development of problem solutions that reconcile diverse views. In tasks of this nature, directive leadership may interfere with group-member participation, and the nondirective, permissive, considerate leader's group may perform better by taking advantage of the abilities and competence of group members. The leader who is permissive and nondirective allows and encourages group members to express their views and contribute their ideas.

In many task groups, the leader must depend on the cooperation of the group since certain jobs, such as moving a piano, cannot be done by one person. In other groups, especially those used in laboratory settings, the leader is a full participant in performing these tasks and the leader may, in fact, be able to do the job alone. Still other tasks require emotional support and interpersonal skills rather than intellectual abilities; for example, restoring the morale of a particular unit or organization or developing the individual member's assertiveness or self-esteem.

Intellectual abilities under certain conditions may be inappropriate or dysfunctional for dealing with tasks of this nature. A "cold, calculating, and intellectual approach" may prevent, rather than assist, the group in achieving these particular goals. Considerate and nondirective leaders may then, perhaps, obtain better results than will directive and structuring leaders. In any event, a stressful leadership situation is likely to divert the leader from applying his or her task-relevant abilities as well as intellectual abilities to the task.

Under relatively stress-free conditions leader and group member abilities correlate with task performance to the extent to which these abilities are required by the task.

Hypothesis Six

Intellectual abilities are not, of course, the only relevant cognitive resources that leaders and group members bring to the organization. As pointed out earlier, a leader also makes use of job-relevant knowledge and previously acquired skills and behavior patterns learned through experience.

We know from a number of studies that people tend to revert to previously learned behavior under the influence of anxiety or stress. Freud (1938) first referred to this phenomenon as regression. A boss clearly represents a potential source of stress in the eyes of most subordinates, and we find that highly experienced leaders are more likely to have previously learned behaviors in their repertoire that enable them to perform more effectively under stress (see Figure 10.2).

When leaders are under stress, their experience rather than their cognitive abilities contribute to group performance.

Hypothesis Seven

Previous research has shown that the leader's personality, reflected by task motivation and relationship motivation (LPC), and the leader's situational control predict the leader's directive behavior (e.g., Fiedler, 1970). This important finding links the contingency model and cognitive resource theory. That is, the same condition which causes some leaders to seek interpersonal support from group members may cause other leaders to become more concerned with the task. Some people become more decisive and challenged by the same stressful conditions that intimidate and immobilize others. Some people are able to think better without pressure,

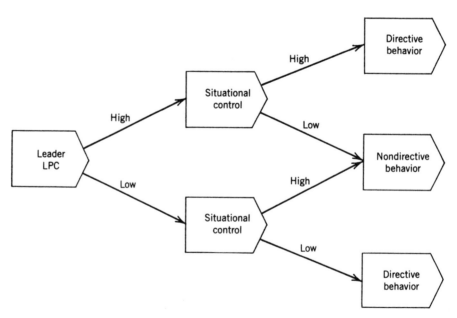

Figure 10.6. Cognitive resource theory hypotheses for tasks requiring intellectual effort. Hypothesis Five.

others must have tight deadlines or a crisis in order to get organized for the job that needs to be done. These findings imply that the leader's personality as well as situational factors strongly influence the manner of managing the group. Therefore, the more leader personality and situational control induce directive behavior, the more likely it is that the leader will effectively use intellectual abilities in the performance of the task. It goes without saying, however, that LPC and situational control account for only part of the variance in directive behavior.

We must also take into consideration that some situations require relatively directive behavior while others require nondirective behavior. The captain of an airliner cannot be nondirective during a difficult landing, and the chairman of a jury cannot be directive during the jury deliberations. Nevertheless, there is considerable variability in directive leader behavior of airline captains and jury formen, reflecting the individual's personality. We are, therefore, concerned not only with the absolute directiveness of a leader but also with the relative directiveness, given the particular situation. Hence, Hypothesis Seven states,

The leader's directive behavior is predicted by the contingency model elements: the leader's task- or relationship-motivation and situational control (see Figure 10.6).

The next chapters present preliminary support of cognitive resource theory.

CHAPTER ELEVEN

Stress, Cognitive Resources, and Performance

The effects of stress are well known to those who have suffered from stage fright or examination anxiety. They know all too well that stress decreases their ability to think on their feet or to answer exam questions. And those who have participated in athletic events know that stress increases competitive performance. In brief, stress depresses performance on new or complex tasks and increases performance on overlearned and simple tasks (Zajonc, 1965). The first part of this chapter asks how stress affects the contribution of the leader's intellectual abilities to task performance. The second part asks how stress affects the contribution of job-related experience to performance.

EFFECTS OF STRESS ON THE EFFECTIVE USE OF INTELLIGENCE

Hypothesis One of cognitive resource theory states that the leader's intellectual abilities are diverted from the task in stressful conditions and therefore can be applied to the task only when the leader does not feel under stress.

Boss Stress, Leader Intelligence, and Performance

While job stress is often seen as part of the work, interpersonal stress, especially stress with one's boss, is much more difficult to accept and considerably more unsettling. It affects our ability "to think straight." The leader who has a stressful relationship with the boss is likely to worry more about this relationship than about the job. This does not necessarily result in poor performance. After all, high intelligence is not required for every job. Also, as we shall see, leaders might have learned from extensive experience how to deal with various situations without having to think about them. If intellectual effort is required, however, a stress-free leadership environment is likely to let the leader concentrate on the job. A series of studies examined this relationship.

Squad Leaders. Fiedler and Leister (1977) studied 128 U.S. Army infantry squad leaders whose performance had been rated by their two superiors, the platoon leader and the platoon sergeants. Also available were intelligence scores, time in service, relations with group members, self-ratings of motivation, and various measures of stress.

The sample was divided into those above and below the median on a simple eight-point bipolar scale asking them to rate how much stress they felt in the relationship with the boss ("stressful–nonstressful"). The correlation between leader intelligence and performance for those reporting low stress was .40 ($n = 72$) $p < .01$ compared to .07 ($n = 56$, ns) for squad leaders with high boss stress, a significant difference.

Company Commander–First Sergeant Dyads. Knowlton (Fiedler, Potter, Zais, & Knowlton, 1979) investigated the effect of stress in 45 dyads consisting of army company commanders and their first sergeants (FSG). The FSG is the senior enlisted man and principal advisor on matters related to enlisted personnel in the army company. He is considered to be the key to effective company performance. The relationship between company commander and FSG, then, is a crucial element in how the army company functions.

First sergeants and company commanders in this sample were asked to rate the stressfulness of their relationship with each other using a 25-item scale adapted from the Leader Behavior Description Questionnaire-Form XII (LBDQ; Stogdill, 1963). Intelligence was measured with the Wonderlic Personnel Test (Wonderlic, 1977). The battalion commander and battalion executive officer, who are the immediate superiors of the company commander, made three performance ratings. They separately evaluated the performance of the FSG's superior, that is, the company commander, the entire company, and the company commander–FSG dyad.

The study considered only those company comander–FSG dyads in which both members reported that they had relatively low stress in their relationship and those in which both reported high stress. Intelligence scores of the FSG (not the company commander) were then correlated with performance of his company commander, the company, and the company commander–FSG dyad. The results in Table 11.1 show that the

Table 11.1. Correlations Between First Sergeant
Intelligence and Performance in Company
Commander–First Sergeant Dyads That Reported
Low Stress and High Stress

Performance Rating of	Stress in Dyad	
	Low (13)	High (8)
Company commander	.71*	.06[a]
First sergeant–company commander dyad	.78*	−.04[a]
Company performance	.51	.24

[a] Differences between correlations in the high and low stress columns are significant ($p < .05$).

FSG's intellectual ability contributed to his boss's and his unit's performance only when the relationship in the dyad was not stressful. These correlations are unusually high, especially since the criteria were the performance of the entire company and of the company commander as well as of the dyad.

Army Company Commanders and Battalion Staff Officers. A third study by Zais (Fiedler, Potter, Zais, & Knowlton, 1979) used the company commanders and staff officers from the same units on which the first sergeant study had been based. The performance of company commanders and staff officers was rated by their battalion commanders and executive officers. The company commander's stress with boss was measured with a set of LBDQ items for describing the stressfulness of the relationship with the immediate superior. A multiple regression analysis, accounting for 27 percent of the variance, showed that the stress experienced by the subordinate leader was highest if the boss pushed the subordinate for high performance (Beta = .32) while at the same time giving him little freedom to act (Beta = .37).

The correlation between intelligence and performance company commanders under conditions of low and high boss stress ($\pm$1SD) were respectively .56 ($n = 7$, ns) and .06 ($n = 13$, ns). The corresponding correlations for staff officers were .17 ($n = 9$, ns) and −.56 ($n = 9$, ns). Although these correlations were not significant, they were again in the negative direction when stress with boss was high. (Mean scores on intelligence, stress, experience, and performance were almost identical, and not significant.)

As can be seen from Figure 11.1, under low stress, intelligence correlated with the performance of company commanders but not staff officers. Under high stress, the more intelligent staff officers performed worse than those with lower intelligence. One explanation for these negative correlations is that many battalion staff officers' jobs tend to be routine and primarily require knowledge and strict adherence to army regulations. Highly intelligent individuals are apt to seek new methods and new solutions to

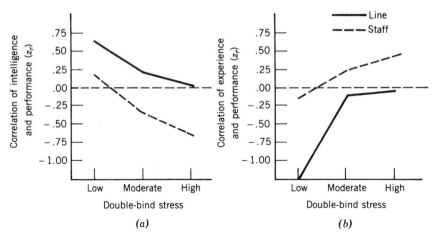

Figure 11.1. The effect of production stress on correlations of company commanders' and staff officers' performance with intelligence and experience. [Reprinted with permissions from F. E. Fiedler, E. H. Potter, M. M. Zais, & W. A. Knowlton (1979). Organizational stress and the use and misuse of managerial intelligence and experience. *Journal of Applied Psychology, 64,* 635–647. Copyright American Psychological Association.]

problems. But creativity and unusual shortcuts are likely to get the staff officer and his boss into difficulties. For example, the results would be disastrous if every staff officer in the thousands of battalions were to create his or her own system of record keeping or requisitioning.

Coast Guard Staff. A study by Potter and Fiedler (1981) investigated the entire staff of a coast guard headquarters consisting of 130 officers, petty officers, and civilians in responsible staff positions. Most of these subjects headed offices or staff sections. Intelligence was measured with the Wonderlic Personnel Test. The stress with boss that appeared to have the strongest effect on the use of intelligence and experience was obtained from a scale which measured "double-bind stress." This 34-item scale focused on the degree to which the respondents felt production pressure from a boss who at the same time withheld needed support, guidance, and information. This type of stress was similar to the stress with boss described by company commanders. Staff personnel also described their specific staff functions and the amount of time devoted to each of these functions.

The sample was divided into those reporting relatively low and relatively high stress with boss. Performance was rated by the immediate supervisor, using the Bons (1974) scale. It is important to note that the supervisor's rating of the subordinate, and the subordinate's rating of his or her stress with the supervisor, were uncorrelated ($-.07$, $n = 102$). As in the other studies, superiors either were unaware of the stress their subordinates experienced in relating to them, or they did not let it affect their evaluations. We are inclined to believe they were unaware, since most supervisors have a rather unrealistic picture of how they appear to their subordinates (e.g., as patient, forgiving, and always open to suggestions).

Correlations were obtained between the intelligence of staff personnel and their performance separately for those reporting relatively low stress with boss and those reporting high stress. Since there was considerable variation in time of service, the sample was also divided into those with less than 10 years, between 10 and 20 years, and more than 20 years of service. The effects of stress were much greater for those with relatively less time in service than for those who had been in the Coast Guard for an extended period of time. The more experienced subjects presumably had become less vulnerable to stress with their immediate superiors as they acquired friends in high places, gained indispensable knowledge about their job, or reached a more secure position in the service. The correlations obtained for job stress indicate that the effects of job stress were relatively small when compared with those of stress with boss (see Table 11.2).

The results in Table 11.2 also support the notion that the contribution of intelligence to leader performance is diminished by boss stress. In fact the negative correlation between intelligence and performance suggests that high levels of boss stress may create conditions in which intelligent leaders misuse their cognitive resources. As already suggested, this misuse may come about because the individual focuses attention on avoiding the stressful situation rather than on performing the task; the more intelligent leaders are probably more effective in these efforts. But another hypothesis should also be considered: the more intelligent leaders might be better

Table 11.2. Correlations Between Intelligence and Performance Under Low and High Boss Stress and Job Stress for Coast Guard Staff

Time in Service	Low Boss Stress	High Boss Stress
All subjects	.16 (60)	−.27* (51)
Less than 10 years	.73* (13)	−.43# (16)[a]
10–20 years	−.23 (21)	−.28 (14)
More than 20 years	.24 (16)	.24 (14)
Time in Service	Low Job Stress	High Job Stress
All subjects	.05 (42)	−.04 (45)
Less than 10 years	.18 (13)	−.11 (8)
10–20 years	.24 (14)	−.33 (16)
More than 20 years	.57 (6)	−.09 (18)

[a] Differences between correlations in the high and low boss stress columns are significant ($p < .001$).

able to visualize the consequences of failure than less intelligent leaders, and this vivid picture of failure might make them unable to function, while others are "too dumb to know better." More tests are needed to determine which hypothesis best accounts for the negative correlations.

Infantry Division Leaders. A large study of nine combat infantry battalions (Borden, 1980) further investigated the effect of stress on the contribution of leader and staff intelligence to performance. Five different leadership levels of the military chain of command were represented in this study: 45 company commanders, 43 executive officers, 106 platoon leaders, 42 first sergeants, and 163 platoon sergeants (all males). All available personnel, with the exception of three noncommissioned officers who had reading difficulties, participated in the study.

Intellectual ability was measured with Form V of the Wonderlic Personnel Test. The measure of experience was time in military service (TIS). Stress with boss was measured by having subjects respond twice to each question on a 30-item questionnaire. The first indicated how much stress a particular behavior of the boss caused ("My boss is unfriendly and unapproachable"); the second indicated frequency of the behavior. This measure thus weights the stressfulness of a behavior with the frequency of its occurrence. Thus if a certain behavior is very stressful but infrequent it will receive a lower score than one that is both stressful and frequent.

A minimum of two, and a maximum of four, superiors independently rated each leader's performance on a modification of the Bons (1974) scale described earlier. Mean intelligence scores of officers were significantly higher than those of NCOs, while the latter had more time in service. Other variables in this study did not differ significantly among different job groups (i.e., platoon sergeant, platoon leader, first sergeant, company commander, company executive officer).

The officers and NCOs in each job category were divided into those with low, moderate, and high stress ratings, and correlations were then computed between their intelligence and performance scores. The results supported the hypothesis: in each of the six job classes, the correlation between intelligence and performance was higher under the low boss stress condition than under the high boss stress condition (see Table 11.3). The results were again less clear when samples were divided on the basis of job stress with which leaders seem better able to cope. This cross-validation leaves little doubt that we are dealing with reliable results. Whether similar results would be obtained for markedly different types of jobs still needs to be examined.

In contrast to the coast guard and company commander studies, the intelligence of staff officers in the combat infantry division study did not correlate negatively with performance under low stress. We need to ask why these results are inconsistent with those reported in the Fiedler, Potter, Zais, and Knowlton (1979) study. A number of explanations are

Table 11.3. Correlations between Leader
Intelligence and Rated Leader Performance
in the Infantry Division Study

Sample	Stress with Boss		
	Low	Moderate	High
Platoon sergeants	.19 (49)	.25# (37)	$-.38^*$ (33)^a
First sergeants	.56 (14)	.22 (14)	$-.08$ (13)^a
Platoon leaders	.64* (32)	.32# (32)	$-.20$ (30)^a
Company executive			
officers	.42 (10)	.86** (8)	$-.12$ (9)^a
Company commanders	.70* (12)	.29 (14)	$-.40$ (10)
Means	.52	.45	$-.08$

^{a}Differences between correlations in the high and low stress with boss
columns are significant.

possible. One of these is that the staff officers in the infantry division
were substantially more experienced, and many of these officers held
major's rank. As the coast guard study showed, the more experienced
leaders and staff officers do not react as strongly to boss stress, probably
because they are more secure or more accustomed to interpersonal stress
of this type. Second, the infantry staff officers' jobs may have been less
routine and structured than those in the Zais study (Fiedler, Potter, Zais,
& Knowlton, 1979) in which the subjects came from medical, transportation,
and artillery battalions, with only one infantry battalion. This problem
needs to be explored further.

STRESS, LEADER EXPERIENCE,
AND PERFORMANCE

Hypothesis six states that the leader's experience correlates with performance under conditions of interpersonal stress. As before, we here
define experience as time in service or time on the job on the assumption
that time is one essential element required for informally acquiring job-
relevant skills, knowledge, and behavior patterns. We assume that a
leader who has dealt successfully with certain problems many times in
the past will deal with these problems in an almost automatic manner
if the situation is stressful.

The studies presented in the first section of this chapter contained
measures indicating time in service and time on the job. These studies
permitted us, therefore, to determine the effect of stress on the relationship
between these experience measures and leadership performance.

Squad Leaders. As will be recalled, the study by Fiedler and Leister (1977) investigated the effect of stress on the correlation between intelligence and performance and found a positive correlation under conditions of low stress but no relationship under high stress conditions. However, time in service correlated with the leader's performance only under conditions of very high boss stress, that is, $+1$ SD $(.40, n = 27, p < .05)$. When boss stress was low, the time in service was uncorrelated with performance $(.09, n = 28)$.

Company Commander–First Sergeant Dyads. This study (Fiedler, Potter, Zais, & Knowlton, 1978) measured experience on the job, that is, specifically, the amount of time the first sergeant had held that position. As will be recalled, this study was concerned with dyads in which both the company commander and the first sergeant (FSG) described the relationship either as very stressful or as relatively stress-free. This study also found that the company commander–FSG dyad's rated performance, as well as the company's performance, correlated with the FSG's years on the job only under high stress conditions (see Table 11.4).

Company Commanders and Battalion Staff Officers. Separate analyses were conducted for line and staff officers in order to determine the relationship of experience to performance for each of these jobs when the officer reported high or low stress with his boss. The company commander's time in service was significantly correlated in the negative direction with performance when he had a stress-free relationship with his boss $(-.86, n = 8, p < .01)$; experience was uncorrelated with performance when stress with boss was high $(-.05, n = 12, ns)$. The staff officers' experience was uncorrelated with performance when stress with the boss was low $(-.13, n = 9, ns)$ but it was positively correlated with performance when stress with the boss was high $(.42, n = 9, ns)$. In other words, when stress was low, the company commanders in this study were rated effective if they had high intelligence but relatively low time in

Table 11.4. Correlations Between
Experience and Performance Under Low
and High Boss Stress for Company
Commander–FSG Dyads

	Boss Stress	
Performance Rating of	**Low**	**High**
Company Commander	.00	.51
Company Commander–FSG	−.09	.66*[a]
Company Performance	−.20	.39

[a] Differences between correlations in the high and low boss stress columns are significant $(p < .05)$.

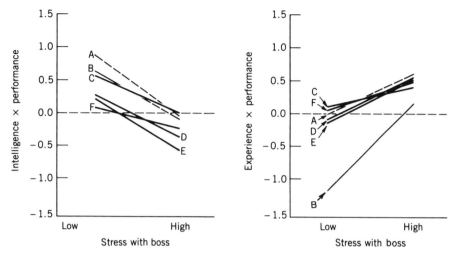

Figure 11.2. Summaries of correlations between leader intelligence and performance and between organizational experience and performance in the (A) first sergeant, (B) company commander, (C) squad leader, (D) Coast Guard member (high on intellectual tasks), (E) staff officer, and (F) Coast Guard member (low on intellectual tasks). Note: All graphs show correlations as z'.

service. When stress was high, they benefited from neither their intelligence nor their experience. Staff officers benefited from neither their intelligence nor their experience when stress was low; but when stress was high, staff officer performance benefited from relatively low intelligence but high experience. These complex relations are best seen by referring to Figure 11.1.

Coast Guard. In this study, as mentioned before, leaders varied considerably in the time they had spent in the organization. Time in service ranged from 15 months to 38 years. The study showed that double-bind stress had a major effect on the relative newcomer to the organization. An old-timer, however, is likely to have learned how to find other sources of information, or he may have developed routines for handling many of the problems in his job. Last but not least, the old hand probably learned how to manage his boss, and how to duck when an unpleasantness looms on the horizon. We would expect, therefore, that the more experienced staff person would perform more effectively than one who is less experienced in obtaining information or assistance. This hypothesis was supported. Experience correlated with performance only under relatively high stress ($r = .44$, $n = 48$, $p < .01$). Under low double-bind stress, the leaders' job experience was not related to the effectiveness of staff personnel ($r = .03$, $n = 60$, ns).

Figure 11.2 summarizes the correlations between leader intelligence and performance and between organizational experience and performance in the squad leader, the company commander–first sergeant dyad, the company commander and staff officer, and the Coast Guard studies. The magnitude of the correlations (z') is indicated on the vertical axis, and low and high stress with boss is shown on the horizontal axis. As can be seen, the two sets of correlations appear to mirror each other.

Infantry Division Leaders

Borden's (1980) study of combat infantry battalions also provided data on time in service, and this measure was correlated with leadership performance under low, moderate, and high stress conditions. Table 11.5 demonstrates that the correlations were, on the whole, relatively high when stress was high, but low or even negative when stress with boss was low, thus supporting previously obtained data.

The means of the correlations between intelligence and performance and between time in service and performance, are plotted in Figure 11.3. As can be seen, the correlations between intelligence and performance and between time in service and performance are practically mirror images of each other. This finding suggests that intellectual abilities and organizational experience may be incompatible or may interfere with each other.

Fire Service Officers. Our research raises the question whether boss stress and job stress or stress from subordinates have similar influence on the effective use of cognitive resources. We also need to know whether such different indices of the leader's experience as time in the organization, time in the job, or time in a particular work unit yield similar findings. We addressed these questions in a study of fire department companies of a large urban fire department (Frost, 1981).

The sample consisted of 110 fire lieutenants and 66 fire captains. Each of these officers directed a fire company of two to five men. Captains and

Table 11.5. Correlations Between Infantry Leaders' Time in Service and Performance Under Conditions of Low, Moderate, and High Boss Stress

Sample	Boss Stress		
	Low	Moderate	High
Platoon sergeant	−.25[#] (51)	−.11 (40)	.59* (35)
First sergeant	.18 (14)	.05 (14)	.59 (13)
Platoon leader	−.05 (32)	−.34* (35)	.53* (30)
Company executive officer	.18 (10)	.24 (8)	.49 (9)
Company commander	.49[#] (12)	.34 (14)	.46 (10)
Means	.12	.04	.54

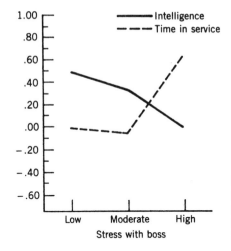

Figure 11.3. Average correlations (z-transforms) between leader intelligence and performance and the leader's time in service and performance under conditions of low, moderate, and high stress with boss.

lieutenants have similar responsibilities for their companies, but captains have the additional duty of administering the fire station, and if no battalion chief is present, the captain, as the senior officer, is in charge at the scene of the fire. The officers' performance was evaluated by their battalion chief, using a behaviorally anchored scale which had been designed for the fire department.

We were able to obtain from each officer the time spent in the fire service, time as an officer, and time in his particular company. All officers come up through the ranks, and practically all have had the same training and have held the same or similar duties in the course of their career. Fire department officials, therefore, consider time in service and relevance of experience as essentially identical.

The various experience measures were analyzed separately for captains, who as a group had more tenure than lieutenants. Table 11.6 shows that

Table 11.6. Intercorrelations Between Experience Measures and Intelligence for Fire Department Lieutenants (n = 110) and Captains (n = 66)

	Intelligence	Time in Fire Service	Time as Fire Officer	Time in Unit
Lieutenants				
Intelligence		−.27	−.05	−.15
Time in fire service			.40*	.36*
Time as fire officer				.47*
Captains				
Intelligence		−.23	−.09	−.05
Time in fire service			.69*	.42*
Time as fire officer				.42*

the various indices were moderately correlated with one another but uncorrelated with intelligence.

To ascertain the effect of the various experience measures on performance, the lieutenants and captains were divided into those with relatively high and low experience. The various experience measures as well as the Wonderlic intelligence score were correlated with rated performance and are shown in Table 11.7. The most striking findings in this table are the high negative correlations between performance and the time in service as well as time in leadership position (time as officer) and between performance and the most general measure of life experience, namely age, when stress with boss is low. These correlations were nonsignificant but in the positive direction when stress with boss was high.

Again we find that the results, although in the same direction, were considerably weaker when the sample was divided on the basis of job stress. Perceived boss stress seems to have a stronger effect on the use of cognitive resources than does job stress. This was also found in the coast guard study. Fire department officials suggested the following two explanations. The poorer performance of the more experienced leaders under low stress may reflect the higher expectations that superiors have of their experienced subordinates. The more favored explanation by fire officers

Table 11.7. Correlations Between Various Experience Measures and Rated Performance of Fire Department Company Officers Who Reported Low or High Boss Stress, Stress with Subordinates, or Job Stress

Correlations Between Performance and:	Lieutenants			
	Boss Stress		Job Stress	
	Low (26)	High (29)	Low (31)	High (24)
Age	−.56*	.40	−.13	−.07
Time in Fire Department	−.47*	.38	−.13	.08
Time as Fire Officer	−.33	.10	−.16	−.11
Time in Present Unit	.17	.39*	.00	.57*
Intelligence	.11	−.15	.16	−.20

Correlations Between Performance and:	Fire Captains			
	Boss Stress		Job Stress	
	Low (17)	High (16)	Low (15)	High (18)
Age	−.63*	.44	−.48	.24
Time in Fire Department	−.55*	.50	−.38	.28
Time as Fire Officer	−.13	.44	.13	.22
Time in Present Unit	−.37	.25	.24	.03
Intelligence	−.13	−.05	.10	−.17

was that the more experienced leaders under low stress performed poorly because they had become bored and jaded. The latter explanation seems more plausible.

It is particularly interesting that age correlated so highly with performance under stress. In fact it correlated more highly with performance than specific measures of job-related experience such as time in the unit or holding the job of lieutenant or captain. It seems doubtful that the older officers are necessarily more competent than younger officers, but they may feel more confident in relating to their younger colleagues. This does not completely answer why they perform worse when stress with boss is low and better when stress with boss is high. This is another interesting question that remains unresolved.

Intellectual abilities were not significantly correlated with performance in this particular study for two possible reasons. First, the performance of a fire service officer is evaluated largely by how well he or she performs under stress; under stressful conditions, intellectual abilities do not correlate highly with performance. Second, the fire service requires extensive drills and training, and the emphasis is on application of the training, not on creativity—certainly not at the scene of a fire.

We raised the question whether the stress rating of the experienced officers might reflect their boss' higher expectations. This study gave us a unique opportunity to provide an answer since it was possible to obtain an objective measure of job stress in this study. This stress measure follows the fire department's assumption that the leader is under most stress at the scene of the fire. At that time he is responsible for the protection of property and, more important, for the lives and safety of his subordinates and those who might be trapped in a burning building. On advice of senior fire department officials, Frost (1981) divided fire companies into those which logged relatively many hours at the scene of fires, that is, companies operating in city districts with many fire calls and presumably high job stress, and fire companies which logged relatively few hours at the scene of fires, which typically came from suburban areas with few fire calls or mostly kitchen and garbage fires (low job stress).

Figure 11.4 shows the average performance scores for experienced and relatively less experienced fire captains of companies which logged relatively many and relatively few hours at the scene of fires. The strong and statistically significant interaction, indicates that the fire captains with many years of service performed better in the stressful districts while the fire captains with relatively less time in service performed better in the less stressful districts. Statistically significant but somewhat weaker findings were obtained for lieutenants. These results show that job stress moderates the correlations between time in service and performance in the same manner as interpersonal stress, and seemingly does so to a greater extent than self-reported job stress.

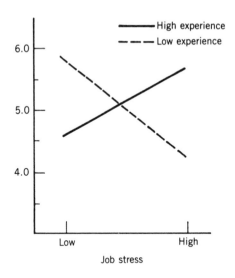

Figure 11.4. Mean performance ratings for relatively experienced and less experienced (time in service) fire department captains of companies in districts with high or low incidence of fire (interaction significant).

Concluding Comments

The results of this series of studies show that stress, and particularly interpersonal stress, strongly moderates the correlations of intelligence and job-related experience with performance. The more intelligent leaders performed better only in situations in which stress with their boss was low. The more tenured and presumably more experienced leaders seem to cope better than inexperienced leaders with high interpersonal stress, supporting Hypothesis Six of cognitive resource theory.

One explanation for these findings is based on social facilitation theory. Zajonc (1965) has shown that overlearned tasks are best performed when there is a critical audience present. Conversely, a critical audience (e.g., a stress-producing boss) interferes with performance on new or complex tasks. Insofar as we can define experience as the equivalent of "overlearned tasks," social facilitation theory may be seen as a plausible explanation for these results.

Intellectual ability correlated with task performance only under conditions of low boss stress. It correlated negatively with performance when stress was high. Two hypotheses were suggested to account for the latter results. One is that the more intelligent persons are better able to project the consequences of failure, and these, in turn, cause the individual to "freeze up." A second hypothesis suggests that stress distracts the individual's intellectual focus from the task. Both of these hypotheses may well be correct under given conditions.

One study of coast guard cadets (Barnes, Potter, & Fiedler, 1983) supports the second hypothesis. Cadets are selected for admission in part on the basis of the Scholastic Aptitude Test (SAT), and their intellectual per-

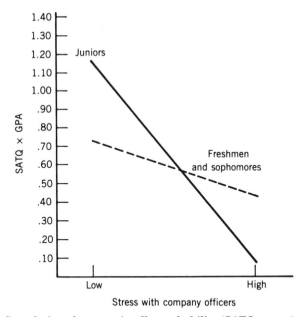

Figure 11.5. Correlations between intellectual ability (SATQ scores) and academic performance (GPA) for cadets reporting high and low levels of stress in their relationships with their company officers at different stages in their Coast Guard Academy career. [Reprinted with permission from V. E. Barnes, F. H. Potter, & F. E. Fiedler (1983). Effects of interpersonal stress on the production of academic performance. *Journal of Applied Psychology, 68*, 686–697. Copyright American Psychological Association.]

formance can be measured by their cumulative grade point average (GPA). If intellectual ability is effectively used we would expect a high correlation between the SAT and GPA scores. The correlation between these two measures for the coast guard cadets is in the range of .45 to .50.

The Barnes et al. study divided the group of cadets in the sophomore and junior classes into those who reported low, moderate, or high stress with their military superiors. When this was done, the study found that the correlation between cadet SAT and GPA is quite high for cadets with low stress (.72) but low and nonsignificant (.20) for the group of cadets who reported high stress with their superior officer. Subsequent interviews showed that the cadets who reported stress felt under pressure from their superiors to perform their military duties, and these duties distracted them from their academic work. This relationship between SAT and GPA is shown in Figure 11.5.

To summarize, the results of these studies indicate that leaders depend on their previous job experience but not on their intelligence when they have stressful relationships with their boss. They depend on their intelligence but not on their job experience when they have a relatively stress-free interpersonal work environment.

CHAPTER TWELVE

Directive Behavior and Intellectual Abilities: Preliminary Tests of Cognitive Resource Theory

This chapter describes preliminary empirical tests of cognitive resource theory in five different studies. The first part of this chapter describes the five test studies on various relevant dimensions. The second part details the three field studies. The third part details two laboratory experiments. Since the studies were not specifically designed to test cognitive resource theory, many measures are approximations of what we would ideally like to have had, since approximate measures are likely to be weaker than those obtained with measures especially designed for the purpose. The results, therefore, are likely to err on the conservative side. The present discussion focuses on the contribution of the leaders' and the members' intellectual abilities.

DESCRIPTION OF THE FIVE TEST STUDIES

The five studies we shall discuss in this chapter differ in several major dimensions, and these differences are important in interpreting the findings. As already pointed out, three are field studies and two are highly controlled laboratory experiments. The first study, of army mess halls by Blades and Fiedler (1973), dealt with leaders who have high position power and must depend on their subordinates' cooperation for the effective operation of the mess hall. The leaders are, however, relatively independent of their immediate superiors.

In the squad leader study by Bons and Fiedler (1976) the leader also had strong position power, but he was closely supervised and much more dependent on his immediate superiors than on the recruits he supervised. The public health volunteer study by Fiedler, O'Brien, and Ilgen (1969) dealt with small, informally organized groups that conducted public health work in Honduras and Guatemala in 1966. Leaders were not appointed by the organization but emerged as the group began its work. They had relatively little formal power, and many groups operated in a relatively stressful environment.

In the two laboratory experiments formal leaders were appointed by the experimenter. In the decoding study by Chemers, Rice, Sundstrom, and Butler (1975), situational control was experimentally varied by giving half of the leaders "technical" training in how to approach the task, while the other half did not receive relevant training. In the ROTC creativity study by Meuwese and Fiedler (1965), teams worked on creative tasks under three experimentally induced stress conditions. Not surprisingly, there are important differences between the findings from the various studies, but we are here primarily concerned with the consistencies which emerged despite the considerable differences among studies.

The problem of identifying the conditions under which various cognitive resources contribute to performance is highly complex. We suffer from the dilemma common to most studies of leadership. There are never enough groups that perform identical tasks under comparable conditions. Data from different studies, therefore, have to be aggregated to give us confidence that the results are stable. Results in support of a hypothesis may well be nonsignificant in one or more studies and yet be consistent and significant when we consider the aggregated results from all five studies.

To facilitate interpretation of the results, we describe the five studies on various dimensions. The first table (Table 12.1) compares the five studies on the leader's situational control dimension. The task structure score is based on ratings of the groups' primary task by five independent judges. The task in the decoding study was rated for trained as well as untrained leaders. (See p. 145.)

Differences among the studies in degree of stress and type of task are shown in Table 12.2. Table 12.3 shows the cognitive resource variables as well as variables related to the group characteristics. It should be noted that we were not able to obtain complete data for all subjects or all groups. Some subjects failed to answer all questionnaire items and some data were lost in transit from Central America. The analyses are based on all available data.

Table 12.1. Situational Control in Studies Described in This Chapter

Study	Leader–Member Relations	Task Structure	Task Structure Score[a]	Position Power
Mess hall	Good to poor	High	15.4	High
Decoding with training	Moderate to poor	High	11.2	Low
Squad leader	Good to poor	High	10.2	Moderate to high
Public health	Good to poor	High to low	4.6[b]	Low
Decoding without training	Moderate to poor	Low	2.1	Low
ROTC creativity				
Payproposal	Good to poor	Low	1.4	High to low
Fable		Low	0.8	High to low

[a] Task structure scores based on five expert ratings.
[b] Task structure rating for the community development task.

Table 12.2. Type and Degree of Stress Encountered by Leaders in the Studies Described in This Chapter

Study	Stress Source	Stress Degree	Type of Task
Mess halls	Subordinates	Low to moderate (not measured)	Routine tasks
Squad leader	Superior, subordinates	Low to high	Routine tasks
Public health	Environment, subordinates	Low to high	Community work
Decoding	Group members	Moderate to high	Puzzle tasks
ROTC creativity	Experimental conditions	Low to high	Creative tasks

Table 12.3. Cognitive Data Available in the Various Studies Described in This Chapter

Study	Sample Size	Size of Group	Leader Intelligence	Member Intelligence	Tech Competence	Experience
Mess halls	41	3–8	X	X	X	X
Squad leader	138	8–10	X		X	X
Public health	38	2–4	X	X		
Decoding	40	3	X	X		
ROTC creativity	54	3	X	X		

FIELD STUDIES

The Mess Hall Study

The Leadership Situation. The first study (Csoka, 1974; Blades & Fiedler, 1973) dealt with 51 army mess halls that were headed by a senior noncommissioned officer. The mess steward's task is relatively routine and structured. A host of regulations prescribes the maintenance of sanitary conditions, the preparation of food, and the management of the facilities and buildings. Menus are prescribed by the post or still higher headquarters.

The mess steward rules over a fairly independent fiefdom. While he is responsible to the commander of the company the mess hall serves, there is very little interference in the way the mess steward runs his mess hall. On the other hand, the mess steward is dependent on the support of his cooks whose cooperation is essential for the operation of the mess hall.

Tests and Measures. The mess stewards' and cooks' intelligence scores were based on a 42-item version of the Henman–Nelson (Lamke, Nelson, & French, 1973) test. Mess stewards also provided information on the length of their service in the army, their training in food service and mess management, and the length of time they had been mess stewards.

We measured the cooks' support of the mess steward on a 10-item group atmosphere (GA) scale, and divided the mess halls at the median of the GA scale into the relatively supportive and less supportive groups. Cooks also rated the directiveness of the mess steward on an eight-point scale which read, "He decides what shall be done, and how it shall be done."

Performance Measures. The mess hall and its food service are frequent topics of discussion among enlisted men, and their complaints about poor meals soon come to the attention of the company commander. Deficiencies in sanitary conditions are also brought to the attention of the company commander and the food service officer and are considered grave problems that need immediate attention. Since mess halls vie with one another for excellence, there is an almost constant evaluation of their performance.

For purposes of this study, the commander of each company rated the effectiveness of his mess hall and the performance of the mess steward. These ratings were also obtained from the brigade food advisor, a specialist who periodically inspects all mess halls and provides technical supervision of food services in the brigade. The agreement between these two ratings was .76, and the correlation between ratings of the mess hall and of the mess steward was .91 ($n = 51$).

The rating of the mess hall is more likely to take into consideration various circumstances beyond the mess steward's control, that is, the quality of equipment and the number and competence of personnel assigned to the mess hall. Any rating of the mess steward is likely to be influenced

Table 12.4. Correlations Between Performance and Leader and Member Intelligence and Technical Competence (Amount of Training and Experience) in Groups with Relatively Directive and Nondirective Leaders[a]

Performance Predictor	Leader Directiveness		
	High (10)	Moderate (25)	Low (13)
Mess steward intelligence	.30	.15	$-.26^b$
Mess steward training	.42	.21	$-.60^{*b}$
Mess steward job experience	.24	.22	$-.17$
Cook intelligence	.01	.22	$-.34$

[a] Analysis of variance (ANOVA) comparing differences in mean performance was not significant.

[b] Differences between correlations in the high and low directiveness column are significant at ($p < .05$).

by the mess steward's ability to make a good impression on superiors, and for this reason, the results are based on ratings of the entire mess hall.

Results. Hypothesis One of the cognitive resource theory could not be tested in this study since no stress measures had been obtained. Hypothesis Two stated that directive leaders utilize their cognitive resources more effectively than do nondirective leaders. This hypothesis was tested by dividing the mess halls into upper, middle, and lower thirds on the leader directiveness item since curvilinear trends have sometimes been found in studies of this nature.* Table 12.4 compares mess halls with relatively directive, moderately directive, and less directive mess stewards. The correlations between the cognitive resource variables and mess hall performance permit us to infer the contributions of the mess steward's and the cooks' intelligence to performance. For purposes of comparison this table also presents correlations with a measure of the mess steward's training and on-the-job experience. Mess steward intelligence for the entire sample was uncorrelated with performance (.00, $n = 50$).

As the table shows, the mess steward's intellectual abilities as well as experience and training (i.e., job-relevant knowledge) were more effectively utilized when the leader was directive than nondirective. Cognitive resource scores correlated *negatively* with performance when leader directiveness was low: groups with brighter, more experienced, and better trained but nondirective leaders tended to perform less well than groups whose leaders were relatively less bright, experienced, and trained. It is important to note in this connection that none of the various cognitive measures cor-

* Splitting the samples into thirds or at the medians in this and the other studies frequently results in subsamples which vary somewhat in size. These differences in subsamples occur because of tied scores, for example, in directiveness or stress ratings, or missing data.

related with one another over .35. In other words, these relatively independent cognitive resource measures yielded very similar results. The mess steward's directiveness did not affect the cook' intellectual contribution to mess hall performance.

Hypothesis Three predicted that the leader's intelligence correlates more highly with performance if the leader is directive and the group is supportive than if the group is unsupportive. Hypothesis Four predicted that the members' abilities correlate with group performance if the group is supportive and has a nondirective leader. To test these hypotheses the sample was subdivided on the basis of the cooks' group atmosphere score (a measure of group support) as well as the leader's directiveness. Correlations were then computed between performance and the mess steward's and cooks' intelligence scores as well as the mess steward's training and experience.

Table 12.5 permits us to see that the leader's intelligence was well utilized only when the leader was directive and had a supportive group. Note that the correlations between group performance and the mess steward's job experience and training were negative and significantly so for training when the leader was nondirective and did not have high group support. This suggests as one possibility that the leaders in this situation attempted to do the job by themselves, and that the nonsupportive cooks might well have wanted to show the more competent leader that he "isn't all that smart" and that he needed the cooperation of his cooks. A second explanation suggests that the highly competent leader becomes so engrossed in the details of the task that he fails to give direction and lets the team

Table 12.5. Correlations Between Member Intelligence and Leader Cognitive Resources with Group Performance in Mess Halls with Relatively Directive and Nondirective Mess Stewards, and High or Low Ratings of Group Support (Cooks' GA)[a]

	Leader's Directiveness			
	High		Low	
Correlations with	Group Atmosphere		Group Atmosphere	
Group Performance	High (13)	Low (13)	High (11)	Low (11)
Mess steward intelligence	.56*[b]	−.09	−.21	−.05
Mess steward job experience	.44	.26	−.08	−.37
Mess steward training	.25	.08	.24	−.65*[b]
Mess steward time in service	.18	.36	−.43	−.31
Cook intelligence	−.06	.16	.45	−.25
Mean performance[a]	124.8	100.7	116.9	123.6

[a] ANOVA of performance means was not significant.
[b] Differences between correlations in the high and low group atmosphere columns are significant ($p < .05$).

fall apart. Interestingly enough, the average performance of mess halls did not differ from condition to condition. We shall return to this point.

The highest correlation (although not statistically significant) between the cooks' intelligence scores and the performance criteria occurred in the hypothesized condition, that is, when the leader was nondirective but had the support of the group. As we shall see, similarly weak results were obtained in other studies.

Table 12.5 also permits us to address Hypothesis Five, that leader abilities correlate with task performance to the extent that they are required by the task. One might have expected that the highly task-relevant measures, represented by mess steward's technical training, would have correlated more highly with performance than did the more general measure of intelligence. In fact, the opposite seemed to be true, though the results were not significant. Assuming that training does reflect technical competence, these results suggest that general intelligence is more important for good leadership than is the leader's technical competence and knowledge.

In brief, Hypothesis Five was not supported. When the leader was nondirective, the correlations between the intelligence of supportive group members and performance was somewhat (albeit not significantly) higher than the correlations obtained for group members who were not supportive. The intelligence of directive leaders, and especially that of leaders also supported by the group, correlated more highly with group performance than intelligence of nondirective or unsupported leaders. There also was evidence that the more specific task-relevant cognitive resources (e.g., training, experience) detract from group performance of the nondirective leader who is not supported by his group.

The Squad Leader Study

The Leadership Situation. A second test of cognitive resource theory was based on data of the previously mentioned study of 138 squad leaders of nine army battalions (Bons & Fiedler, 1976). The squad leaders had the task of training their squad in accordance with detailed schedules and instructions. As mentioned earlier, squad leaders are closely supervised by their superiors, a platoon leader and a platoon sergeant. Stress with one or both of these superiors, therefore, must have a considerable impact on the lives of these leaders. The subordinates in this instance were young recruits who looked at their squad leaders with some awe, or at least with respect or fear.

Test and Measures. Group support was measured by a group atmosphere scale (GA), here completed only by the squad leader, since group member scores were not available. The squad leader, also completed a one-item scale which read, "Describe your relationship with the boss," and then contained an eight-point bipolar semantic differential bounded by the adjectives "stressful–nonstressful." Another single item scale read, "In relation to all other jobs you have had (or know about), rate your job in terms of overall stress to you."

(greatest)   8   7   6   5   4   3   2   1   (least)

The two stress measures were essentially uncorrelated (.18, $n = 130$, $p < .05$); boss stress and job stress were correlated with the GA score .23 and .08 respectively. These low correlations indicate that the three measures are dealing with three different types of stress. Intellectual ability measures were based on the Army General Classification Test, a part of the army's classification battery with a standardized mean of 100, SD = 10. The mean score of squad leaders in this sample was 105.4 (SD = 14.56).

The squad members described their squad leader on items from the Leader Behavior Description Questionnaire (LBDQ XII; Stogdill, 1963). Two factors emerged. One of these, which we refer to as directive behavior, consisted of items from the structuring and production emphasis scales. The other factor contained items from the consideration and tolerance of freedom scales.

Performance Ratings. Squad leader effectiveness was measured on the 16-item, five-point rating scale developed by Bons (1974). Performance was rated by the squad leader's two superiors. Their ratings indicated a factor of task performance (mission accomplishment) and a second factor of personnel performance (rapport, morale, and discipline). A comparison of task performance and personnel performance will be used for testing Hypothesis Five, that intellectual abilities contribute to performance to the extent to which these abilities are required by the task. The average correlation between the two raters was .65 (.79 corrected for attentuation). An independent measure of squad performance was not available in this study.

It is perhaps self-evident that intellectual abilities in this study were more relevant to task accomplishment than to the personnel performance criterion of maintaining high morale and discipline and good relations with squad members. This was also indicated by a rating made in another context by experienced military officers.

Results. Table 12.6 addresses the question raised by Hypothesis One, whether the intellectual abilities of leaders contribute to the task only in nonstressful situations. The table shows that this hypothesis was supported primarily when stress was generated by the boss. The correlations were weaker when the groups were divided on the basis of job stress. These findings probably indicate that one cannot cope intellectually or rationally with a boss who makes unreasonable demands or is hostile;

Table 12.6. Correlations Between Squad Leader Intelligence and Performance Under Conditions of Low and High Perceived Boss and Job Stress[a]

Leader Intelligence Correlated with	Boss Stress			Job Stress		
	Low (46)	Moderate (41)	High (37)	Low (47)	Moderate (41)	High (37)
Task performance	.43**[b]	.27	−.01[b]	.26[#]	.27[#]	.20
Personnel performance	−.03	−.03	.14	.10	−.16	.14

[a] ANOVAs not significant.
[b] Differences between correlations in the high and low boss stress columns are significant ($p < .05$).

the individual focuses attention on his or her own anxieties rather than the task. Individual intellect, therefore, will not contribute to the task.

On the other hand, a job may be stressful because it involves very difficult problems. In this case, the leader's attention will be focused on the task, and his or her intellectual abilities will increase performance. As a result, we might not see the same attentuation of the relationship between leader intelligence and performance that we see when interpersonal stress is present.

Hypothesis Two predicted that the intellectual abilities of directive leaders will correlate more highly with performance than those of less directive leaders. To test this hypothesis, the sample was divided into upper, middle, and lower thirds on the directiveness measure, and correlations were then computed between the leader's intelligence and performance. Table 12.7 supports Hypothesis Two, that the intelligence of directive leaders correlates more highly with leadership performance than does the intelligence of less directive leaders. Table 12.6 and Table 12.7 also show that intelligence is correlated somewhat more highly (although not significantly so) with the task performance than the personnel performance criterion, thus supporting Hypothesis Five.

Table 12.7. Correlations Between Task and Personnel Performance and Intelligence of Leaders Rated as Highly, Moderately, or Relatively Low in Directiveness[a]

	All Leaders (132)	Directive Behavior		
		High (36)	Moderate (38)	Low (35)
Task performance	.24*	.49**	.29	.01[b]
Personnel performance	.02	.33[#]	−.23	.08

[a] ANOVAs not significant.
[b] Differences between correlations in the high and low directiveness columns are significant ($p < .05$).

Table 12.8. Correlations Between Intelligence and Task Performance of Directive and Nondirective Leaders in Relatively Less Stressful and More Stressful Situations[a]

	Directiveness			
	High		Low	
Situational	Situational Control		Situational Control	
Control Measure	High	Low	High	Low
Leader GA	.49** (27)	.38# (24)	.13 (26)	−.03 (30)
Boss stress[b]	.58** (29)	.10 (26)[b]	.15 (25)	.14 (24)
Job stress[b]	.63** (22)	.11 (31)[b]	.28 (33)	.17 (20)
Mean performance	321.5	299.2	305.3	302.1

[a] ANOVA not significant.
[b] Differences between correlations in high and low situational control columns are significant ($p < .05$).

Hypothesis Four, which concerns the effect of group member abilities, could not be tested since group member intelligence scores were not available. However, Table 12.8 presents the correlations between leader intelligence and task performance in groups with relatively directive and nondirective leaders and groups perceived by the leader to be relatively supportive and nonsupportive. As in the mess hall study, the correlation between leader intelligence and task performance was significant only in groups with directive leaders and supportive squad members.

The table also shows the correlations between leader intelligence and performance when the groups were subdivided on the basis of low or high stress with boss or low and high job stress. It is interesting to note that leader GA, boss stress, and job stress had almost identical moderator effects on the correlations between leader intelligence and performance, even though the three measures were practically uncorrelated.

Personnel performance presumably requires interpersonal skills rather than intellectual abilities. As predicted by Hypothesis Five, leader intelligence did not correlate with personnel performance in any of the analyses.

To summarize the results of this study, we found that leader intelligence predicted task performance best when leaders were directive, they had a supportive group or low stress with their boss, and the task demanded intellectual abilities rather than interpersonal skills.

The Public Health Team Study

The studies of mess halls and army infantry squad leaders dealt with groups in which the leader had a structured task and high position power. We now turn to teams with emergent leaders, in which group members informally decided among themselves who was to perform various leadership functions. The informal leader was identified in this study by means of sociometric questionnaires administered at the end of the three-week tour.

The Leadership Situation. The study was based on 41 small teams of volunteer public health workers (Fiedler, O'Brien, & Ilgen, 1969). The teams were composed of 16- to 19-year-old high school students who established and administered vaccination and innoculation programs and performed community development work. The teams lived and worked in small rural villages in Honduras and Guatemala under spartan conditions.

Tests and Measures. Intelligence of all team members was assessed by a short vocabulary and information scale administered by the organization. Leader directiveness (using structuring items from the Leader Behavior Description Questionnaire, LBDQ; Stogdill, 1963) was rated by team members at the termination of their tour in Central America. The measure of group support consisted of group atmosphere ratings by group members (MGA). The stressfulness of the job environment depended largely on the degree to which villagers and village officials were supportive and cooperative or hostile and uncooperative. Stress was quite high in villages in which the local medical practitioner or priest felt threatened, or rumors circulated about the supposedly nefarious motives of the organization which sponsored the program. In most villages, problems of this nature were relatively minor, but the abysmal poverty and primitive living conditions in the villages created culture shock in some volunteers. This "village stress" was measured by an 11-point rating scale, completed by the project director and his staff.

Performance Measures. The principal measure, for purposes of our analysis, is the team's success in performing community development work (e.g., literacy training, building a park, repairing a school). These projects reflected the team members' own initiative and resourcefulness, and as a result, were relatively demanding of intellectual effort.

The project director and his staff also evaluated each team on "clinic administration," which involved highly standardized procedures for innoculating and vaccinating children and keeping appropriate records. A third criterion, maintaining good interpersonal relations among team members ("maintaining group harmony"), required socioemotional skills rather than intellectual ability.

The presence of two types of criteria again allows us to test Hypothesis Five, that intellectual abilities are more highly related to intellectually demanding tasks than to less demanding tasks. The three criteria correlated as follows: community development with clinic administration and group harmony, .65 ($p < .01$) and .26 ($p < .10$); clinic administration and group harmony, .46 ($p < .01$, $n = 41$). As mentioned earlier, some data were lost in transit or could not be obtained for all teams.

Results. Hypothesis One stated that the correlations between leader intelligence and performance on intellectually demanding tasks would be lower under stressful than under nonstressful conditions. The teams were divided into those operating in villages in which stress was relatively low, moderate, or high. Under high stress conditions, the correlations between leader intelligence and performance on all three criteria were in the negative direction but did not support Hypothesis One (see Table 12.9). Further research is needed to determine whether these weak correlations between leader intelligence and performance were due to the informal nature of the groups and low position power of the leader, or, rather, to the generally stressful nature of the conditions under which these teams worked (see Table 12.10). As predicted in Hypothesis Four, however, correlations between member intelligence and performance were higher in groups with nondirective leaders.

To test Hypothesis Two, we divided the teams into those in which the informal leaders were rated by teammates as relatively high, moderate, or low in directive behavior. We then correlated leader intelligence with performance (see Table 12.10). The data support Hypothesis Two at a statistically significant level in the case of the intellectually demanding community development criterion.

The data in Table 12.10 also give some support to Hypothesis Five. For directive leaders, the correlation between leader intelligence and the intellectually demanding community development criterion was somewhat

Table 12.9. Correlations Between Leader and Member Intelligence and Performance in Relatively Stressfree and Stressful Villages[a]

	Village Stress		
	Low (15)	Moderate (11)	High (14)
Leader intelligence			
Community development	.21	.22	−.16
Clinic administration	−.21	.01	−.32
Group harmony	.06	.05	−.52[#]
Member intelligence			
Community development	−.22	.36	.49[b]
Clinic administration	−.06	−.03	.51[#]
Group harmony	−.34	.83**	.04

[a] ANOVAs not significant.
[b] Differences between correlations in the high and low village stress columns are significant ($p < .05$).

Table 12.10. Correlations Between Leader and Member
Intelligence and Performance Measures in the Public
Health Study[a]

	Leader Directiveness		
	High (12)	Moderate (14)	Low (13)
Leader intelligence			
Community development	.61*	.16	−.23[b]
Clinic administration	.22	.24	−.39
Group harmony	−.28	−.05	−.19
Member intelligence			
Community development	−.26	.21	.38
Clinic administration	.00	.02	.27
Group harmony	−.21	−.40	.51[#b]

[a] ANOVAs testing differences between means were not significant.
[b] Differences between correlations in the high and low leader directiveness cqlumns
are significant ($p < .05$).

higher than the correlation between leader intelligence and the intellectually less demanding clinic administration. This correlation was significantly higher than the correlation between leader intelligence and the
group harmony criterion, which primarily required interpersonal rather
than intellectual skills. The correlations between leader intelligence and
performance for nondirective leaders were again in the negative direction,
although not significantly so. In contrast, group member intelligence
scores correlated negatively with the group harmony criterion in groups
with directive and moderately directive leaders. These correlations tended
to be positive when the leader was nondirective. While these correlations
were not significant, they support the widely held belief that member
participation encouraged by nondirective leadership results in group
member satisfaction.

Hypothesis Three stated that the intellectual abilities of leaders correlate
with group performance when the leader is directive and the group is
supportive. Hypothesis Four stated that the intellectual abilities of group
members predict group performance on intellectually demanding tasks
if the leader is nondirective and the group members are supportive. We
tested these hypotheses by dividing the groups into those with directive
or nondirective leaders and supportive and relatively less supportive groups
(high vs. low member GA). We examined these groups in relation to the
intellectually demanding task of community development. Table 12.11
shows that the correlation between leader intelligence and community
development was marginally significant in the case of directive leaders
with supportive groups, but again, the correlation for groups with directive
leaders and nonsupportive groups was almost as high. On the other hand,
correlations between leader intelligence and performance were in the

Table 12.11. Correlations Between Leader and Member Intelligence and Performance on Community Development Tasks Under Directive and Nondirective Leaders with High and Low Member Group Atmosphere Scores[a]

	Leader Directiveness			
	High		Low	
	Member Support		Member Support	
	High	Low	High	Low
Leaders	(10)	(10)	(8)	(10)
Community development	.56[#]	.43	−.58	.06
Clinic administration	.38	.34	−.68[#]	.00
Group harmony	−.09	−.30	−.38	.27
Members				
Community development	−.05	.26	.13	.35
Clinic administration	.40	−.54[b]	.14	.21
Group harmony	−.29	−.10	.39	.02

[a] ANOVAs not significant.
[b] Differences between correlations in the high and low member support columns are significant ($p < .05$).

negative direction in groups with nondirective leaders but high group support. Clearly member intelligence was unrelated to performance in the subgroups specified by the hypothesis.

Let us also consider the correlations between intelligence and performance in relatively stressful and stress-free work situations, as shown in Table 12.12. None of the correlations reached statistical significance.

Table 12.12. Correlations Between Leader and Member Intelligence and Performance of Public Health Teams Under Directive or Nondirective Leaders in Relatively Stressfree and Stressful Villages[a]

	Leader Directiveness			
	High		Low	
	Village Stress		Village Stress	
	Low	High	Low	High
Leaders	(10)	(7)	(10)	(7)
Community development	.51	.33	−.40	.13
Clinic administration	.09	−.41	−.42	−.41
Group harmony	.30	−.23	−.24	−.39
Members				
Community development	−.42	.43	.06	.66
Clinic administration	−.30	.14	.10	.39
Group harmony	−.19	−.24	.05	.67

[a] ANOVAs not significant.

It is interesting to note, however, that the positive correlations between leader intelligence and group performance occurred mainly in the condition in which the leader was directive and group stress was low. In contrast, the correlations between member intelligence and performance were negative when leaders were directive and the situation as relatively nonstressful but positive in all other conditions, that is, the conditions in which either group members were free to use their abilities since the leader did not give directions, or stress diverted the leader's attention from the task. All of these correlations must be considered as highly tentative by themselves.

It should be recalled that the public health teams constitute an unusual set of groups. These were teen-aged volunteers working in small groups without formal leadership. One task was quite routine (clinic administration); another required creativity and initiative (community development). A third required interpersonal skills. It is surprising that the results with the community development criterion are so consistent with those from formal teams and teams having highly structured tasks. These findings speak to the generalizability of cognitive resource theory.

LABORATORY EXPERIMENTS

The Decoding Study

The Leadership Situation. The decoding study (Chemers, Rice, Sundstrom, & Butler, 1975) was a highly controlled laboratory experiment in which 40 three-man teams deciphered as many coded messages as possible in 30 minutes. The messages were incomprehensible until the correct letters had been substituted. In effect, these were convergent thinking tasks in the form of cryptogram puzzles.

As mentioned earlier, 20 relationship-motivated and 20 task-motivated Reserve Officer Training Corps (ROTC) cadets served as leaders of teams consisting of two ROTC cadets and one psychology student. The leaders were randomly assigned either to a training condition or to a no-training condition. The leaders in the training condition learned a well-established method for deciphering simple codes.

It is important to note that the groups operated under relatively stressful conditions. This study was part of a ROTC leadership course, and at the time of the study there was considerable antagonism between the ROTC and social science students. Group atmosphere scores (GA) were significantly below the mean of those obtained in other studies. For this reason, analyses using member group atmosphere scores would not be meaningful. In contrast to the previously discussed studies of military groups, but in common with the public health teams, the leaders of these groups had relatively low formal position power. The leaders who had received training did have "expert power" because of their special competence.

Tests and Measures. Chemers et al. administered a brief intelligence scale consisting of vocabulary and quantitative items. Leaders completed group atmosphere scales indicative of perceived group support. The leader described his "personal reaction to the experience of working in your group." The GA scale included the items "stressful–unstressful" and "tense–relaxed," which were used together as the measure of stress. Again, the situation was relatively stressful for all leaders.

A scale was administered at the end of the task that included members' descriptions of the leader's behavior. One eight-point bipolar item was indicative of the leader's tendency to behave in a directive manner:

When people are appointed as the leader of a group, they differ in the degree to which they exercise their authority and control the group. Some people are strong leaders in such situations while others exercise little control and allow the group members to do what they want. To what extent did the appointed leader of your group exercise his authority and control the group?

Did not   Completely
control the   controlled
group at all   __ __ __ __ __ __ __ __   the group
                 1   2   3   4   5   6   7   8

Leaders and group members also described various other behaviors of interest. These included the leader's concern with having good interpersonal relations as opposed to good task performance ("relationship-orientation"), and the degree to which subjects were motivated to perform the task.

As already discussed in Chapter 8, the training condition in the Chemers et al. study was intended as an experimental manipulation in order to test whether increasing situational control affects the performance of high- and low-LPC leaders in the predicted manner. This prediction was confirmed. Training also increased task structure. Leaders with training reported less stress than those without training ($-.27$, $n = 40$, $p < .10$). This condition, therefore, provided higher situational control than was enjoyed by the leaders who had not received training.

Results. Table 12.13 addresses Hypothesis One, which asks whether correlations between leader intelligence are higher in groups in which leaders experience moderate stress than in those in which they experienced high stress. The correlations between leader intelligence and performance conformed to our expectations, that is, lower in the more stressful than in the less stressful condition. But the correlation was low, even in the relatively low stress situation; this finding is consistent with the description by Chemers et al. of the study as being abnormally stressful for their subjects.

Hypothesis Two predicted that directive leaders use their intellectual abilities more effectively than nondirective leaders. We divided the groups,

Table 12.13. Correlations Between Leader and Member
Intelligence and Number of Cryptograms in Groups Perceived
by the Leader as Relatively Low, Moderate, or High in Stress[a]

	Leader-Perceived Stress[b]		
	Low (13)	Moderate (15)	High (12)
Leader intelligence	.21	−.53*[c]	−.19
Member intelligence	.24	−.03	−.10

[a] ANOVA not significant.
[b] None of the groups were considered to operate under low stress conditions (Chemers et al., 1975).
[c] Differences between correlations in the moderate and low stress columns are significant ($p < .05$).

as well as the data allowed, into upper, middle, and lower thirds on the previously described directive behavior scale item, "controls group", and correlated the leader's and the group members' intelligence scores with performance. The data in Table 12.14 show once more that directive leader behavior was associated with effective use of leader intelligence, while members' intelligence was unrelated with performance. The correlation between the nondirective leader's intelligence and performance was negative at a marginally significant level. In addition, the correlations between leader intelligence and performance run in the opposite direction from those between member intelligence and performance.

The correlations between leader intelligence and performance in relatively less stressful and more stressful conditions were more pronounced when we also considered the directiveness of the leader. The results of this analysis are shown in Table 12.15. Note the high negative correlation of −.72 between leader intelligence and performance in supportive groups with nondirective leaders. It is obvious in this case that the leader's directiveness in conjunction with moderate stress had a very marked

Table 12.14. Correlations Between Leader and Member
Intelligence and Performance for Leaders Rated
Relatively High or Low on the Directiveness Item,
"Controls the Group's Behavior"[a]

	Directive (Controlling)		
	High (11)	Moderate (17)	Low (12)
Leader intelligence	.20	−.58*	−.56#[b]
Member intelligence	−.18	.37	.22

[a] ANOVAs not significant.
[b] Differences between correlations in the high and low directiveness columns are significant ($p < .05$).

Table 12.15. Correlations Between Leader and Member Intelligence and Performance of Teams with Directive and Nondirective Leaders in Moderate or High Stress Conditions

	Leader Directiveness			
	High		Low	
	Stress		Stress	
	Moderate (11)	High (8)	Moderate (11)	High (10)
Leader intelligence	.62*	.28	−.72**	−.10
Member intelligence	−.17	−.14	.29	−.05

effect on the contribution of his intelligence to performance. The convergent task of this study seemingly required a highly directive leader who kept the group on track. With a relatively nondirective leader, group members may well have become involved in arguments on procedure and on the preferred solutions.

Another index of the leader's security and ability to complete the task is provided by training. This is seen by the substantially higher task structure ratings in Table 12.1, and the somewhat lower stress ratings by leaders who had received training than those without training. The leader with training knew how to proceed and could immediately tell the group members what to do. The leader therefore had the advantage of knowing the methods and procedures for accomplishing the task. Table 12.16 demonstrates, however, that only directive, intelligent leaders were able to capitalize on the technical knowledge their training provided. Nondirective leaders who had technical competence failed to take advantage of their intellect. In addition, the more intelligent nondirective leaders performed significantly less well than those who were less intelligent.

Table 12.16. Correlations Between Performance and Leader and Member Intelligence, and Member Intelligence for Directive and Nondirective Leaders With and Without Training[a]

| | Leader Directiveness | | | |
| | High | | Low | |
	Training (11)	No Training (8)	Training (9)	No Training (12)
Leader intelligence	.59*	.03	−.62#	−.57*
Member intelligence	.19	−.33	−.22	.32

[a] ANOVA not significant.

The ROTC Creativity Study

The Leadership Situation. The least structured leadership situation is found in the ROTC creativity study (Meuwese & Fiedler, 1965) in which 54 three-man teams of Reserve Officer Training Corps (ROTC) cadets participated. These teams performed two divergent thinking tasks under three experimentally induced stress conditions. Leaders were randomly assigned to stress conditions and on the basis of their LPC scores. One of the conditions was designed to generate a minimum of stress. The cadets were told to come in civilian clothes, and that the purpose of the study was to investigate the creative process, although it was important that they perform as well as possible. A second condition generated internal group conflict by first assigning two Army and one Navy ROTC students to the same team and then designing tasks that created conflict between army and navy cadets. In the third "external" stress condition, three army cadets in uniform performed the task while a high ranking officer (lieutenant colonel or colonel) sat across the table from the group members and rated their behavior. There was a highly significant difference in stress reported between the control condition and the other two conditions.

All groups were assigned the following fictional tasks consisting of (a) developing an equitable pay schedule ("Payproposal") for army, navy, and airforce cadets (the Navy ROTC received higher pay at that time), and (b) inventing a fable ("Fable") for elementary school children to illustrate the need for a large peacetime army rather than a large navy. Since the teams in the "internal stress" condition consisted of two cadets from the army program and one from the navy program, conflict inevitably occurred in these groups. Performance on the two tasks correlated .32 ($n = 54$, $p < .02$).*

---

* *Payproposal Task.* "The BOLTE Commission recently proposed to Congress that the ROTC program benefits be standardized. Specifically the present system of financing the ROTC programs [in 1960] provides for tuition, books, and a $50 monthly allowance for four years while Army and Air Force ROTC cadets do not receive comparable benefits, especially during the first two years. According to the Commission's report, this has attracted many exceptionally capable individuals to the Navy program purely for the financial benefits which it offers, although only 25% of these men remain in the service.

" 'Your committee has been appointed to write a brief proposal to be submitted to the Joint Chiefs of Staff. The proposal should recommend a fair and equitable implementation of this policy, without exceeding the total of currently available funds for ROTC training, and justifying the recommendations as convincingly as possible.

" 'You will have 25 minutes to complete your proposal."

Fable Task. "A nation-wide program has been instituted to alert the nation to our defense problems. The ROTC has been assigned the task of helping elementary school children to understand our current national defense problems. Your committee has been instructed to compose a fable or story for 8 to 10-year-old children which clearly shows the need for a large army in peacetime. The fable or story must be clear to these young children

Tests and Measures. One week prior to the experimental sessions, all cadets took the Psychological Corporation Multi-Aptitude Scale (Cureton & Cureton, 1955), and the Plot Titles and Alternative Uses tests of creativity (Guilford, Berger, & Christensen, 1954). The Plot Titles Test requires the subject to think of clever titles for short story plots; the Alternative Uses Test requires the subject to think of unusual uses for such common objects as a brick or a coat hanger. According to the authors, the Plot Titles test taps "divergent production of semantic units and transformations"; the Alternative Uses test taps "divergent production of semantic classes of objects." The Plot Titles and Alternative Uses tests correlated .30 ($p <$ .05) with each other, with the intelligence scale .31 ($p < .02$), and .18 (ns, $= 54$). At the end of each task, the leaders and members of each team rated one another's behavior, using items from the structuring dimension of the Ohio State LBDQ to indicate directive behavior.

The Alexander and Husek (1962) scale of situational anxiety was administered prior to the study as an indication of the individual's anxiety level related to the experiment. The use of this test enables us to ask a question which arose in connection with studies of squad leaders, fire service officers, and coast guard staff: Is the "objective" job stress as detrimental to leader's ability to utilize intellectual abilities as interpersonal stress? Experimentally induced stress can here be compared with the subjectively felt stress, that is, anxiety, in determining how these affect the leader's intellectual contribution to performance.

Performance Evaluations. Independent ratings of team performance were made by three judges on the Payproposal task and by five judges on the Fable task. Interrater agreement averaged .67 (corrected for number of raters, .87).

The study had the usual limitations of laboratory experiments. The ad hoc groups worked on contrived tasks, but the group members did seem to become deeply involved in trying to find good answers to the problems these tasks posed. The leaders participated actively in the process and wrote the final version of the payproposal and fable. Their own ideas as well as their style of writing undoubtedly influenced the judges' evaluations of the team's performance.

This study involved the performance of divergent thinking tasks, which require imagination and creativity. Committees are frequently asked to propose a compromise, to develop a new method of dealing with a problem,

---

and as interesting and original as possible. Your main point should be that a large, trained, land army is the most important element in the protection of a country, even if it is not engaged in a major war, and when it must also protect its coast line.

" 'Write down the complete fable or story including an appropriate title. Remember that the story will be used with elementary school children.

" 'You will have 25 minutes to complete this story.' "

Table 12.17. Correlations Between Leader and Member Intelligence
and Performance Under Experimentally Induced Conditions
of Stress

	Leaders' Experienced Stress			Members' Experienced Stress		
	Low (18)	Moderate (18)	High (18)	Low (18)	Moderate (18)	High (18)
Intelligence and payproposal	.27	.20	.10	−.42	−.19	.80**[a]
Intelligence and fable	.39	.02	.30	−.18	−.41	.48*[a]

[a] Differences between correlations in the high and low experienced stress columns are significant.

or to establish a new procedure. The Payproposal task resembled the typical committee task in requiring a solution which would be acceptable to various parties in conflict. This conflict was most salient in the "internal stress" situation in which one navy cadet participated along with two army cadets, although reconciling different views remained important to the other groups as well. The Payproposal task was somewhat more focused and familiar than the Fable task (Shirakashi, 1980), which proved unstructured and divergent in character and similar to such tasks as the development of new products, plays, or advertising campaigns.

Results. Hypothesis One was first tested by comparing correlations between leader and member intelligence and performance of groups with different levels of experimentally induced stress. Table 12.17 illustrates that the effect of this manipulation was weak as far as this test is concerned. The main findings are the large and significantly positive correlations between group member intelligence and performance in the high stress condition, while the corresponding correlations under low stress were negative, suggesting that the group members could contribute only when the leader was distracted by high stress.

Table 12.18 shows the effect of experimentally induced stress on the way in which leaders utilize their intelligence. As can be seen, the effects are similar to those observed in the other studies. It is interesting to note, however, that group member intelligence contributed highly only in the low stress condition. This suggests that leader stress interfered with the ability of members to use their intelligence.

As Chapter 3 pointed out, the same objective situation may seem very stressful and distracting to one person and not to another. This is seen when we determine the effect of varying levels of anxiety on the effective use of intellectual abilities. It should be noted in this connection that leader anxiety was uncorrelated with stress (.09) or group member support (.01), and group support was uncorrelated with stress (−.14, all $n = 54$). Table 12.19 shows the expected significant positive correlations between

Table 12.18. Correlations Between Task Performance and Leader
and Member Intelligence in Various Experimentally Induced
Stress Conditions for Leaders Who are Relatively Directive
or Nondirective

	Highly Directive Leader			Nondirective Leader		
	Stress			Stress		
	Low (9)	Moderate (10)	High (8)	Low (9)	Moderate (8)	High (10)
Leader intelligence						
Payproposal	.24	.71*	.35	.09	−.09	.34
Fable	.77*	.49	.14	.00	−.47	.46
Member intelligence						
Payproposal	.81*	−.29	−.49**	.86*	.03	−.61#†
Fable	.50	−.66*	−.27	.48	.23	.03

** $p < .01$; † $p < .001$; differences between correlations in the high and low stress conditions
are significant.

the directive leader's intelligence and performance in the low anxiety
group and low correlations in the high anxiety group. The table suggests,
therefore, that the utilization of intelligence depends more on the absence
of anxiety than on low levels of "objective" stress. Group member abilities
were effectively used when the leader was stressed by the job or the
situation, but not when the leader's anxiety directed attention (and perhaps
the attention of the group) away from the task. High external stress
induced the leader to rely on group members; high anxiety may simply
prevent the leader from giving sensible directions that enable the group
to function in an organized way.

Table 12.19. Correlations Between Leader and Member Intelligence
and Creativity, and Performance in Groups with Leaders Who
Report Low, Moderate, or High Anxiety

	Leaders			Members		
	Leader Anxiety			Leader Anxiety		
	Low (18)	Moderate (19)	High (17)	Low (18)	Moderate (19)	High (17)
Intelligence and payproposal	.45#	.35	−.13[a]	.00	.09	.16
Intelligence and fable	.50*	.47#	.14	−.60	−.10	.06

[a] Differences between correlations in the high and low leader anxiety columns are significant
($p < .05$).

Table 12.20. Correlations Between Leader and Member Intelligence and the Team's Performance Under Directive and Less Directive Leaders

	Leaders			Group Members		
	Leader Directiveness			Leader Directiveness		
	High (20)	Moderate (16)	Low (18)	High (20)	Moderate (16)	Low (18)
Intelligence and payproposal	.24	.21	.14	.23	.02	.05
Intelligence and fable	.12	.57*	−.10	.00	.28	.39

Hypothesis Two concerned the effect of the leader's directive behavior on the effective utilization of leader and group member intellectual resources. The correlations between leader intelligence and creativity and performance on the two tasks, Payproposal and Fable, are shown in Table 12.20 for groups divided into upper, middle, and lower thirds on the leader directiveness ratings. The leader's intellectual ability did not contribute more to performance when the leaders were relatively directive rather than nondirective. The results are somewhat clearer when the leaders were divided into just two groups, that is, those falling above and below the median in rated directiveness. These correlations for the Payproposal and Fable tasks were, for directive leaders, respectively, .36 and .46 ($n = 27$, $p < .10$ and $p < .05$), and for nondirective leaders, .10 and −.01 ($n = 27$). These data support Hypothesis Two. The contribution of the group members' intellectual abilities was not affected by leader directiveness.

Hypotheses Three and Four are examined in groups with directive or nondirective leaders and high or low group support in Table 12.21. As

Table 12.21. Correlations Between Performance and the Intelligence of Leaders and Members in Groups with Directive or Nondirective Leaders and High or Low Group Support[a]

	Leader Directiveness			
	High		Low	
	Group Atmosphere		Group Atmosphere	
	High (13)	Low (14)	High (12)	Low (15)
Leader				
Intelligence and payproposal	.55*	.34	.48[#]	−.17
Intelligence and fable	.80**	−.17**	.52[#]	−.29*
Member				
Intelligence and payproposal	.22	.38	.07	.10
Intelligence and fable	−.34	−.05	.29	.27

[a] ANOVAs not significant.
* $p < .05$; ** $p < .01$; differences between correlations in the high and low group atmosphere columns are significant.

can be seen, the leaders utilized their intellectual abilities in performing the task only when they were directive and felt supported by the group. The members' intelligence did not contribute more to performance in teams of nondirective leaders and supportive group members. We thus find that the ROTC study supported Hypothesis Three but not Four.

COGNITIVE RESOURCE THEORY AND CONSIDERATE BEHAVIOR

We have had very little to say about the second major category of leader behavior, variously known as consideration, socioemotional behavior, or group maintenance. We did compute correlations in each of the studies between intelligence and performance for leaders who were rated high or low in considerate behavior. Only in the ROTC study did the leader's considerate behavior seem to affect the correlations between intelligence or time in service with performance. However, as Table 12.22 shows, the correlations between intelligence and performance were more affected by stress than by the leaders' considerate behavior.

We would expect the leader's considerate behavior to have greatest impact on the group members' contributions to the task when the leader is considerate and not anxious or under stress. But Table 12.22 shows that the contribution of member intelligence occurred in the low stress

Table 12.22. Correlations Between Task Performance and Leader and Member Intelligence for Leaders Who Are Relatively Considerate or Inconsiderate and Had High, Moderate, or Low Stress (ROTC Study)

	High Consideration Stress			Low Consideration Stress		
	Low (7)	Moderate (13)	High (8)	Low (13)	Moderate (5)	High (10)
Leader						
Payproposal and Intelligence	.14	.60*	.40	.03	−.15	.20
Fable and Intelligence	.62*	−.41	.17	−.24	−.56	.51
Member						
Payproposal and Intelligence	.87*	−.32	−.87*[a]	.78*	−.37	−.17*[a]
Fable and Intelligence	.85*	−.29	−.19[a]	.13	−.67	−.19

[a] Differences between correlations in the high and low stress columns are significant ($p <$ .05).

condition regardless of considerate leader behavior. Correlations between member intelligence and performance were negative under moderate and high stress, regardless of the leader's considerate behavior. The leader's own intelligence contributed to performance only when the leader was considerate and stress was low or moderate. This suggests that the considerate behavior may serve a more useful function for the leader than for the group members, at least insofar as performance is concerned. These correlations are, of course, based on small samples and on groups in which leaders could participate fully, and to some extent ignore the contributions of group members. In general, correlations involving the consideration behaviors were less than exciting, although it is perhaps too early to abandon research on their role in determining the utilization of cognitive resources.

CHAPTER THIRTEEN

Directive Behavior and Cognitive Resource Utilization: Summary of Empirical Findings

To what extent do the five "test studies" in Chapter 12 support the propositions of cognitive resource theory? This chapter summarizes the results relevant to Hypotheses One to Four.

STRESS AND USE OF INTELLIGENCE

The first hypothesis stated that stress, and especially stress with one's boss, results in low correlations between leader intelligence and group performance. As pointed out earlier, we generally assume that the leader's intellectual abilities are focused on the performance of the task. This is not always the case. Perceived stress—in particular, interpersonal stress—tends to focus the leader's attention on his or her own agenda and away from the assigned task (e.g., Sarason, 1975).

Under stressful conditions, a leader may worry more about how he or she will deal with the boss or appear in the eyes of others rather than how the task is to be done. The leader's plans, decisions, and action strategies may then be misdirected. This was illustrated by Figure 10.2. Hypothesis One predicted, therefore, that the correlations between leader intelligence and performance will be higher under conditions of low stress than high stress. Table 13.1 shows somewhat higher correlations between

Table 13.1. Summary of Correlations Between Leader Intelligence Scores and Performance Under Conditions of Low, Moderate, and High Stress

Study[a]	Criterion	Low	Moderate	High
			Stress	
Squad Leader[c]	Performance leader:			
	Stress with boss	.43** (46)	.27 (41)	−.01(31)
	Job Stress	.26 (46)	.27 (41)	.20 (31)
Public health	Rated performance on			
	community development	.21 (15)	.22 (11)	−.16 (14)
Decoding	Number of cryptograms			
	correctly solved	.21 (13)	−.53* (15)	−.19 (12)
ROTC creativity[c]	Rated team performance:			
	Payproposal	.27 (18)	.20 (19)	.10 (17)
	Fable	.39 (18)	.02 (19)	.30 (17)
Mean correlation[b]		.30	.23	.02

[a] Stress measures were not available for the mess hall study and all conditions in the decoding study were relatively stressful, according to Chemers et al.

[b] In this and all subsequent tables, mean correlations were obtained by transforming r into z.

[c] Correlations for study were averaged.

leader intelligence and performance in the low than in the high stress conditions in each of the studies. And although the differences between correlations were generally small, they were consistent throughout the five studies.

DIRECTIVENESS AND USE OF INTELLIGENCE

Hypothesis Two of cognitive resource theory states that leaders must communicate their plans and action strategies in order to implement them if their intellectual abilities are to have influence on the performance of the task. One important way of communicating these plans and action strategies is directive behavior. Table 13.2 supports this hypothesis. The correlations between the intelligence of directive leaders are higher in each study than those for nondirective leaders.

The joint effect that the leader's directiveness and stress have on the utilization of leader intelligence is seen in Table 13.3. This table indicates by sign-test alone (a test of the direction of the correlation) that the intellectual abilities of directive leaders contributed more highly to performance than did those of less directive leaders. Table 13.3 and Figure 13.1 present the correlations between leader intelligence and performance in groups in which the leader was relatively directive or nondirective and the situation was relatively stressful or nonstressful. We find here that the leader's intelligence correlates only in nonstressful situations in which

Table 13.2. Summary of Correlations Between Leader Intelligence Scores and Performance for Relatively Directive, Moderately Directive, and Nondirective Leaders

Study	Criterion	Leader Directiveness		
		High	Moderate	Low
Mess hall	Performance	.30 (10)	.15 (25)	−.26 (13)
Squad leader	Performance of leader	.49** (36)	.29 (38)	.01 (35)
Public health	Rated performance on community development	.61* (12)	.16 (14)	−.23 (13)
Decoding	Correctly solved	.20 (11)	−.58* (17)	−.56* (12)
ROTC creativity[a]	Rated team performance:			
	Payproposal	.24 (20)	.21 (16)	.14 (18)
	Fable	.12 (20)	.57* (16)	−.10 (18)
Mean Correlations		.35	.16	−.11

[a] Correlations for study were averaged.

the leader was directive. In the nonstressful groups with nondirective leaders, the leader's intelligence correlated negatively with performance in the public health and decoding studies, in which the leader had low position power. This may be a relationship worth further exploration.

DIRECTIVE LEADERS WITH SUPPORTIVE GROUPS

Hypothesis Three, first advanced by Blades (Blades & Fiedler, 1973), states that the leader's intelligence contributes to performance when the

Table 13.3. Correlations Between Leader Intelligence Scores and Performance for Conditions in Which the Leader is Directive or Nondirective, Under Relatively Low and High Stress

Study[a]	Stress Measure	Directive Behavior			
		High		Low	
		Stress		Stress	
		Low	High	Low	High
Squad leader[b]	Boss stress	.58* (29)	.10 (26)	.15 (25)	.14 (24)
	Job stress	.63* (22)	.11 (31)	.28 (33)	.17 (20)
Public health	Vill stress	.51 (10)	.33 (7)	−.40 (10)	.13 (7)
Decoding	Rept stress	.62* (11)	.28 (8)	−.76** (11)	−.10 (10)
ROTC creativity[c]					
Payproposal	Experimental stress	.24 (9)	.35 (8)	.09 (9)	.34 (10)
Fable	Experimental stress	.77* (9)	.14 (8)	.00 (9)	.46 (10)
Mean correlations		.57	.07	.00	.03

[a] Stress measures were not available for the mess hall study.
[b] Correlations for study were averaged.
[c] Stress in ROTC study based on control condition and "external stress" from superior officer.

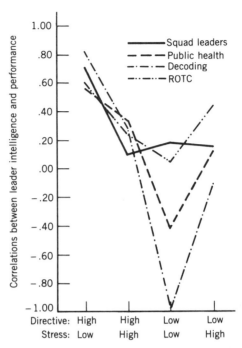

Figure 13.1. Correlations (z') between leader intelligence and performance in relatively stressful and nonstressful leadership situations from four different studies.

leader is directive and group support is high, and this hypothesis was supported when group atmosphere (GA) scores were used as measures of group support. As documented in Table 13.4 and Figure 13.2, the results of this set of analyses are strikingly similar to those in which groups were divided on the basis of stress reported by the leader or stress generated by the environment (i.e., in the Public Health study). This suggests that these two moderator variables have the same effect on the leader's ability to use intellectual abilities. Note again that the stress measures and GA scores were uncorrelated in these studies. As pointed out earlier, GA scores were the best available index of group support; more precise measures of group support would have been helpful at this point. The GA scores left some questions unanswered: Is it critical, for instance, that the group members support the leader as a person or that group members support the group's goals? Is it more important that the leader feels supported or that the group in fact supports the leader?

In some types of groups, support by group members did not appear to be critically important. This was the case in the ROTC and public health studies, in which the leader not only supervised but actively participated in the work and, therefore, directly affected the performance of the task.

Table 13.4. Correlations Between Leader Intelligence Scores and Performance for Conditions in Which the Leader is Directive or Nondirective, with High or Low Group Support

Study	Situational Control	Directive Behavior			
		High		Low	
		Group Support		Group Support	
		High	Low	High	Low
Mess hall	Cooks' GA	.56* (13)	−.09 (13)	.21 (11)	−.05 (11)
Squad leader	Leader GA	.49** (27)	.39# (24)	.13 (26)	.03 (30)
Public health	Member GA	.56# (10)	.43 (10)	−.58 (8)	.06 (10)
Decoding[b]	Leader GA		−.29 (8)		−.68* (12)
ROTC creativity[a]	Leader GA:				
	Payproposal	.58* (13)	.27 (14)	.12 (12)	.16 (15)
	Fable	.75** (13)	.06 (14)	.23 (12)	−.21 (15)
Mean correlations		.58	.19	.14	−.18

[a] Correlations for study were averaged.
[b] Group support was low in all teams in the decoding study.

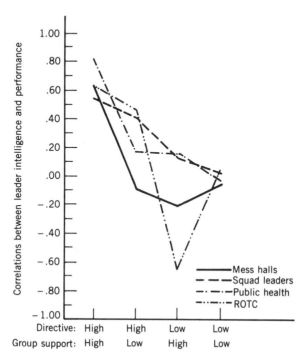

Figure 13.2. Correlations (z′) between leader intelligence and performance in supportive and nonsupportive groups from four different studies.

Although redundant with Tables 13.3 and 13.4, Figures 13.1 and 13.2 show somewhat more clearly that the leaders' intellectual abilities contributed consistently in only one fourth of the groups within each study. In the three other types of groups the intellectual abilities of leaders had little or no direct influence on the outcome of the group task, and in nearly half the groups, high intellectual abilities of the leader may even be slightly detrimental to group performance.

Leaders who experience stress or do not enjoy high group support apparently will not, or cannot, apply their intellectual abilities to the task in an effective manner, and their abilities do not correlate with performance. A high correlation between leader intelligence and performance does not necessarily mean that these particular groups are more effective than other types of groups in which the leader is less directive or is under stress, or the members are less supportive. We must recall that a high correlation presents a "good news–bad news" message: leaders who are relatively intelligent perform well but leaders who are relatively unintelligent perform poorly.

Intelligence and Level of Performance

We need to ask whether the *average* performance of teams with bright and directive leaders was higher than the *average* performance scores of teams with less bright or less directive leaders. This is a quite different question from the one we ask of correlational data. A hypothetical illustration makes this clear. Assume that we correlate the intelligence scores with a knowledge test for elementary school children of grades one to four and for graduate students. This correlation will be high for elementary school students, since older and brighter children will know much more than younger and duller children. The correlation will be quite low for graduate students since all will have relatively high intelligence scores. But graduate students will, of course, have considerably higher knowledge scores than will elementary school students.

In contrast to the previous tables and figures in this chapter which showed correlations between intelligence and performance, Table 13.5 and Figure 13.3 show average performance (expressed in standard scores) for groups in each study which fell into the six categories: leaders with relatively high or low intelligence, high or low directiveness, and high or low group support.

According to our data, leaders should be directive if they are intelligent; they should be nondirective if they are relatively less intelligent. In other words, if you are bright, speak up; if you are not so bright, let other people do the talking!

Table 13.6 shows the performance averages for directive and nondirective leaders with high and low intelligence regardless of group support, and for leaders with high or low group support regardless of intelligence. As

Table 13.5. Mean Performance (Indicated by z scores) of Groups with Leaders Who Had Relatively High or Low Intelligence, High or Low Directiveness, and High or Low Group Support

	Leader Directiveness			
	High		Low	
	Group Support		Group Support	
Study	High	Low	High	Low
High Intelligence				
Mess hall	.582	−.197	−.449	.000
Squad leader	.516	.436	.039	−.385
Public health				
Community development	.393	.417	−.689	−.440
Clinic administration	.000	.069	−1.010	−.346
Decoding[a]		.560	−.109	−.455
ROTC creativity				
Payproposal	.533	.055	.191	−.185
Fable	.522	.569	.073	.411
Medians	.516	.243	−.109	−.385
Low Intelligence				
Mess hall	−.225	.446	.083	−.397
Squad leader	.045	−.339	.091	.050
Public health				
Community development	−.287	−.264	.286	−.159
Clinic administration	−.287	−.202	.681	.118
Decoding	.000	−.213	.133	1.286
ROTC creativity				
Payproposal	−.470	−.381	.499	.184
Fable	−.212	.243	−.540	.000
Medians	−.225	−.213	.083	.050

[a] Stress substituted for Member GA since all GA scores were low in this study. First cell has only one case.

might be expected, the effect of intelligence is more pronounced than that of group support.

THE CONTRIBUTION OF GROUP MEMBER INTELLIGENCE

A question too rarely addressed in small group research concerns the intellectual contribution that group members make to organizational performance. Hypothesis Four, based on Blades' study (Blades & Fiedler, 1973), predicts that group member intelligence contributes to performance if the leader is nondirective and the group members support the leader.

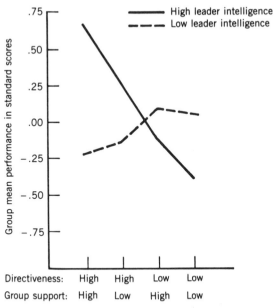

Figure 13.3. **Mean performance scores of relatively intelligent and less intelligent leaders in four different types of group situations. Leaders were either directive or nondirective, and groups were either supportive or nonsupportive.**

Group support was inferred from members' group atmosphere scores, or those of the leader in studies for which member GA scores were not available. If the leader is nondirective, group members should be able to contribute more to the task. This was not the case. If the leader is nondirective, the group's performance will depend in part on the group's willingness to perform the planning and executive components of the

Table 13.6. **Average Performance Scores of Groups with Directive or Nondirective Leaders with High or Low Intelligence and High or Low Group Support**

Leader Directiveness			
High		**Low**	
Intelligence		Intelligence	
High	**Low**	**High**	**Low**
.379	−.274	−.219	.066
Group Support		Group Support	
High	**Low**	**High**	**Low**
.145	.015	−.013	−.167

task. The group that does not support the leader's or the organization's goals will simply not care, and neither the leader's nor the group members' intellectual abilities will contribute to task performance. We first show in Table 13.7 the correlations between group member intelligence and performance for groups with relatively directive, moderately directive, and nondirective leaders without regard to group acceptance of the leader. These correlations were low and nonsignificant.

Contrary to our original expectations, Table 13.7 shows that leader directiveness had little influence on the degree to which the intellectual abilities of group members contributed to performance. In fact, Table 13.8 shows that the correlations are not substantially higher when we further divide the groups into those with supportive or nonsupportive group members. The third column in Table 13.8 contains the groups in which leaders were nondirective and had the support of their groups, and each of the correlations in this column was positive, although relatively low. The five studies thus give only very limited support to Hypothesis Four.

THE RELATION OF LEADER AND MEMBER ABILITIES

Do the best groups have the brightest leaders and the brightest group members? In other words, do intellectual abilities of leaders and group members enhance or interfere with one another? A comparison of the correlations of performance with leader and member intelligence shows that the situations in which the leader's abilities contribute most strongly to group performance are frequently the ones in which group member abilities correlate negatively with performance. The reverse is also true.

Table 13.7. Summary of Correlations Between Member Intelligence Scores and Group Performance for Relatively Directive, Moderately Directive, and Nondirective Leaders

| Study | Criterion | Leader Directiveness | | |
		High	Moderate	Low
Mess hall	Performance	.01 (10)	.22 (25)	−.34 (13)
Public health	Rated performance on community development	−.26 (12)	.21 (14)	.28 (13)
Decoding	Number of cryptograms correctly solved	−.18 (11)	.37 (17)	.22 (12)
ROTC[a] creativity	Rated team performance			
	Payproposal	.23 (20)	.02 (16)	.05 (18)
	Fable	.00 (20)	.28 (16)	.39 (18)
Mean correlations		.00	.23	.14

[a] Correlations for the ROTC tasks have been averaged.

Table 13.8. Correlations Between the Intelligence Scores of Group Members and Performance in Groups in Which the Leader Is Directive or Nondirective and the Group Members Are Supportive or Nonsupportive

| | Directive | | Nondirective | |
| | Group Support | | Group Support | |
Study	High	Low	High	Low
Mess hall	−.06	.16	.45	−.25
		.26		
Public health	−.05		.13	.35
Decoding[a]		−.66		.18
ROTC Creativity[b]				
Payproposal	−.06	.23	.39	.22
Fable	−.47	.13	.19	.42
Mean correlations	−.18	.10	.25	.14
Sample Size in Corresponding Cells				
Mess halls	13	13	11	11
Squad leader	27	24	26	30
Public health	10	10	8	10
Decoding		8		12
ROTC creativity	13	14	12	15

[a] None of the groups had high group support scores.
[b] Correlations for the two ROTC tasks have been averaged.

It appears, therefore, that the intellectual abilities of leaders and group members may be incompatible or antagonistic factors in determining group performance.

In some types of team situations it is difficult to ascertain whether the leader and member abilities both contributed to group performance. This is a problem in such groups as those in the public health study, the decoding study, and the ROTC creativity study. In these studies the leader was a full partner in performing the task. This makes it difficult to separate the leader's contribution from that of the members. The mess hall study was the cleanest in this respect since the leader was clearly in charge of the cooks and temporary help and had many responsibilities different from those of the cooks.

Figure 13.4 shows the correlations (z') between leader intelligence and performance. The magnitude of the correlations is indicated on the vertical axis and the group situation (directive vs. nondirective leaders, high vs. low group support) is indicated on the horizontal axis. The correlations between leader intelligence and performance are represented by the solid line, those between group member intelligence and performance by the broken line. This figure shows quite clearly that leader intelligence contributes positively to performance in situations in which member intel-

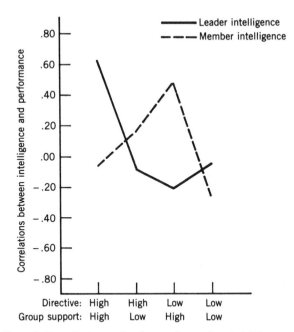

Figure 13.4. **Correlations between leader and member intelligence and mess hall performance in supportive and nonsupportive mess halls with directive and non-directive leaders.**

ligence detracts from performance, and member intelligence contributes positively to performance in situations in which leader intelligence detracts from performance.

The findings based on the other three studies in which member as well as leader intelligence scores were available are less clear, although they follow the same trend. See, for example, the same analyses for the Public Health study, shown in Figure 13.5, and the ROTC study, shown in Figure 13.6.

The question is why leader intelligence and member intelligence should interfere with each other in contributing to effective team performance. We suggest that highly intelligent people like to make use of their ability and to advance their ideas vigorously. If this is done by leaders as well as by group members, it is highly probable that there will be considerable discussion, and perhaps also argument, about the best way to proceed, and there may be some rivalry about whose ideas are to be implemented. This conflict would almost certainly require time for discussion and compromise, or it may lead to an impasse with hurt feelings or grudging compliance. It is easy to see that the time loss and lack of cooperation would result in less effective performance. These hypotheses require further investigation.

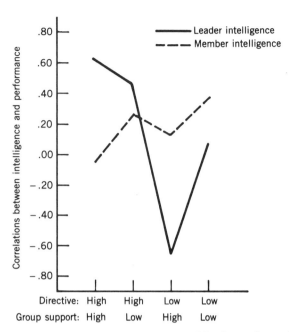

Figure 13.5. Correlations between performance and leader and member intelligence in supportive and nonsupportive public health teams with directive or nondirective leaders.

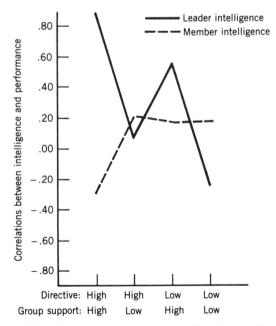

Figure 13.6. Correlations between performance and leader intelligence in supportive or nonsupportive groups with directive or nondirective leaders (ROTC creativity study).

168

INTELLIGENCE AND EXPERT KNOWLEDGE

It's obvious that intellectual abilities cannot be the only cognitive resource variables that play a part in leadership performance. We must also consider, for example, the leader's job-relevant knowledge and technical competence. The evidence is as yet scanty, but two of our studies do provide some data that may be of interest to investigators wishing to explore this problem. Since expert knowledge is generally acquired by formal or on-the-job training, the question has considerable implications for the training and development of leaders.

In the mess hall study the mess stewards were asked to report the number of weeks of their formal training in schools and courses devoted to mess management and food service as well as the number of months each had been a mess steward, which presumably provides on-the-job-training. The correlation between these two measures was .38 ($n = 52$, $p < .01$), and intelligence correlated with these two variables .25 ($p < .10$) and .35 ($p < .01$). The sum of the standardized measures of training and mess steward experience was here interpreted as a rough index of technical competence.

In the decoding study Chemers and his associates gave training in decoding to the leaders of 20 groups. These leaders were taught how a simple code can be broken, and they therefore had some "expert knowledge." The leaders of the other 20 groups did not receive training.

The groups in the three studies were divided into those with directive or nondirective leaders, and having high or low expert knowledge. Table 13.9 shows the average performance scores (z) for the four types of groups. As can be seen, the differences between means falls short of being statistically significant, although the groups with directive leaders who had expertise might turn out to be somewhat more effective in more highly controlled studies.

Table 13.9. Average Performance (in Standard Scores) of Groups with Relatively Directive or Nondirective Leaders with High or Low Expert Knowledge (Training and On-the-Job Experience)

	Leader Directiveness			
	High		Low	
	Expert Knowledge		Expert Knowledge	
Study	High	Low	High	Low
Mess halls	.582 (9)	.017 (15)	−.215 (13)	−1.000 (9)
Decoding	.240 (10)	−.344 (9)	.096 (8)	−.064 (13)

Table 13.10. Correlations Between Leader and Member Intelligence and Performance in Mess Halls with Relatively Directive or Nondirective Leaders with Relatively Much or Little Expert Knowledge[a]

	Directiveness			
	High		Low	
	Expertness		Expertness	
Study	High	Low	High	Low
Leader intelligence				
Mess halls	.62[#] (9)	.10 (15)	−.10 (13)	−.26 (9)
Decoding	.59[#] (10)	.03 (9)	−.62[#] (8)	−.57* (13)
Member intelligence				
Mess halls	.19 (9)	−.33 (15)	−.22 (13)	.32 (9)
Decoding	−.24 (10)	.18 (9)	−.03 (8)	.31 (13)

[a] ANOVA of group means not significant.

We next asked whether the more intelligent leaders are better able to capitalize on expert knowledge than leaders with less intelligence. This question is vital for the appropriate utilization of leadership training. The groups were divided into those with directive and nondirective leaders who had relatively high or low expert knowledge. We then correlated the leader's intelligence score with performance. Correlations between member intelligence and performance are also listed as a matter of interest. Table 13.10 shows the results.

As Table 13.10 shows, expert knowledge and directiveness allowed the more intelligent leaders to perform well. Intelligent leaders performed less well if they were nondirective, even if they did have expert knowledge. The two studies for which we have data suggest that directiveness and intellectual abilities are needed in order to capitalize on technical competence and expertise. The results obtained in the mess hall study were weak but consistent with those obtained in the decoding study.

If these results are confirmed by further research, they will have major implications for leadership selection and training. In effect, they tell us that the selection on the basis of technical competence has utility only for directive leaders with intellectual ability. For those with low intellectual ability, training or selection on the basis of expertise may well be wasted. Those who are not very bright may not have sufficient judgment in applying what they know or have been taught. And the leader's expertise can be applied to the task only if they are directive. How to obtain directive behavior from leaders is the topic of the next chapter.

SUMMARY

The five studies support the proposition that the effective utilization of leader intelligence requires directive leaders and supportive or stress-free leadership situations. The predictions related to the effective use of group member intelligence were not supported. This may well be because we used the average intelligence of group members rather than another index. It may also be that the intelligence of group members is less important than their technical competence, or that we need to look at the key member of the group rather than the average. This remains a problem for future research. The comparison of the intellectual contributions of leaders and group members indicates that they are inimical in their effects on group performance. In situations in which high leader intelligence contributes to good performance, high member intelligence contributes to poor performance, and vice versa. Finally, we showed that directive behavior contributes to the performance of relatively intelligent leaders. Less intelligent leaders tend to be more effective if they manage their group in a nondirective manner.

CHAPTER FOURTEEN

Cognitive Resource Theory and the Contingency Model

This chapter explores the connection between the contingency model and cognitive resource theory. One important link is suggested by Hypothesis Seven, which states that the contingency model's elements, LPC and situational control, predict not only leadership performance but also the leader's directive behavior. And as we have seen, directive behavior in turn determines how intellectual abilities contribute to the task. This chapter first reviews some relevant studies on how directive leadership behavior is affected by the situation, by the leader's personality, and the personality–situation interaction. It then discusses this link as it applies to the studies described in Chapter 12.

Directive leadership behavior has been a natural focus of research in the field of leadership. According to Webster's Dictionary (Gove, 1971), to lead means to direct. In fact, most employees want to be told in fairly specific terms what they are supposed to do and what is expected of them. Giving vague instructions and failing to make clear what is expected of the employee are major causes of interpersonal conflict in working settings (personal communication, Robert A. Baron, 1986). This is especially interesting when we consider that the human relations movement in the field of management very strongly favored nondirective and participative leadership.

The human relations movement, as articulated by such writers as Mayo (1933), McGregor (1944), and Likert (1967), gained a considerable following in the academic community in the 1950s, although the empirical support for this position was mixed. It seems fair to say that the principles and precepts of nondirective leadership were more frequently honored in word than in deed. Nevertheless, the human relations movement had a profound influence on managerial thinking during the 1950s and 1960s, and it continues to be important. Whether nondirective behavior is appropriate for all groups is another question. We will now briefly summarize some relevant studies that predict directive behavior.

RELEVANT STUDIES ON DIRECTIVE BEHAVIOR

Situational Factors Affecting Directive Leader Behavior

Many employees in business, industry, and the public sector may wish to be asked for their opinion or suggestions, but most also want clear directions from their boss and explicit standards by which their work will be judged. Although there are always exceptions, highly directive behavior obviously is inappropriate in such groups as committees, boards, councils, and juries. This point is also made by Vroom and Yetton (1973), whose normative decision model tells the leader when to direct, when to consult with subordinates, and when to let group members participate. Thus leaders are advised to encourage group participation when they do not have all the information about a problem or when different points of view need to be represented, as is the case in the typical committee meeting. Indeed, in many group situations, tradition and logic require that every member must be consulted and given an equal voice in the group's decision. *Robert's Rules of Parliamentary Law and Order* (Roberts, 1979), which govern most groups of this type, prohibit highly autocratic leader behavior. There are also cultural norms and traditions that demand nondirective leadership. The Quaker meeting and the Japanese quality circle are examples of groups that require consensus by discussion and patient examination of the issues before action is taken.

Several empirical studies have identified situational factors that affect directive leader behavior. Korten (1968) showed that leaders were more directive if the work was practical (i.e., more structured than unstructured); Selznik (1957) and Blankenship and Miles (1968) reported more directiveness at lower than at higher levels of the management hierarchy (i.e., in situations having high task structure). Emery and Trist (1965) and Lawrence and Lorsch (1967) also reported more directive behavior when the task was structured than when it was unstructured.

Personality Factors and Directive Behavior

As one would expect, personality also influences directive leader behavior. Some people are "naturally" more bossy and directive than their coworkers;

others are more hesitant to give orders, less confident of being right, less willing to give directions. The psychological literature has identified "authoritarians" who are inclined to be directive and sure of themselves (Adorno, Frenkel-Brunswick, Levinson, & Sanford, 1950) when they are in charge, as well as being more submissive toward authority figures. Heller (1969) and others found that leaders behaved in a more directive manner if they felt that they were more intelligent or more competent than their subordinates. There is also evidence that persons with low LPC scores tend to be somewhat more directive than those with high LPC scores (Fiedler, 1978a; Rice, 1978b).

In general, however, an individual's personality is not the only determinant of directive behavior. The bulk of the evidence shows that directive or nondirective behavior varies considerably from situation to situation (Bass, 1981; Michaelson, 1973; Shaw & Blum, 1966). For example, the test–retest correlations for structuring behavior in a longitudinal analysis of the squad leader study (Bons & Fiedler, 1976) was only .10 ($n = 109$) over a six to eight month interval. This indicates that the individual's tendency to be generally directive or nondirective is very slight.

The Person–Situation Interaction and Directive Behavior

Chapter 7 pointed out that the directiveness of high- and low-LPC leaders depends on their situational control and whether they feel anxious or under stress. These differences in behavior of high- and low-LPC leaders have been the basis for interpreting LPC as a measure of motivational structure. It implies that high- and low-LPC leaders set a different value for such goals as task accomplishment and close interpersonal relations. We assume that the person whose behavior focuses on the task sets a higher priority on task accomplishment at that point in time than on good interpersonal relations; a person who focuses on interpersonal relations sets a higher priority on good relations with coworkers than on the task. Since high-LPC leaders focus on the task when they have high control, but on the relationship when their control is lower, we assume that the immediate goals of the individual have shifted from the task to the relationship. The low-LPC leader is primarily concerned with the relationship when situational control is relatively high, but with task accomplishment when control is low. We assume therefore that the goal of task accomplishment is more pressing for the low-LPC leader when the accomplishment of the task is uncertain.

By definition, the high-control situation makes it more likely that the basic goal can be accomplished. For this reason the high-LPC leaders, who already have good relations with their group, no longer need to concentrate on their primary goal of close relations with coworkers, and focus their attention on their secondary goal of accomplishing the task.

In the high-control situation the low-LPC leaders can be reasonably certain that they will accomplish their primary goal of completing the task since the task is structured and the group is supportive. Hence they are able to focus on accomplishing their second-ranking goal of having good relations with coworkers. This interpretation is based on Maslow's (1954) well-known dictum that satisfied needs no longer motivate. Two laboratory experiments illustrate this hypothesis. The first shows the effect of task structure on the directive behavior of high- and low-LPC leaders. The second shows the effect of stress and anxiety on the leader's behavior.*

The Sample and Wilson Experiment.   Sample and Wilson (1965) conducted an ingenious laboratory experiment in a large introductory psychology class to show that the behavior of high- and low-LPC leaders changes in different directions as the task becomes more structured. They assigned students to groups each consisting of one leader appointed on the basis of his high or low LPC score and three team members, as well as one observer. The task consisted of running, planning, and reporting a maze-learning experiment using a white rat. The observer rated the leader's behavior in each of these three phases on the basis of Bales' (1950) Interaction Process Analysis categories, that is, as making primarily socioemotional comments or comments concerned with the task.

The Sample and Wilson data were subsequently reinterpreted by Shirakashi (1980), who pointed out that the planning function constituted the least structured subtask while running the experiment according to a predetermined schedule constituted a highly structured subtask, hence relatively higher situational control. Shirakashi plotted the mean behavior scores for high and for low LPC leaders, as shown in Figure 14.1. This figure shows performance on the vertical axis and three degrees of task structure, corresponding to running, reporting, and planning the study. As can be seen, in the most structured task phase (running the experiment), the high LPC leaders made more comments about the task than did low LPC leaders; in the highly unstructured planning phase, the relationship-motivated (high LPC) leaders were more concerned with the relationship while task-motivated (low LPC) leaders were more concerned with the

---

* An alternative but related interpretation has been offered by Rice (1978b) and Chemers (personal communication, 1983). In their view, leader behavior reflects the basic orientation of the high-LPC leader's high value for interpersonal relations and the low-LPC leader's high value for task accomplishment. According to this interpretation, the high- and low-LPC leaders do not change their goals. Rather, they adopt the behavior that will most effectively accomplish their particular goals in a particular leadership situation. Which of these two interpretations is to be preferred needs to be determined by empirical tests. Both interpretations allow us to hypothesize that the high- and low-LPC leaders behave differently depending on whether the situation provides high, moderate, or low control or creates stress and anxiety for the leader.

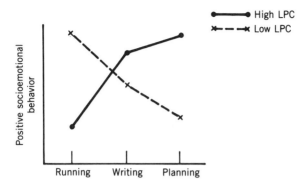

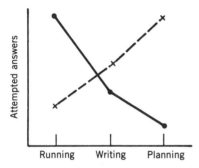

Figure 14.1. Sample and Wilson data, reanalyzed by Shirakashi. Comparison of behaviors by relationship-motivated (high LPC) and by task-motivated (low LPC) leaders in the phases of an experimental task involving a class project of running a rat maze study. [Reprinted with permission from F. E. Fiedler (1972b). Personality, motivational systems, and behavior of high and low LPC persons. *Human Relations*, *25*, 391–412.]

task. The Sample and Wilson experiment thus demonstrated that the same leaders changed their behavior as the situation changed, and that these changes followed the prediction of the contingency model.

Highway Engineering Department Managers. Larson and Rowland (1973) asked whether stress would affect the behavior of high- and low-LPC leaders. The authors conducted an in-basket experiment during a management training program for a county department of highways. The participating managers were divided into those with high- and low-LPC scores and randomly assigned to a high- or a low-stress condition. The low-stress group was told that the test was an experimental version for which the investigators wanted the trainees' opinions and reactions. Man-

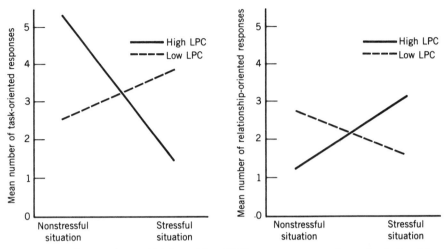

Figure 14.2. Comparison of high and low LPC managers on task- and relationship-oriented responses to in-basket items in stressful and nonstressful situations. [Adapted with permission from L. L. Larson, & K. M. Rowland (1973). Leadership style, stress, and behavior in task performance. *Organizational Behavior and Human Performance, 9,* 407–420.]

agers in the high-stress group were given to understand that the test was a good measure of administrative ability, and that it might be used in a forthcoming reorganization of the department. (This stress manipulation was effective as shown by palmar sweat measures taken before and after the experiment, as well as by a postsession questionnaire.)

The task consisted of making decisions about various management and personnel problems that the managers presumably found in their in-baskets. The responses showed that task-motivated managers were more concerned with interpersonal relations in the low-stress condition but more concerned with the task in the high-stress condition. The behavior of high-LPC managers was exactly in the opposite direction (Figure 14.2). Similar findings were obtained by Green, Nebeker, and Boni (1976), who conducted a study in which students were asked to give verbal reports to simulated management problems.

In brief, several studies, including those by Sample and Wilson (1965) and by Larson and Rowland (1973), found that high-LPC leaders were more directive when their situational control was relatively high; low-LPC leaders were more directive in situations in which their situational control was relatively low (Fiedler, 1970). However, some studies have yielded inconsistent results (Ayer, cited in Shirakashi, 1980). Shirakashi, who reviewed all then-available data on the subject, concluded that task structure played the principal role in determining the directive behavior of high- and low-LPC leaders.

Table 14.1. Average Ratings (Standard Scores) of Leader Directiveness in Supportive and Nonsupportive Groups with High and Low Task Structure

Study	Task Structure	Group Support			
		High		Low	
		Leader LPC		Leader LPC	
		High	Low	High	Low
Mess hall	High	.429 (14)	−.331 (9)	.099 (10)	−.256 (15)
Squad leaders	High	.204 (29)	−.061 (28)	.099 (27)	−.264 (32)
Public health	Low	−.258 (11)	.235 (7)	.010 (11)	.016 (10)
ROTC creativity	Low	−.168 (19)	.116 (7)	−.287 (9)	.216 (19)

In retrospect this conclusion makes eminent sense. Task structure is clearly one of the most important factors in determining the leader's directive behavior (e.g., Korten, 1968). A leader who knows exactly what needs to be done is expected to tell subordinates what to do. This suggests that leader behavior would differ between groups with structured task assignments and those with relatively unstructured task assignments. The studies in Chapter 12 allow us to test this hypothesis.

LPC, STRUCTURE, AND DIRECTIVE LEADER BEHAVIOR

Table 14.1 shows the mean directiveness ratings in standard scores for high and low task structure (see Table 12.1). The studies were further divided into those with high and low group support (GA) and high or low leader LPC scores.*

These data are shown in graphic form in Figure 14.3 for supportive groups (high GA) and in Figure 14.4 for nonsupportive groups (low GA). It requires no statistical sophistication to see that relationship-motivated and task-motivated leaders differed markedly in directive behavior under different group–task conditions, supporting Shirakashi's (1980) conclusion. The effect of group support was considerably weaker.

Table 14.2 presents these same results in nonstatistical terms. It shows that these results are compatible with those previously suggested. High-LPC leaders become nondirective and probably concerned with their interpersonal relations when these are jeopardized by their lack of control.

---

* The decoding study had to be deleted from this analysis because group atmosphere scores were uniformly low and task structure was experimentally manipulated by task-relevant training.

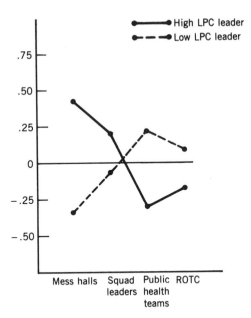

Figure 14.3. Average directiveness scores of high and low LPC leaders in supportive groups.

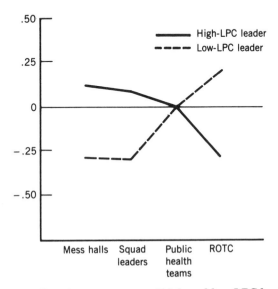

Figure 14.4. Average directiveness scores of high and low LPC leaders in nonsupportive groups.

Table 14.2. Conditions in Which Relationship-Motivated and Task-Motivated Leaders Are Directive in Various Situations

	Leader LPC			
	High		Low	
	Task Structure		Task Structure	
Group Support	High	Low	High	Low
High	High	Low	Low	Moderately high
Low	Moderately high	Low	Low	High

In turn, task motivated leaders become concerned with the task when task accomplishment is jeopardized by their lack of control. This causes them to behave in a directive and structuring manner toward group members.

In brief, there seems to be a fairly strong relationship between the leader's directive behavior and the contingency model's variables—LPC, group support, and task structure. The suggested link between the contingency model and cognitive resource theory is shown below:

LPC and situational control $\longrightarrow$ Leader behavior $\longrightarrow$ Leader cognitive resource use $\longrightarrow$ Performance

Intelligence and Directive Behavior

Its important place in cognitive resource theory also leads us to consider the role of intelligence in determining directive behavior. Additional analyses were, therefore, made by further dividing groups on the basis of leader intelligence. Table 14.3 shows the average directiveness scores for each of these subgroups. This table and Figures 14.5, 14.6, 14.7, and 14.8 which graphically depict these data, suggest that the additional factor of intelligence accentuates the differences in the behavior of high- and low-LPC leaders in the various conditions. This is particularly apparent in groups that are not highly supportive. The data suggests that the intelligent, task-motivated leader with an unstructured task may wish to take complete control of the group process in order to accomplish the job. The less intelligent, relationship-motivated leader may well give up in situations in which the task is ambiguous and the group is nonsupportive.

Contingency Model Predictions

Before going further, we should ask whether the performance of the groups in the five test studies was consistent with the contingency model

Table 14.3. Mean Leader Directiveness (Standard Scores) in Groups with High- and Low-LPC Leaders with Relatively High and Low Intelligence

Study	Intelligence			
	High		Low	
	LPC		LPC	
	High	Low	High	Low
High Group Support				
Mess hall	.538 (10)	−.410 (4)	.156 (4)	−.279 (6)
Squad leader	.391 (8)	−.039 (17)	.132 (21)	−.098 (10)
Public health	.330 (3)	.320 (7)	−.168 (5)	.043 (3)
ROTC creativity[a]	−.156 (3)	.088 (6)	−.125 (9)	−.180 (9)
Low Group Support				
Mess halls	−.221 (7)	−.134 (6)	.852 (2)	−.453 (9)
Squad leaders	.059 (13)	−.497 (18)	.134 (15)	.035 (14)
Public health	.088 (6)	.281 (4)	−.862 (4)	−.072 (5)
ROTC creativity[a]	−.133 (10)	1.103 (4)	−.996 (4)	−.063 (9)

[a] Member GA scores were used in these calculations.

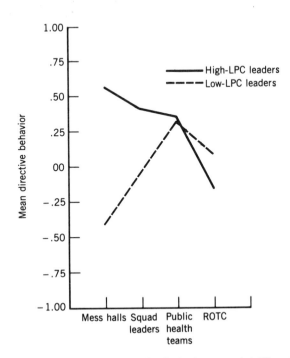

Figure 14.5. Mean directive behavior of relatively more intelligent high and low LPC leaders in supportive groups.

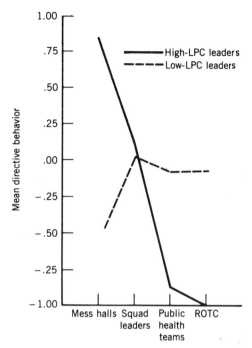

Figure 14.6. Mean directive behavior of relatively less intelligent high and low LPC leaders in nonsupportive groups.

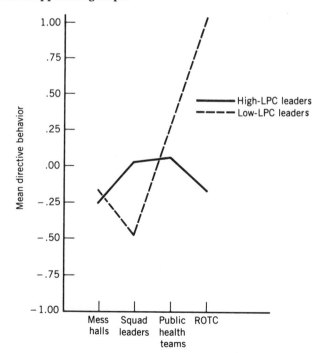

Figure 14.7. Mean directive behavior of relatively more intelligent high and low LPC leaders in nonsupportive groups.

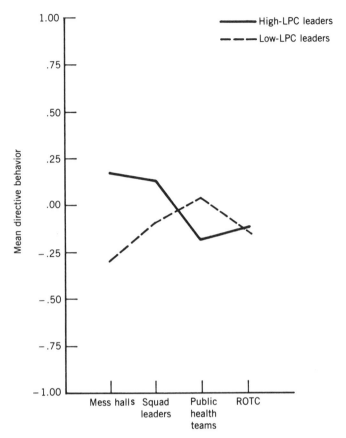

Figure 14.8. Mean directive behavior of relatively less intelligent high and low LPC leaders in supportive groups.

predictions. Table 14.4 presents correlations between leader LPC scores and the performance of groups classified as falling into the high, moderate, and low situational control zones. This classification was based on group support, task structure, and position power. The last row on the table indicates the ratio of correct and incorrect predictions. The contingency model was supported in eight of the twelve sets of correlations from the five studies.

As pointed out in Chapter 6, several writers have averred that group performance in the lower situational control zone tends to be lower than in the high and moderate control zone. The data from the five test studies show that this is not the case. Mean performance scores (z) were computed for the studies classified as falling into the high, moderate, and low situational control zones. These means were almost identical: .033, −.058,

Table 14.4. Correlations Between Leader LPC and Performance in Supportive and Nonsupportive Groups[a]

	Situational Control		
Study	High	Moderate	Low
Mess hall	−.34 (28)	.06 (24)	
Squad leader[b]	−.20 (61)	.07 (65)	
Public health			
Clinic Administration	−.04 (18)	.46 (21)	
Community Development		−.40 (22)	.18 (21)
Decoding[c]		−.39 (20)	−.18 (20)
ROTC creativity			
Payproposal		−.14 (28)	−.16 (26)
Fable		−.07 (28)	−.52* (26)
Predictions correct/incorrect[d]	3/0	3/3	2/1

[a]Member GA indicated situational control except for squad leaders, for whom member GA was unavailable. Task structure and position power were essentially identical for groups within each of the studies.

[b]Squad leader GA used since member GA not available.

[c]Leader's rating of stress and tension used since GA scores were uniformly low. ROTC study results were counted only once in each condition.

[d]Where more than one correlation was obtained in a study, the mean was used in determining the direction of the relationship.

and −.004, and they show that the groups in the low situational control zone perform about as well as those in higher situational control zones.

DISCUSSION

Several issues raised in this chapter require some further comment. First, we need to ask what directive leader behavior really means. Although directive and structuring leader behaviors are extensively measured and discussed in the leadership literature, it is not completely clear what these terms imply. Directive behavior may occur when the leader feels confident about what must be done and therefore tells people what do do. Alternatively, directive behavior occurs when the leader feels insecure and in need for control. Nondirective behavior probably indicates that the leader feels that the task is being performed, and there is no need to intervene. The second interpretation fits with the hypotheses of path–goal theory as well as the goal hierarchy interpretation of LPC, but further research is called for to clarify this point.

One problem that also needs attention is the report by a number of studies that members' judgments of leader behavior tend to be relatively unreliable (e.g., Mitchell, 1970a). To what extent does this make the findings based on directive behavior suspect? There is no question that ratings of leader behavior are relatively unreliable. One likely reason for low agreement among raters is that the same leader may relate to group members differently (Graen, 1976). Second, most individuals are not very accurate judges of behavior. And third, judgments of leader behavior may be influenced by preconceived notions of effective leadership (Lord, Binning, Rush, & Thomas, 1978; Phillips & Lord, 1981). Nevertheless, ratings of leader behavior have proven highly useful in many studies because the reliability of ratings increases when, as in our studies, the observations of two or more raters are combined. In addition, the reliability of behavior ratings increases with the rater's opportunity for observing the leader on different occasions (Epstein, 1979). This would be the case in natural groups. Finally, we could not have obtained consistent significant results for directive behavior if the rating measures were invalid. Exactly how ratings of directive leader behavior should best be interpreted deserves further research (Gioia & Sims, 1985).

One other finding of our studies presents an apparent dilemma. The results show that low-LPC leaders of groups with structured tasks (mess halls and squads) were successful, but they were also nondirective and therefore did not use their intelligence effectively. This finding seems counterintuitive unless we recall from Chapter 11 that in routine jobs which require a high degree of technical knowledge, the brighter leaders performed less well than did the less intelligent leaders.

We must remember that most laboratory studies of leadership have used intellectually demanding tasks. Perhaps we have been too willing to assume that these findings would be representative of all types of tasks, including those that do not demand high intellectual effort from the leader.

SUMMARY

This chapter shows that the directive behavior of leaders can be predicted from the interaction of personality and situation—that is, from the contingency model. The task-motivated leaders tend to be directive in situations that provide relatively low control; relationship-motivated leaders tend to be directive in situations characterized by relatively high control, but even this formulation is considerably oversimplified.

The evidence has shown thus far that the contingency model predicts the leader's directive behavior, and that directive behavior and intelligence predict performance of supportive groups. We now consider Hypothesis Five of cognitive resource theory, relating task requirements to the leader's cognitive resources.

CHAPTER FIFTEEN

Critical Task Requirements and Cognitive Resource Utilization

This chapter addresses Hypothesis Five: the abilities of the leader and of group members contribute to the performance of tasks which require these abilities. Specifically, intellectual abilities will correlate more highly with problem solving tasks that are intellectually demanding than with interpersonal conflicts that require interpersonal skills.

Research on small groups (e.g., Hackman & Morris, 1975; McGrath & Altman, 1966) has stressed the need for a better understanding of task characteristics. In response, several classification systems have been proposed in an effort to systematize our knowledge of group tasks (e.g., Fleishman & Quaintance, 1984; Hackman, 1968; Shaw, 1973; Steiner, 1972).

While these taxonomies have been important contributions to the field, our own research indicates that the same task may require different leader abilities under different conditions. As Chapter 11 showed, the leader's intellectual abilities contribute to task performance only in situations that are relatively free of interpersonal stress. In stressful leadership situations, however, the identical task may require organizational experience rather than intellectual ability. This chapter examines more closely how the characteristics of the task affect the leader's and members' abilities to contribute to group performance. These points are here illustrated.

Coast Guard Staff

This study (Potter & Fiedler, 1981) (described earlier in Chapter 11) shows that an individual's intellectual abilities contribute to the task to the degree to which the task is intellectually demanding. The 130 officers, petty officers, and civilians held responsible staff positions, and almost all of them were in charge of an office or a staff section. They were asked to estimate the proportion of time they devoted to each of 10 important staff functions. The intellectual demand of the 10 staff functions was rated independently by five Coast Guard officers. The staff functions shown in Table 15.1 are listed in the order of the intellectual demands they make of the job holder.

We expected that the brighter people will perform better on intellectually demanding tasks than will those with less intellectual ability; this was the case for situations in which stress with boss was low. However, exactly the opposite occurred for situations in which stress with boss was high. Here the more intellectually demanding the task, the *poorer* was the performance of the more intelligent staff personnel (see Table 15.1).

As can be seen, boss stress moderated the correlation between intelligence and performance. In fact, if we rank order the intellectual demand rating of the staff function and rank order the magnitude of the correlation between intelligence and performance, we obtain a correlation of .78 ($n = 10$, $p < .05$) for the low stress condition, but a correlation of $-.35$

Table 15.1. Correlations Between Intelligence and Performance Under Low and High Stress in the Coast Guard Study, on Tasks Listed in Order of Their Intellectual Demand

	Stress	
	Low	**High**
Intellectually demanding tasks		
Advising	.27 (30)	−.46* (22)
Making decisions	.11 (21)	−.47 (13)
Inspecting	.20 (16)	−.36 (10)
Engineering	.38 (20)	−.16 (21)
Administration	.35 (25)	−.47* (25)
Mean correlations	.26	−.39
Intellectually less demanding tasks		
Paper work	−.01 (25)	−.25 (21)
Training	.11 (26)	−.17 (21)
Public relations	.04 (26)	−.36 (16)
Attending meetings	.28 (23)	−.28 (24)
Supervision	.07 (29)	.04 (18)
Mean correlations	.10	−.21

Table 15.2. Correlations Between Time in Service
and Performance Under Low and High Stress in
Coast Guard Staff Assignments

	Stress	
	Low	High
Intellectually demanding tasks		
Advising	.06 (35)	.43* (22)
Making decisions	.01 (23)	.47 (14)
Inspecting	−.07 (20)	.60* (12)
Engineering	.30 (22)	.13 (22)
Administration	.06 (31)	.40* (26)
Mean	.07	.41
Intellectually less demanding tasks		
Paperwork	−.28 (27)	.44* (22)
Training	−.09 (31)	.42 (23)
Public relations	−.09 (27)	.55* (18)
Attending meetings	.06 (23)	.53** (26)
Supervision	−.06 (31)	.41 (19)
Mean	−.12	.47

($n = 10$, ns) for the high stress condition. In other words, under low stress, the more demanding the task, the higher was the correlation between intelligence and performance. Under high stress, the tendency was, if anything, in the opposite direction.

Table 15.2 considers the effect of organizational experience (time in service) on performance. It shows that the individual's time in service correlated with performance only under stress, regardless of the intellectual demands made by the task.

Combat Infantry Division Leaders

As will be recalled, Borden (1980) investigated combat leaders at five organizational levels of an infantry battalion. His study permits us to determine the contribution of intelligence and organizational experience to the performance of tasks that make various demands of the leader. Data were collected on platoon sergeants, platoon leaders, first sergeants, company commanders, and executive officers (see Chapter 11).

A group of 13 officers and senior NCOs rated the degree to which good performance on the five leadership jobs requires intellectual ability, technical competence, and the ability to "manage the boss" and keep him out of trouble. The further steps in this analysis were as follows. We first ordered the five leadership jobs on the degree to which they were rated as making intellectual demands. Second, the leaders in each job group were divided into those reporting low or high boss stress. The final step consisted of plotting the correlations between intellectual ability and performance and between time in service and performance for each of the positions. Identical procedures analyzed the task's requirement for technical competence and for ability to manage relations with the boss.

The results of these analyses are best seen in graphic form. Figure 15.1 shows the correlations between the Wonderlic Test Score and leadership performance for each leadership position in the study. The vertical axis shows the magnitude of the correlation between intelligence and performance (in z scores); the horizontal axis shows the five jobs arrayed in order of intellectual demand (from low on the left side of the graph to high intellectual demand, at the right). These correlations generally increase in magnitude with the increasing demands for intellectual effort of the job. The greater the job's critical requirement for intellectual effort, the greater was the contribution of the leader's intellectual ability to performance—but only for leaders who reported low boss stress. Correlations between intelligence and performance and between time in service

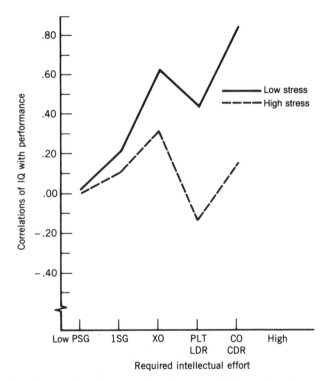

Figure 15.1. Correlations between intellectual ability and performance of leaders in different army infantry jobs under conditions of high or low stress due to stress when jobs are ordered on the basis of intellectual effort required of the leader. Key: PSG = platoon sergeant; 1SG = first sergeant; XO = company executive officer; PLT LDR = platoon leader; CO CDR = company commander.

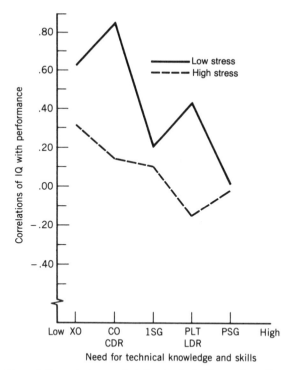

Figure 15.2. Correlations between intellectual ability and performance of leaders in different army infantry jobs under conditions of high or low stress due to stress when jobs are ordered on the basis of the required technical competencies of the leader. (Key same as Figure 15.1.)

and performance are not shown since these were low and not meaningfully interpretable.

Figure 15.2 shows the analogous correlations when jobs were ordered on the basis of the technical competence required of the leader. Technical competence, in this context, means knowledge and skill needed to do a job (e.g., how well does the squad leader know how to assemble a rifle, or how well must the company commander know how to repair a truck). We are concerned here with the degree to which the various jobs require the *leader* to have technical competence and knowledge of the job his group members must perform, and to what extent high intellectual ability contributes to performance on these jobs.

The correlations between intelligence and task performance were inversely related to the technical competence the job requires: The greater the need for technical competence, the less did the leader's intelligence contribute to performance. We must remember, however, that technical competence implies knowledge of existing methods and procedures for performing the task, and not the development of new methods or procedures.

Nevertheless, it is something of a surprise that jobs requiring technical competence do not seem to benefit from intellectual abilities.

The third categorization of tasks was based on the need to manage the interpersonal relationship with the boss, that is, to "manage" in the sense of keeping him or her organized and out of trouble, and if necessary keeping the boss off one's own back. When arrayed on this basis, the correlations between leader intelligence and performance were low and negligible under low- and high-stress conditions and are not shown. These low correlations are not surprising since intellectual abilities did not correlate with interpersonal performance in other studies (e.g., the public health study or the squad leader study). However, when the leader felt high job stress, the correlations between time in service and performance increased as the job required more management of interpersonal relations with the boss (see Figure 15.3). This suggests that interpersonal skills of this nature are learned from experience. There is also the possibility, of course, that those who have these interpersonal skills are more likely to

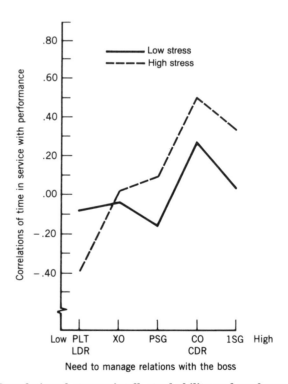

Figure 15.3. Correlations between intellectual ability and performance of leaders in different army infantry jobs under conditions of high or low stress due to stress when jobs are ordered on the basis of required ability of the leader to deal with the boss. (Key same as Figure 15.1.)

survive. This explanation seems somewhat less plausible in military settings since it is very difficult to "fire" such people as first sergeants.

In support of Hypothesis Six, the data from the infantry division study suggest that the nature of the task determines what abilities are needed from the leader. However, the important points in this case, as well as in the coast guard study, are, first, that intellectual abilities correlated more highly with performance as the intellectual demand of the task increased. Second, intellectual abilities did not contribute to jobs requiring high technical skill and competence. In this case, of course, high technical skill was confounded with intellectual demand of the task. This finding therefore cannot be taken at face value until further studies are conducted in other settings. Third, we are inclined to place more credence in the finding that jobs that demand a high level of interpersonal skill may well be performed more effectively by individuals with long job tenures. These particular interpersonal skills may indeed be acquired by experience.

INTELLIGENCE AND CREATIVITY

How essential is it for a leader to have the abilities which are specifically required by the task? This is an important question for leadership selection and training. As may be recalled from the mess hall study, the correlation between performance and the mess steward's technical competence (i.e., training and experience) on Table 12.5 was slightly but not significantly lower than the correlation between performance and his general intelligence. The ROTC creativity study (previously described in Chapter 12) provides an opportunity to compare the contribution of the leader's general intelligence and of the highly task-specific creative ability to his group's performance.

The Guilford, Berger, and Christensen (1954) Plot Titles and Alternative Uses tests of creativity were administered in the pretest of the ROTC study. These tests were moderately correlated (.36) and the standardized scores were summed to provide a combined "creativity" measure. Although intellectual ability and creativity are not highly related, we had assumed that the two ability measures should yield somewhat similar results when correlated with performance. In fact we had expected that the task-relevant creativity score of the directive leader would correlate more highly with group creativity than the general intelligence score. Separate correlations were computed for nondirective leaders. Table 15.3 presents the correlations between intelligence and performance and between creativity and performance of groups with directive or nondirective leaders and high or low group support (Member GA). Figures 15.4 and 15.5 show these same findings in graphic form.

These results were unexpected. Every correlation between the directive leader's intelligence and performance was positive; every correlation be-

Table 15.3. Correlations Between Performance and Leader and Member Creativity Scores in Groups with Directive and Nondirective Leaders, and High or Low Group Support

| Task | High Leader Directiveness | | | |
| | High Group Support | | Low Group Support | |
	Intelligence (14)	Creativity (13)	Intelligence (14)	Creativity (13)
	Leader			
Payproposal	.58*	−.18	.27	−.58*
Fable	.75**	−.08	.06	−.51#
	Members			
Payproposal	−.06	.02	.23	−.20
Fable	−.51#	−.21	.13	−.12

| Task | Low Leader Directiveness | | | |
| | High Group Support | | Low Group Support | |
	Intelligence (14)	Creativity (13)	Intelligence (14)	Creativity (13)
	Leader			
Payproposal	.12	.08	.16	.46#
Fable	.23	.36	−.21	.09
	Members			
Payproposal	.35	.23	.22	.03
Fable	.19	.20	.42	.08

tween creativity scores and performance was negative. Thus directive leaders could be effective in two ways. They could have high intelligence and high member support—in which case they could manage the group process—or they could have low creativity and low member support, leaving the creative process to others. Group member intelligence and creativity did not correlate highly with group performance. Very similar results were obtained when groups were divided on the basis of the leader's directiveness and low and high leader anxiety scores. Thus anxiety, based on pretest measures, appeared to have very similar effects on the leader's cognitive function as low group support. While this could mean that high anxiety caused low group support this seems unlikely since group support and leader anxiety were uncorrelated in this study ($-.01$, $n = 54$).

We interpret the findings shown in Table 15.3 as indicating that the intellectual ability of the leader is used to direct and monitor the group process, and perhaps also to integrate the ideas of other group members. High leader creativity may then get in the way of these important leadership functions. The creative leader may be more interested in contributing a multitude of ideas rather than in keeping the group process on track. A free flow of ideas also may interfere with the leader's ability to direct the

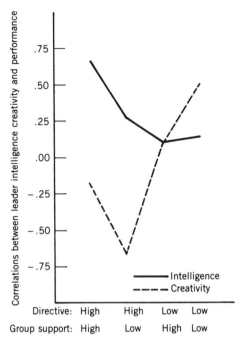

Figure 15.4. Correlations between leader intelligence and performance and leader creativity and performance in the Payproposal task.

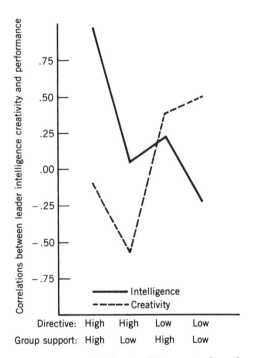

Figure 15.5. Correlations between leader intelligence and performance and leader creativity and performance in the Fable task.

group's work in a logical manner. This, in turn, may cause the discussion to get out of hand.

This hypothesis finds some support in the Dutch creativity study by Fiedler, Meuwese, and Oonk (1961), in which 32 four-man groups invented stories based on two pictures from the Henry Group TAT Test (Murray, 1943). Leader and group member intelligence was measured with a Dutch version of the Miller Analogies Test (Miller, 1926). The team's performance was rated by two independent judges. We compared the 10 groups with the most congenial group climates and the 10 groups with climates described as most tense and antagonistic. The group discussions were recorded and the participants' verbal contributions were then content-analyzed.

In the more congenial groups we found a positive correlation between creative performance and the leader's analogies test score (.60, $p < .10$), but a high negative correlation ($-.72, p < .01$) between performance and the number of original ideas produced by the group. We also found a negative correlation between performance and the total number of comments ($-.64, p < .05$). This finding suggests that the effective leaders of the congenial groups maintained a high degree of control over the group process by limiting the number of ideas and general conversation. Similar but somewhat lower correlations were obtained in the more stressful groups between performance and the leader analogies and performance (.42) and between performance and number of new ideas ($-.43$).

We suggest that the creative groups were successful if the leader had the intellectual ability to monitor and control the group process, and the ability to eliminate all but the more fruitful ideas. The Dutch data thus lend further support to the notion that the leader's creativity and logical thinking ability play markedly different roles in the group process.

SUMMARY

The results of these studies highlight the importance of critical task requirements as well as of stress in predicting when the leader's and the members' cognitive resources contribute to group performance. Put simply, when stress is low, leader intelligence is likely to contribute to group success provided that the task requires intellectual effort. Intelligence will not contribute strongly to the success of the leader of a social club. When stress is high, job tenure and general experience enable the leader to perform better, and perhaps especially in jobs requiring interpersonal skill.

A high level of creative ability specific to the task appears to interfere with performance of groups with directive leaders since it may keep the leader from attending to the noncreative leadership functions. Intelligence appears to be required for the management of the group and the monitoring of the group process. However, the match between intellectual tasks and mental abilities is of little importance under conditions of high stress, and intellectual ability may then result in poor performance.

Future leadership research efforts should consider the need for classifying the abilities required by the leader as well as those required for individual performance. The development of a more specific taxonomy should have theoretical value as well as practical significance for the selection and training of leaders.

CHAPTER SIXTEEN

Finished Business and Unfinished Business

What are the theoretical and practical implications of cognitive resource theory, and what are some of the research problems the theory suggests?

THEORETICAL IMPLICATIONS OF COGNITIVE RESOURCE THEORY

The Role of Intellectual Abilities

Cognitive resource theory throws new light on the function of directive and structuring behavior. The theory points out that directive behavior results in good performance only if linked with high intelligence in a supportive, nonstressful leadership environment. This hypothesis, suggests the not surprising conclusion that directive leaders who are stupid give stupid directions, and if the group follows these directions, the consequences will be bad.

This hypothesis, which seems well supported by our studies, provides a much needed explanation of how intellectual abilities contribute to the leadership process. A major surprise has been the negligible part played by considerate behavior in determining group performance. Only the ROTC study provided any evidence that considerate behavior affected performance, and not even in that study were the relations uniformly strong. With the exception of the work of Podsakoff and his associates (Podsakoff, Todor, Grover, & Huber, 1984; Podsakoff, Todor, & Schular, 1983), investigators in the leadership area may have paid too little attention to the control behaviors of rewarding and punishing that leaders employ to keep their group members in line. A beginning was made in the Bons and Fiedler (1976) study, and more highly focused research should yield useful results. In addition, we must consider that directive and structuring behavior includes instructions on how to perform a certain task, who is to perform it, and what standards are to be observed. These more subtle aspects of the term "directive" may well have various effects that still need to be determined. Moreover, one can be considerate in order to get a job accomplished, that is, ingratiating, and one can be considerate for its own sake. One may be directive in telling subordinates what to do or directive in structuring the interpersonal relations so that the group will be harmonious. We need to consider these problems in more detail.

There has been almost no research in recent years on the contribution of group members' intellectual abilities to organizational performance. Blades (Blades & Fiedler, 1973) hypothesized that group members are able to contribute to the task only if the leader is nondirective and the group members are motivated and supportive. The results have been weak. It is far too early to discard the hypothesis.

We must also consider that the average of the group members' intelligence scores may be a poor index for studying the intellectual contributions of group members. For example, the disjunctive tasks described by Steiner (1972) may require that we correlate group performance with the score of the most influential or the most intelligent group member. In another type of task we may need to consider the variance of group member intelligence or the task-relevant abilities rather than group member intelligence.

The finding that the correlations between leader intelligence and performance and the correlations between member intelligence and performance ran so frequently in opposite directions was serendipitous and unexpected. These results suggest that either the leader's or the group members' intelligence, but not both, contributed to performance. Thus there may be room for only one planner and idea generater in a particular group. Having bright leaders and bright members might result in an overload of ideas or rivalry between group leader and group members as to whose ideas get implemented. We now need to ask whether this finding is fairly universal or whether there are at least some group structures or conditions that allow two or more idea persons to contribute on a creative task.

We also need further research to determine why the correlations between leader intelligence and performance and between the same leaders' performance and their creativity scores run in the opposite directions. We suggested that the highly creative leader may devote too much intellectual effort to developing original ideas and not enough effort to directing, monitoring, and controlling the group process. This explanation certainly fits some of our everyday observations. The case of Stephen Jobs, former chief executive officer of the Apple Computer Corporation, is a good example, since Jobs devoted his efforts to the development of a new computer, the MacIntosh, rather than to managing. And many highly committed researchers who become department heads or administrators either resent the burden of managerial duties or pay too little attention to their administrative jobs. It is also said that the best technicians do not necessarily make the best shop foremen. The adage that "those who can, do; those who can't, teach" probably oversimplifies the issue. It does appear, however, that the contributions of the leader's creative and intellectual abilities are at best marginally related, and that they may be negatively related.

These findings run counter to the widely held notion that the supervisor must know as much about the job as each employee. We must remember, of course, that these findings surfaced only in two laboratory studies in which artificial groups were given short and contrived tasks, and that the high correlations showed up primarily in groups with directive leaders. We now need to see whether field studies lead to the same results.

Cognitive resource theory is based on the assumption that the more intelligent leaders develop better plans, decisions, and action strategies than do less intelligent leaders, that is, plans and decisions more likely to result in effective performance. The assumption seems axiomatic, but the few data which bear on it are far from overwhelming. We need more empirical data to support this belief.

Most of our studies have been based on very simple measures of intellectual ability. More sophisticated measures of intellectual ability should now be employed in following up the results we have obtained thus far, and there is good reason to expect that more specialized intelligence scales and job specific measures of technical competence will provide further insight into the role of various cognitive resources in affecting the leadership process.

The Role of Job-Relevant Experience

Job experience is one of the most important factors in hiring and promoting managerial personnel. In the military services, governmental agencies, and many private sector jobs, "time in rank," seniority, or tenure is prerequisite for promotion, and in some instances this may be the only real criterion. It is amazing, therefore, that so little research has been done on this important variable.

Our research has dealt mainly with such simple experience measures as time in service, time on the job, or number of different jobs, although some of our studies have used relevance of experience as variables. These studies have consistently shown that job experience pays off primarily, if not exclusively, under stressful conditions. In fact, under low stress conditions, the performance of the more experienced leaders tends to be less effective. These findings are consistent with Zajonc's (1965) social facilitation theory. The studies also suggest that even better results could be obtained with more sophisticated measures. Bettin's (1983) operational definition of relevant experience is one such step in the right direction. His results were similar to those we obtained with a simple index but sufficiently different to warrant pursuing further.

Equating experience with overlearned behavior seems a reasonable working hypothesis for further research but there may well be more to experience than meets the eye. We do not know at this time exactly how task-relevant experience is acquired, when it is retrieved, and how it is used. Knowledge gained through experience may be related to state-dependent learning, that is, learning which occurred in a particular emotional state. We often learn from experience under stressful conditions, and we may well retrieve what we learned from experience only under similarly stressful conditions. This hypothesis gains credence when we ask our friends to recall something they learned from experience, and then ask them whether this incident was pleasant or unpleasant, stress-free or stressful. The answer is almost invariably that it was stressful and usually also that it was unpleasant. The state-dependent learning theory presents a very intriguing hypothesis in this context.

Why are the correlations between leader intelligence and performance so consistently in the opposite direction from the correlations between job experience and performance? One would think that the more intelligent leaders are better able to learn from experience. H. C. Triandis (1979) has suggested that the interference between intelligence and experience is similar to the interference of conscious thought and habit. Recall the fable about the centipede who could no longer walk when he started to think about his feet. This is also true of people who think about the position of their feet while they are dancing, or of their hands while playing tennis. This is presumably because their active thought processes interfere with long-established and overlearned habits. And if we want to develop new work processes, we usually look for an outsider or someone new to the organization who can bring a "fresh point of view" to the problem, that is, who is not bound by long-established habits.

This hypothesis is consistent with recent work indicating there are two types of cognitive processes operating (Schneider & Shiffrin, 1977; Shiffrin & Schneider, 1977), the controlled and automatic, in making social judgments (Lord & Smith, 1983; Nisbitt & Ross, 1980; Smith & Lerner, 1986) and in storing and utilizing information in memory (Hasher & Zacks, 1979). How these processes relate to leader intelligence and experience seems worth further investigation.

A better understanding of experience and job tenure is closely related to the entire question of how to interpret leadership research in laboratory settings, especially since the latter comprise a substantial number, if not the great majority of leadership studies reported in the literature. There are obvious advantages and disadvantages to both field and laboratory research. The virtues of the well-controlled laboratory experiment are too well known to require elaboration. However, experimentally controlled findings often differ from those obtained in the admittedly less controlled field studies. One major reason for these differences may well be in the varying amount of experience leaders bring to the job in field studies. The leader in real-life groups typically has had previous exposure to the task and to the organization and has had time to establish stable working relations with his or her boss as well as subordinate group members. Three major differences between the laboratory experiment and the field study seem particularly relevant to leadership research. These concern the leader's role, the status of the group in an organization and in particular the relationship of the leader to the next higher superior, and the ad hoc group's life span, which is shorter than that of the one-day fly. These issues have been well presented in other contexts. We have already shown that the leader's boss plays a very important role in determining how the leader uses his or her cognitive resources. We wish to point to the difficulties in interpreting data which come from short-lived groups. The temptation is always very strong to disconfirm a theory on the basis of a study that may be based on no more than 25 college sophomores.

The danger of ignoring the effect of job experience and tenure in studies of task groups is well illustrated by our study of infantry squads. We obtained data when these squads were newly formed, and again after the squads had become combat-ready, some six to eight months later. Table 16.1 illustrates the substantial differences in the correlations between leader intelligence and performance at these two periods in the squad's life. But even in these newly formed squads the men had been living and working together for one to three weeks—a considerably longer period of time than the participants in laboratory experiments ever spend together. This example clearly shows that data obtained shortly after a group has been formed will not necessarily be similar to those obtained after a group has been in existence for some time. One of the most important tasks in this area of research is the development of a theory that explains exactly what happens as the leader and the group continue to work together.

Table 16.1. Correlations Between the Intelligence of Directive and Nondirective Squad Leaders and Performance in Newly Formed and Combat-ready Squads

	Infantry Squads			
	Newly Formed		Combat Ready	
	Directiveness		Directiveness	
	High (59)	Low (59)	High (55)	Low (55)
Task Performance	.14	.38**	.44**	.04
Personnel Performance	−.11	.14	−.13	.08

The Role of Stress

Hypothesis One stated that leaders who experience stress with which they cannot cope in a rational, logical manner will be distracted from the assigned task so that their intellectual abilities do not contribute to the task. Hence the intellectual abilities of leaders correlate with group performance primarily in situations which the leader perceives as nonstressful. Focusing on such task-irrelevant problems as concern with the consequences of failing, losing face, and so on, presumably results in negative correlations between intelligence and performance. While the correlations tend to be small, they are usually in the negative direction and sometimes substantial and significant.

We now need to determine which specific cognitive abilities, intellectual factors, or modes of information processing are affected by various types of stress. Sarason's studies on test anxiety (1984) and the Barnes, Potter, and Fiedler study (1983) at the U.S. Coast Guard Academy suggest that the major reason for our results might be the stress-related distraction from the main task.

Table 16.2. Summary of Major Findings and Conclusions and Level of Confidence in Their Generalizability

Hypothesis	Special Limitations	Confidence
Intelligent leaders make better plans and decisions	In low stress conditions	Probable
Directive leaders utilize their intellectual abilities more	In high control situations	High
Leaders' intelligence does not contribute to performance under stress	Especially if stress is interpersonal	High
Intellectual contribution of directive leaders is higher when group is supportive	Under low stress	Low to moderate
Group member intelligence is effectively used when the leader is nondirective and the group is supportive	Under low stress	Low to moderate
Intelligence is expected to contribute more as the intellectual demands of the task increase	General but weak Under low stress	High
Leaders' task-relevant abilities contribute to task performance	Complex	Needs further study
LPC and Situational Control predict leaders' directive behavior	Requires knowledge of task structure and other situational factors	Moderate to high

This explanation, however, does not account in a satisfactory manner for all the negative correlations between leader intelligence and performance under high-stress conditions. We suggest that the more intelligent leader is more successful than the less intelligent leader in effectively pursuing a private agenda that leads the group away from the organization's goals. Also, the more intelligent leader is more persuasive in coopting group members to his or her personal agenda. And third, perhaps the less intelligent leader is "not smart enough to be scared" in considering the consequences of stressful relations with the boss. These alternative hypotheses need to be tested.

Table 16.2 summarizes the major findings and the confidence with which we regard the conclusions.

PRACTICAL IMPLICATIONS OF COGNITIVE RESOURCE THEORY

Using Cognitive Resources to Increase Organizational Performance

Probably most important for the management of organizations are the findings that show that the leader's and the members' abilities contribute to group performance only under certain conditions. When we divided groups into four categories, that is, those with high or low leader directiveness and high or low group support (or low or high stress), leader intelligence correlated with group performance only in one of the four types of groups. How could these findings be applied in practice? Can we assure group support? Can we induce leaders to be directive?

It is certainly possible to enhance a group's support for its leader. The military services and private organizations have done so for centuries by channeling important information through the leader, backing the leader's legitimate actions, giving the leader special titles or insignia of rank, and allowing the leader to mete out rewards and punishment within appropriate limits.

Can we assure that the relatively intelligent leaders will behave in a directive manner? The evidence suggests that we can. Being more knowledgeable, being more intelligent, knowing more clearly how to tackle a task, and being confident of the organization's backing all tend to make leaders more directive, and this seems especially so in the case of relationship-motivated leaders. Tasks that are unstructured and ambiguous tend to bring out directive behavior in task-motivated leaders. No doubt this simplified prescription requires fine tuning, but there is no reason to believe that this problem is unmanageable.

Participative versus Directive Management

This research contributes to the resolution of a long-standing controversy about the presumed benefits of participative and nondirective versus directive and autocratic management styles. Our studies show that bright leaders should be directive and that the less bright leaders should be nondirective. Can we get leaders to accept the fact that they may be relatively less intelligent than their subordinates? Certainly not everyone will accept it, but interestingly enough some preliminary studies suggest that a surprising number of people have no difficulty recognizing that they may not be the brightest or the most expert in their particular group. There are certainly any number of university professors who will openly acknowledge that many of their graduate students outstrip them in intellectual horsepower. And many managers in business and industry also know full well that some of their subordinates may be more intellectually able or more creative. Many managers also realize that they must listen to the advice and ideas of others if their enterprise is to succeed.

We are just beginning to identify the conditions under which group members' abilities contribute to task performance. This should result in more effective employment of group members' abilities, knowledge, and competence. The methods of engineering the appropriate work environment for these potential intellectual contributors are similar to those already successfully employed in Leader Match training.

Selection and Training

Cognitive resource theory has two very important implications for selection and training of managers. Public as well as private sector organizations devote substantial resources to the selection and development of their managers. Our research makes abundantly clear that the power of current selection and training methods could be vastly improved. We need to assure that the abilities and experiences for which we select the skills that we impart by training are applied under conditions in which they can be effectively used. Our research identifies some of these conditions.

The present practice of the personnel officer or the agency in the organization charged with selecting its personnel is based on the assumption that higher scores on ability tests predict better performance. If selecting for an intellectually demanding job, choose the brightest available person. If selecting for an engineering position, choose the student with the highest grades or the most experience.

Our studies show, however, that the selection of leaders would benefit if we were to specify that the person who has been selected will live up to our expectations only under certain conditions. Thus the bets are off if the person is placed with a boss who likes to generate stress in a task that does not require intellectually demanding work. True, we cannot always keep bosses from creating stress, but we can teach leaders appropriate stress management techniques for reducing vulnerability to stress. We can teach them how they can make at least some of their relations with the boss less stressful by reinforcing the boss for nonstressful behavior. Not all of these methods will work all of the time, and some individuals will not be able to benefit from stress management training, but nothing works all the time. We also know that a highly supportive group will buffer the stress generated by the boss, and we can teach leaders how to garner group support.

The few data we have suggest that only the more intelligent leaders can make effective use of the knowledge they gained from training and on-the-job experience. We may need to look for different methods if we are to make better use of the training for the many who do not meet high intellectual standards.

Job Assignment

It is also clear that we must learn how to assign individuals so that they and their organization can capitalize on their particular strengths. A good example of this point was the fire department study which showed that the more experienced fire department officers performed better than inexperienced officers in districts with highly stressful jobs, that is, many hours spent in fire fighting. In contrast, the less experienced fire officers performed better than experienced officers in relatively quiet districts in which there were few fire calls. It would obviously make sense to assign the experienced officers to the more stressful jobs and the relatively inexperienced officers to the less stressful jobs.

Attrition

The effective use of cognitive resources is also of potential importance to the individual's satisfaction and fulfillment in the job. Who has not heard employees or volunteer group members complain that the organization fails to appreciate their abilities or knowledge, or that they are underemployed or not allowed to practice the skills for which they were trained? These frustrations result in poor morale and high attrition. Above all, the performance of the organization could be substantially increased by capitalizing on the talents which are already available. Nor are the penalties for misusing intellectual abilities and competence negligible. It is surely a bad sign when we find negative correlations between leader intelligence and group performance as low as $-.40$, as in the study of coast guard staff officers, or $-.76$, as in the decoding study. Since we tend to listen to the most intelligent people, we are most likely to receive bad advice from these intelligent leaders when they are under stress or untrained.

We can be quite certain that organizations will be more effective if they enable the bright leaders and their supporting staff to make good use of their cognitive resources. This may require that managers at higher levels monitor carefully the stress they generate for their subordinate leaders. In somewhat oversimplified terms, the managers at higher levels may need to consider whether they want the benefits of their subordinates' intellectual abilities or of their subordinates' experience.

As we stressed in our introduction, this book should be read as a progress report. It is most certainly not the ultimate theory of leadership. In fact we have bathtubs full of data that have yet to be analyzed and dozens of questions that await research—as soon as we have some spare time! The study of leadership presents a complex and difficult problem. Cognitive resource theory needs to be related to such other theoretical developments as Bales' (Bales, 1970; Bales & Isenberg, 1982; Bales, Cohen, & Williamson, 1979) work on group behavior, Hollander's (1978) studies on status, Kipnis, Schmidt, Swaffin-Smith, and Wilkinson's (1984) work on power and influence, House's (1977) research on charismatic leadership, Burns (1978) and Bass's (1985) recent studies of transformational leadership, and Yukl's (1981) Multiple Linkage Model.

In brief, there is an abundance of unfinished business in the field of leadership. It is one of the very few arenas in human life in which important interpersonal relations take place in full public view, open to investigation. It is also an area which has major implications for the survival and success of groups as small as committees and as large as nations. Above all the study of leadership is as spellbinding as a good mystery, and as habit-forming as a bowl of peanuts, but considerably more healthful. What more can one ask of life?

Characteristics of Frequently Cited Studies

1. ARMY SQUAD LEADERS

Type of Study: Field study conducted with U.S. Army personnel

Subjects: 138 army infantry squad leaders of newly formed squads of 8 to 10 men (all males)

Intelligence: Army General Classification Test

Experience: Time in service

Stress: Stress with boss, and job stress ratings by squad leader

Group Support: Group atmosphere scores

Behavior: Ratings of directive behavior factor composed of LBDQ structuring and production emphasis items by squad members

Performance: Ratings by leader's immediate superiors, the platoon leader and the platoon sergeant

Reference:
Bons, P. M., & Fiedler, F. E. (1976). The effects of changes in command environment on the behavior of relationship- and task-motivated leaders. *Administrative Science Quarterly, 21,* 453–473.

Fiedler, F. E., & Leister, A. F. (1977). Leader intelligence and task performance: A test of multiple screen model. *Organizational Behavior and Human Performance, 20*, 1–14.

2. THE BELGIAN NAVY STUDY

Type of Study: Laboratory experiment conducted in Belgium

Subjects: 96 three-person teams each consisting of 2 naval recruits and a team leader (48 Belgian navy petty officers and 48 recruit leaders) (all males)

Design:

	Leader (Position Power)	
Group Composition	Petty Officer	Recruit Leader
Homogeneous		
Flemish	12	12
Francophone	12	12
Heterogeneous		
Flemish Leader	12	12
Francophone Leader	12	12

a. Homogeneity: 48 teams homogeneous—all Flemish (Netherlands) or all French-speaking

b. Position Power: 48 with high position power (petty officers); 48 with low position power (recruit leaders)

c. Task structure: each team worked on two tasks, one relatively structured (routing a ship through 10 or 12 ports) one unstructured (writing a recruiting letter)

d. Four high-, four middle-, and four low-LPC leaders in each cell of 12 groups

Intelligence: Short intelligence scale used in Belgium

Experience: Petty officer experience indicated by age since almost all petty officers enter petty officer candidate school at the same age and remain in service for 20 years

Tasks:

1. To find the shortest route for a ship to reach 12 destinations.

2. Compose a recruiting letter directed at Belgian youths.

Situational Control: Cultural homogeneity; position power; task structure

Behavior: Directiveness ratings by group members

Performance:
Routing task: shortest number of "miles"

Recruiting letter: evaluation by judges

Reference:
Fiedler, F. E. (1966). The effect of leadership and cultural heterogeneity on group performance: A test of the contingency model. *Journal of Experimental Social Psychology, 2,* 237–264.

3. THE COAST GUARD STUDY

Type of Study: Field study with U.S. Coast Guard and civilian personnel

Subjects: 130 officers, petty officers, and civilians in responsible staff positions at a large Coast Guard headquarters (123 males; 7 females)

Intelligence: Wonderlic Personnel Test

Experience: Time in service

Stress: Stress with immediate superior as rated by subject (stress with boss).

Performance: Ratings by immediate superior

Reference:
Potter, E. H., & Fiedler, F. E. (1981). The utilization of staff member intelligence and experience under high and low stress. *Academy of Management Journal, 24*(2), 361–376.

4. COMPANY COMMANDERS AND BATTALION STAFF OFFICERS (ZAIS)

Type of Study: Field study with U.S. Army personnel

Subjects: 47 company commanders, 45 battalion staff officers (all males)

Intelligence: Wonderlic Personnel Test

Experience: Time in service

Stress: Stress with boss, job stress reported by subjects

Performance: Ratings by battalion commander and executive officer

Reference:

Zais, M. M. (1979). *The impact on intelligence and experience on the performance of army line and staff officers.* Unpublished master's thesis, University of Washington, Seattle.

Fiedler, F. E., Potter, E. H., III, Zais, M. M., & Knowlton, W. A., Jr. (1979). Organizational stress and the use and misuse of managerial intelligence and experience. *Journal of Applied Psychology, 64*, 635–647.

5. DECODING STUDY

Type of Study: Laboratory study conducted by Chemers et al. (1975) with college students (all males)

Subjects: 40 three-person groups each composed of two ROTC Cadets and one psychology student

Design:

	Leaders	
LPC	Training	No Training
High	10	10
Low	10	10

In 20 groups leader received training in decoding method, in the other 20 groups the leader was untrained. Half of trained and untrained leaders were high- half were low-LPC

Intelligence: Vocabulary scale

Stress: Ratings by group's leaders

Task: Deciphering as many short "coded messages" (cryptograpms) as possible in 30 minutes

Group Support: All teams had very low group atmosphere (GA) score

Situational Control: Manipulated by the experimenter by delivering or not delivering training to the leaders

Behavior: Members' ratings of leader's control of the group

Performance: Number of correct solutions

Reference:
Chemers, M. M., Rice, R. W., Sundstrom, E., & Butler, W. (1975). Leader esteem for the least preferred co-worker scale, training, and effectiveness: An experimental examination. *Journal of Personality and Social Psychology, 31,* 401–409.

6. DUTCH CREATIVITY STUDY

Type of Study: Laboratory experiment conducted in Holland

Subjects: Male Calvinist and Catholic university students from the North and South of Holland, respectively. 32 four-person teams with homogeneous (four Calvinists or four Catholics) or heterogeneous (two Calvinists and two Catholics) composition, and appointed or emergent leadership (all males).

Design:

| | Group Composition | |
Leader Status	Homogeneous	Heterogeneous
Appointed	8	8
Emergent	8	8

Intelligence: Dutch translation of the Miller Analogies

Stress: Ratings of tense atmosphere

Tasks: Tell stories based on 2 Thematic Apperception Test pictures.

Group Support: Frequency of critical comments

Behavior: Frequency of directive, socioemotional and creative comments rated on basis of typed protocol of discussions. Leader and member comments could not be distinguished in recordings.

Performance: Rating of stories by two independent judges

Reference:
Fiedler, F. E., Meuwese, W. A. T., & Oonk, S. (1961). An exploratory study of group creativity in laboratory tasks. *Acta Psychologica, 18,* 100–119.

7. FIRE SERVICE OFFICERS

Type of Study: Field study with fire department captains and lieutenants from a metropolitan fire department

Subjects: 66 fire captains, 110 fire lieutenants (all males)

Intelligence: Wonderlic Personnel Test and Horn's Fluid and Crystallized Intelligence (given to part of sample)

Experience: Time in fire service, time in unit, time on job, time in rank.

Stress: Stress with boss, job stress rated by subjects, and stress defined by hours at scene of fire

Performance: Rating by battalion chief

Reference:
Frost, D. E. (1981). *The effects of interpersonal stress on leadership effectiveness.* Unpublished doctoral dissertation, University of Washington, Seattle.

Frost, D. E. (1983). Role perceptions and behavior of the immediate supervisor: Moderating effects on the prediction of leadership performance. *Organizational Behavior and Human Performance, 31,* 123–142.

8. ILLINOIS FARM SUPPLY STUDY

Type of Study: Field study of midwestern farm supply cooperatives

Sample: 31 general managers and board presidents from 32 farm supply sales cooperative companies of the same federation (all males)

Experience: Time in the organization

Situational Control: Sociometric preference ratings

Performance: Percentage of net income or operating expenses to total sales over three year period

Reference:
Godfrey, E., Fiedler, F. E., & Hall, D. M. (1959). *Boards, management and company success.* Danville, IL: Interstate Press.

9. THE INFANTRY DIVISION STUDY (BORDEN STUDY)

Type of Study: Field study with U.S. Army personnel

Subjects:

	Job Title	Typical Rank
45	company commanders	Captain
43	company executive officers	First lieutenant
106	platoon leaders	Second lieutenant
42	company first sergeants	First sergeant E-7
163	platoon sergeants	Technical sergeant E-6
	(all males)	

Intelligence: Wonderlic Personnel Test

Motivation: Four items related to pleasing boss, looking good to others

Stress: Stress with boss, job stress as rated by subject

Group Support: Group atmosphere scales

Performance: Rating by two to four superior officers

Reference:
Borden, D. F. (1980). *Leader-boss stress, personality, job satisfaction and performance: Another look at the inter-relationship of some old constructs in the modern large bureaucracy.* Unpublished doctoral dissertation, University of Washington, Seattle.

Fiedler, F. E., Jobs, S. M., & Borden, D. F. (1984). *Downward transmission of stress and its effect on the performance of motivated and unmotivated leaders* (Organizational Research Tech. Rep. 84-2). Seattle, University of Washington.

10. LEADER DYADS

Type of Study: Field study with U.S. Army personnel

Subjects: 45 company commander and first sergeant dyads (all males)

Intelligence: Wonderlic Personnel Test

Experience: Time in job of first sergeant

Stress: Ratings by company commander and by first sergeant of stress in their relationship

Performance: Battalion commander's performance rating of company commander, company, and company commander–first sergeant dyad

Reference:
Knowlton, W. A. Jr. (1979). *The effects of causal attributions on a supervisor's evaluation of subordinate performance.* Unpublished doctoral dissertation, University of Washington, Seattle.

Fiedler, F. E., Potter, E. H., III, Zais, M. M., & Knowlton, W. A., Jr. (1979) Organizational stress and the use and misuse of managerial intelligence and experience. *Journal of Applied Psychology, 64,* 635–647.

11. MESS HALL STUDY

Type of Study: Field study with U.S. Army mess hall personnel

Subjects: Mess stewards and two to five cooks of 52 army company mess halls (all males)

Intelligence: Henman–Nelson Ability Test (1972), test of knowledge of cooking and mess hall management

Experience: Mess steward's time in service, time on job

Group Support: Member group atmosphere scores

Behavior: Cooks' ratings of leader directiveness

Performance: Brigade Food Service officer and company commander ratings of mess hall performance

Reference:
Blades, J. W., & Fiedler, F. E. (1973) *The influence of intelligence, task ability and motivation on group performance* (Organizational Research Tech. Rep. No. 76–78).

Csoka, L. S. (1975). Relationship between organizational climate and the situational favorableness dimension of Fiedler's contingency model. *Journal of Applied Psychology, 60,* 273–277.

12. OFFICER EXPERIENCE AND PERFORMANCE (BETTIN)

Type of Study: Field study with U.S. Army infantry personnel

Subjects: 79 officers holding jobs typically assigned to army captains in an infantry division (company commanders and battalion staff officers, all males)

Intelligence: Wonderlic Personnel Test and Horn's Fluid and Crystallized Intelligence tests

Experience: Measures of relevant experience, diversity of experience, and time in service

Stress: Stress with boss and job stress reported by subjects

Situational Control: High versus low task structure and position power

Performance: Ratings by officer's battalion commander and battalion executive officer

Reference:
Bettin, P. J. (1983). *The role of relevant experience & intellectual ability in determining the performance of military leaders: A contingency model explanation.* Unpublished doctoral dissertation, University of Washington, Seattle.

13. PUBLIC HEALTH TEAM VOLUNTEERS

Type of Study: Field study conducted in Honduras and Guatemala with high school student volunteers in public health

Subjects: 38 groups, consisting of two to five persons, either all male or all female, of high school students 16 to 19 years of age who volunteered to establish and administer public health and community development programs in Honduras and Guatemala during their summer vacation

Intelligence: Short verbal and analogies scales used by the organization for selection

Group Support: Leader and member groups atmosphere scales

Situational Control: Ratings of village stressfulness by project director and staff

Performance: Ratings by project director and staff of team's performance in conducting community development work, administering the clinic's vaccination and innoculation program, and maintaining group harmony

Reference:
Fiedler, F. E., O'Brien, G. E., & Ilgen, D. R. (1969). The effect of leadership style upon the performance and adjustment of volunteer teams operating in successful foreign environment. *Human Relations, 22*, 503–514.

14. THE ROTC CREATIVITY STUDY

Type of Study: Laboratory experiment conducted by Meuwese and Fiedler (1965)

Subjects: 54 three-person teams of ROTC cadets (all males)

Design:

	Stress		
LPC	Control (Low)	Internal (Moderate)	External (High)
High	9	9	9
Low	9	9	9

control condition: stress minimized

internal stress: two army, one navy navy cadets

external stress: teams observed by high-ranking officer (LTC or Colonel) during the task

Intelligence: Psychological Corporation Multi-Aptitude Scale (Verbal and Mathematical)

Creativity: Guilford-Christensen Plot Titles, Alternative Uses

Behavior: Ratings by group members, using items from LBDQ structuring scale and items emerging on same factor

Stress: Three experimentally induced conditions of stress

Tasks:
1. Develop a proposal for making pay of army, navy, and airforce cadets more equitable

2. Invent a fable for elementary school children on why country needs a large peace-time army

Group Support: Group atmosphere scores

Performance: Payproposal and Fable evaluated by independent judges

Reference:
Meuwese, W. A. T., & Fiedler, F. E. (1965). *Leadership and group creativity under varying conditions of stress* (Tech Rep.). Urbana: University of Illinois, Group Effectiveness Research Laboratory.

References

Adorno, T. W., Frenkel-Brunswick, E., Levinson, D. J., & Sanford, R. N. (1950). *The authoritarian personality*. New York: Harper.

Alexander, S., & Husek, T. R. (1962). The anxiety differential: Initial steps in the development of measures of situational anxiety. *Educational and Psychological Measurement, 22,* 325–348.

Anderson, C. P. (1977). Locus of control, coping behaviors, and performance in a stress setting: A longitudinal study. *Journal of Applied Psychology, 62,* 446–451.

Anderson, L. R. (1966). Leader behavior, member attitudes and task performance of intercultural groups. *Journal of Social Psychology, 69,* 305–318.

Anderson, L. R., & Fiedler, F. E. (1964). The effect of participatory and supervisory leadership on group creativity. *Journal of Applied Psychology, 48,* 227–236.

Arbuthnot, J. (1968). *Relationships among psychological differentiations and leadership style*. Unpublished master's thesis, Cornell University, Ithaca, NY.

Argyris, C. (1964). *Integrating the individual and the organization*. New York: Wiley.

Ashour, A. S. (1973a). The contingency model of leadership effectiveness: An evaluation. *Organizational Behavior and Human Performance, 9,* 339–355.

Ashour, A. S. (1973b). Further discussion of Fiedler's contingency model of leadership effectiveness. *Organizational Behavior and Human Performance, 9,* 369–376.

Bales, R. F. (1950). *Interaction process analysis*. Reading, MA: Addison-Wesley.

Bales, R. F. (1970). *Personality and interpersonal behavior*. New York: Holt, Rinehart & Winston.

Bales, R. F., Cohen, S. P., & Williamson, S. A. (1979). *SYMLOG: A system for the multiple level observation of groups*. New York: Free Press.

Bales, R. F., & Isenberg, D. J. (1982). SYMLOG and leadership theory. In J. G. Hunt, U. Sekaran, & C. Schriesheim (Eds.), *Leadership: Beyond establishment views*. Carbondale: Southern Illinois University Press.

Bales, R. F., & Strodbeck, F. L. (1951). Phases in group problem solving. *Journal of Abnormal Social Psychology, 46,* 485–495.

Barnes, V., Potter, E. H., III, & Fiedler, F. E. (1983). Effect of interpersonal stress on the prediction of academic performance. *Journal of Applied Psychology, 68*(4), 686–697.

Bass, B. M. (1981). *Stogdill's handbook of leadership*. New York: Free Press.

Bass, B. M. (1985). Leadership—Good, better, best. *Organizational Dynamics, 13*, 28–40.

Bass, R. M., Fiedler, F. E., & Krueger, S. (1964). Personality correlates of assumed similarity (ASO) and related scores. Urbana: University of Illinois, Group Effectiveness Research Laboratory.

Baum, A., Fleming, R., & Singer, J. E. (1982). Stress at Three Mile Island: Applying psychological impact analysis. *Applied Social Psychology Annual, 3*, 217–247.

Beach, B. H., & Beach, L. R. (1978). A note on judgements of situational favorableness and probability of success. *Organizational Behavior and Human Performance, 22*, 69–74.

Bennis, W. G. (1961). Revisionist theory of leadership. *Harvard Business Review, 39*, 26–36, 146–150.

Berkum, M. M. (1964). Performance decrement under psychological stress. *Human Factors, 6*(1), 24–26.

Bettin, P. J. (1982). Leadership experience: The contribution of relevance and diversity to leadership performance. Unpublished master's thesis, University of Washington, Seattle.

Bettin, P. J. (1983). The role of relevant experience and intellectual ability in determining the performance of military leaders: A contingency model explanation. Unpublished doctoral dissertation, University of Washington, Seattle.

Bettin, P. J., & Fiedler, F. E. (1984). *The effects of leadership experience on organizational performance: A review* (Organizational Research Tech. Rep. No. 84–5). Seattle: University of Washington.

Blades, J. W. (1976). *The influence of intelligence, task ability, and motivation on group performance*. Unpublished doctoral dissertation, University of Washington, Seattle.

Blades, J. W., & Fiedler, F. E. (1973). *The influence of intelligence, task ability and motivation on group performance* (Organizational Research Tech. Rep. 76–78). Seattle: University of Washington.

Blake, R. R., & Mouton, J. S. (1964). *The managerial grid*. Houston, TX: Gulf.

Blankenship, L. V., & Miles, R. E. (1968). Organizational structure and managerial decision behavior. *Administrative Science Quarterly, 13*, 106–120.

Bons, P. M. (1974). *The effect of changes in leadership environment on the behavior of relationship and task-motivated leaders*. Unpublished doctoral dissertation, University of Washington, Seattle.

Bons, P. M., Bass, A. R., & Komorita, S. S. (1970). Changes in leadership style as a function of military experience and type of command. *Personnel Psychology, 23*, 551–568.

Bons, P. M., & Fiedler, F. E. (1976). The effects of changes in command environment on the behavior of relationship- and task-motivated leaders. *Administrative Science Quarterly, 21*, 453–473.

Borden, D. F. (1980). *Leader-boss stress, personality, job satisfaction and performance: Another look at the inter-relationship of some old constructs in the modern large bureaucracy*. Unpublished doctoral dissertation, University of Washington, Seattle.

Bray, D. W., Campbell, R. J., & Grant, D. L. (1974). *Formative years in business: A long term AT&T study of managerial lives*. New York: Wiley-Interscience.

Brief, A. P., Aldag, R. J., & Van Sell, M. (1977). Moderators of the relationship between self and superior evaluations of job performance. *Journal of Occupational Psychology, 62*, 278–282.

Broadbent, D. E. (1971). *Decision and stress*. New York: Academic.

Buck, V. E. (1972). *Working under pressure*. New York: Crane.

Burke, M. J., & Day, R. R. (1986). A cumulative study of the effectiveness of managerial training. *Journal of Applied Psychology, 71*, 232–245.

Burns, J. M. (1978). *Leadership*. New York: Harper and Row.

Campbell, J. P. (1973). The cutting edge of leadership: An overview. In J. G. Hunt & L. L. Larson (Eds.), *Leadership: The cutting edge* (pp. 221–246). Carbondale: Southern Illinois University Press.

Campbell, J. P., Dunnette, M. D., Lawler, E. E., & Weick, K. E. (1970). *Managerial behavior, performance, and effectiveness*. New York: McGraw-Hill.

Cascio, W. F., & Valenzi, E. R. (1977). Behaviorally anchored rating scales: Effects of education on job experience of raters and ratees. *Journal of Applied Psychology, 62*, 278–282.

Cattell, R. B. (1951). New concepts for measuring leadership in terms of group syntality. *Human Relations, 4*, 161–184.

Cattell, R. B. (1971). *Abilities: Their structure, growth, and action*. Boston: Houghton Mifflin.

Chemers, M. M. (1970). The relationship between birth order and leadership style. *Journal of Social Psychology, 80*, 243–244.

Chemers, M. M., Rice, R. W., Sundstrom, E., & Butler, W. (1975). Leader esteem for the least preferred co-worker scale, training, and effectiveness: An experimental examination. *Journal of Personality and Social Psychology, 31*, 401–409.

Chemers, M. M., & Skrzypek, G. J. (1972). Experimental test of the Contingency Model of leadership effectiveness. *Journal of Personality and Social Psychology, 24*, 172–177.

Coch, L., & French, J. R. P. (1948). Overcoming resistance to change. *Human Relations, 1*, 512–532.

Cottrell, N. B., & Epley, S. W. (1977). Affiliation, social compassion, and socially mediated stress reduction. In J. M. Sals & R. L. Miller (Eds.), *Social comparison processes*. Washington, DC: Hemisphere.

Cottrell, N. B., Wack, D. L., Sekerak, G. J., & Rettle, R. H. (1968). Social facilitation of dominant response by the presence of an audience and the mere presence of others. *Journal of Personality and Social Psychology, 9*, 245–250.

Crutchfield, R. S. (1955). Conformity and character. *American Psychologist, 10*, 191–198.

Csoka, L. (1975). Relationship between organizational climate and the situation favorableness dimension of Fiedler's contingency model. *Journal of Applied Psychology, 60*, 273–277.

Csoka, L. S. (1974). A relationship between leader intelligence and leader rated effectiveness. *Journal of Applied Psychology, 59*, 43–47.

Csoka, L. S., & Fiedler, F. E. (1972). The effect of military leadership training: A test of the contingency model. *Organizational Behavior and Human Performance, 8*, 395–407.

Cureton, E. E., & Cureton, L. W. (1955). *The multi-aptitude test*. New York: The Psychological Corporation.

Deffenbacher, J. L. (1980). Worry and emotionality in test anxiety. In I. G. Sarason (Ed.), *Test anxiety: Theory, research, and applications*. Hillsdale, NJ: Erlbaum.

Easterbrook, J. A. (1959). The effect of emotion on the utilization and the organization of behavior. *Psychology Review, 66*, 183–201.

Emery, F. E., & Trist, E. I. (1965). The causal texture of organizational environments. *Human Relations, 18*, 21–32.

Epstein, S. (1979). The stability of behavior: I. On predicting most of the people much of the time. *Journal of Personality and Social Psychology, 37*, 1097–1126.

Erdly, W. W. (1986). *A behavioral analysis of leadership performance: Self- and observer ratings of leader behavior compared*. Unpublished masters thesis, University of Washington, Seattle.

Fiedler, F. E. (1951). A method of objective quantification of certain countertransference attitudes. *Journal of Clinical Psychology, 7*, 101–107.

Fiedler, F. E. (1958). *Leader attitudes and group effectiveness*. New York: McGraw-Hill.

Fiedler, F. E. (1964). A contingency model of leadership effectiveness. In L. Berkowitz (Ed.), *Advances in experimental social psychology* (Vol. 1, 149–190). New York: Academic.

Fiedler, F. E. (1966). The effect of leadership and cultural heterogeneity on group performance: A test of the contingency model. *Journal of Experimental and Social Psychology, 2,* 237–264.

Fiedler, F. E. (1967). *A theory of leadership effectiveness.* New York: McGraw-Hill.

Fiedler, F. E. (1970). Leadership experience and leader performance—Another hypothesis shot to hell. *Organizational Behavior and Human Performance, 5,* 1–14.

Fiedler, F. E. (1971a). Note on the methodology of Graen, Orris and Alvarez studies testing the contingency model. *Journal of Applied Psychology, 55,* 202–204.

Fiedler, F. E. (1971b). Validation and extension of the contingency model of leadership effectiveness: A review of empirical findings. *Psychological Bulletin, 76,* 128–148.

Fiedler, F. E. (1972a). Predicting the effects of leadership training and experience from the contingency model. *Journal of Applied Psychology, 56,* 114–119.

Fiedler, F. E. (1972b). Personality, motivational systems, and the behavior of high and low LPC persons. *Human Relations, 25,* 391–412.

Fiedler, F. E. (1973). The contingency model: A reply to Ashour. *Organizational Performance and Human Behavior, 9,* 356–368.

Fiedler, F. E. (1977). A rejoinder to Schriescheim and Kerr's premature obituary of the contingency model. In J. G. Hunt & L. L. Larson (Eds.), *Leadership: The cutting edge.* Carbondale: Southern Illinois University Press.

Fiedler, F. E. (1978a). The contingency model and the dynamics of the leadership process. In L. Berkowitz (Ed.), *Advances in experimental social psychology* (Vol. 11). New York: Academic.

Fiedler, F. E. (1978b). Situational control and a dynamic theory of leadership. In B. King, S. Streufert, & F. E. Fiedler (Eds.), *Managerial control and organizational democracy.* Washington, DC: Winston.

Fiedler, F. E. (1984). *The contribution of cognitive resources and leader behavior to organizational performance* (Organizational Research Tech. Rep. No. 84-4). Seattle: University of Washington.

Fielder, F. E., & Barron, N. M. (1967, December). *The effect of leadership style and leadership behavior on group creativity under stress* (Tech. Rep. No. 25). Urbana-Champaign: University of Illinois, Group Effectiveness Research Laboratory.

Fiedler, F. E., & Chemers, M. M. (1968). *Group performance under experienced and inexperienced leaders: A validation experiment.* Urbana: University of Illinois, Group Effectiveness Research Laboratory.

Fiedler, F. E., & Chemers, M. M. (1974). *Leadership and effective management.* Glenview, IL: Scott, Foresman & Company.

Fiedler, F. E., & Chemers, M. M. (1984). *Improving leadership effectiveness: The leader match concept* (2nd ed.). New York: Wiley.

Fiedler, F. E., Chemers, M. M., & Mahar, L. (1976). *Improving leadership effectiveness: The leader match concept.* New York: Wiley.

Fiedler, F. E., & Fiedler, J. (1975). Port noise complaints: Verbal and behavioral reactions to airport-related noise. *Journal of Applied Psychology, 60,* 498–506.

Fiedler, F. E., & Gillo, M. (1974, December). Correlates of performance in a community college. *Journal of Higher Education.*

Fiedler, F. E., Jobs, S. M., & Borden, D. F. (1982). *Downward transmission of stress and its effect on the performance of motivated and unmotivated leaders* (Organizational Research Tech. Rep. No. 84–2). Seattle: University of Washington.

Fiedler, F. E., & Leister, A. F. (1977). Leader intelligence and task performance: A test of a multiple screen model. *Organizational Behavior and Human Performance, 20,* 1–14.

Fiedler, F. E., & Mahar, L. (1979). A field experiment validating Contingency Model leadership training. *Journal of Applied Psychology, 64*(3), 247–254.

Fiedler, F. E., & Meuwese, W. A. T. (1963). Leader's contribution to task performance in cohesive and uncohesive groups. *Journal of Abnormal and Social Psychology, 67*, 83–87.

Fiedler, F. E., Meuwese, W. A. T., & Oonk, S. (1961). An exploratory study of group creativity in laboratory tasks. *Acta Psychologica, 18*, 100–119.

Fiedler, F. E., Nealy, S. M., & Wood, M. T. (1968). *The effects of training on the performance of post office supervisors.* Unpublished manuscript, Urbana: University of Illinois, Group Effectiveness Research Laboratory.

Fiedler, F. E., O'Brien, G. E., & Ilgen, D. R. (1969). The effect of leadership style upon the performance and adjustment of volunteer teams operating in successful foreign environment. *Human Relations, 22*, 503–514.

Fiedler, F. E., Potter, E. H., III, Zais, M. M., & Knowlton, W. A., Jr. (1979). Organizational stress and the use and misuse of managerial intelligence and experience. *Journal of Applied Psychology, 64*, 635–647.

Fine, B. J., & Kobrick, J. L. (1978). Effects of altitude and heat on complex cognitive tasks. *Human Factors, 20*, 115–122.

Fishbein, M., Landy, E., & Hatch, G. (1969). A consideration of two assumptions underlying Fiedler's Contingency Model for prediction of leadership effectiveness. *American Journal of Psychology, 82*, 457–473.

Fleishman, E. A. (1957). The leadership opinion questionnaire. In R. M. Stogdill & A. E. Coons (Eds.), *Leader behavior: Its description and measurement.* Columbus: Bureau of Business Research, Ohio State University.

Fleishman, E. A., & Quaintance, M. K. (1984). *Taxonomies of human performance.* Orlando, FL: Academic.

Folkman, S. (1984). Personal control and stress and coping processes: A theoretical analysis. *Journal of Personality and Social Psychology, 46*, 839–852.

Folkman, S., & Lazarus, R. S. (1980). An analysis of coping in a middle-aged community sample. *Journal of Health and Social Behavior, 21*, 219–239.

Foa, U. G., Mitchell, T. R., & Fiedler, F. E. (1971). Differential matching. *Behavioral Science, 16*, 130–142.

Fox, W. F. (1967). Human performance in the cold. *Human Factors, 9*, 219–239.

Fox, W. M. (1976). Reliabilities, means, and standard deviation for LPC scales: Instrument refinement. *Academy of Management Journal, 19*, 450–461.

Fox, W. M., Hill, W. A., & Guertin, W. N. (1973). Dimensional analysis of least preferred co-worker scales. *Journal of Applied Psychology, 57*, 192–194.

French, J. R. P., Israel, J., & Ås, D. (1960). An experiment on participation in a Norwegian factory. *Human Relations, 13*, 3–19.

Freud, S. (1938). The history of the psychoanalytic movement. In A. A. Brill (Ed. & Trans.), *The basic writings of Sigmund Freud.* New York: Random House.

Frost, D. E. (1981). *The effects of interpersonal stress on leadership effectiveness.* Unpublished doctoral dissertation, University of Washington, Seattle.

Frost, D. E. (1983). Role perceptions and behavior of the immediate superior: Moderating effects on the prediction of leadership effectiveness. *Organizational Behavior and Human Performance, 31*, 123–142.

Geen, R. G. (1980). The effects of being observed on performance. In P. B. Paulus (Ed.), *Psychology of group influence.* Hillsdale, NJ: Erlbaum.

Geyer, L. J., & Julian, J. W. (1973). Manipulation of situational favorability in tests of the contingency model. *Journal of Psychology, 84*, 13–21.

Ghiselli, E. E. (1963). Intelligence and managerial success. *Psychological Reports, 12*, 898.

Gibb, C. A. (1969). Leadership. In G. Lindzey & E. Aronson (Eds.), *The handbook of social psychology* (2nd ed., Vol. 4). Reading, MA: Addison-Wesley.

Gioia, D. A., & Sims, H. P., Jr. (1985). On avoiding the influence of implicit leadership theories in leader behavior descriptions. *Educational and Psychological Measurement, 45*, 217–232.

Glass, G. V. (1976). Primary, secondary and meta-analysis of research. *Educational Research, 5*, 3–8.

Godfrey, E. B., Fiedler, F. E., & Hall, D. M. (1959). *Boards, management and company success.* Danville, IL: Interstate.

Gordon, M. E., & Fitzgibbons, W. J. (1982). Empirical test of the validity of seniority as a factor in staffing decisions. *Journal of Applied Psychology, 67*, 311–319.

Gove, P. E. (Ed.). (1971). *Webster's seventh new collegiate dictionary.* Springfield, MA: Merriam.

Graen, G. (1976). Role making processes within complex organizations. In M. D. Dunnette (Ed.), *Handbook of industrial and organizational Psychology.* Chicago: Rand McNally.

Graen, G., Alvares, K., Orris, J. B., & Martella, S. A. (1970). Contingency model of leadership effectiveness: Antecedent and evidential results. *Psychological Bulletin, 74*, 285–296.

Graen, G., Orris, J. B., & Alvares, K. M. (1971). Contingency model of leadership effectiveness: Some experimental results. *Journal of Applied Psychology, 55*, 196–201.

Green, S. C., Nebeker, D. M., & Boni, M. A. (1976). Personality and situational effects on leader behavior. *Academy of Management Journal, 19*, 184–194.

Gruenfeld, L. W., Rance, D. E., & Weissenberg, P. (1969). The behavior of task-oriented (low LPC) and socially oriented (high LPC) leaders under several conditions of social support. *Journal of Social Psychology, 79*, 99–107.

Grusky, O. (1970). The effects of succession: A comparative study of military and business organizations. In O. Grusky & G. A. Miller (Eds.), *The sociology of organizations.* Glencoe, IL: Free Press.

Guilford, J. P., Berger, R. M., & Christensen, A. (1954). A factor analytic study of planning: Vol. 1. Hypothesis and description of tests. University of Southern California, Psychological Laboratory, Los Angeles, CA.

Guion, R. M. (1965). *Personnel testing.* New York: McGraw-Hill.

Hackman, J. R. (1968). Effects of task characteristics on group products. *Journal of Experimental Social Psychology, 4*, 162–187.

Hackman, J. R., & Morris, C. G. (1975). Group tasks, group interaction process, and group performance effectiveness: A review and proposal integration. In L. Berkowitz (Ed.), *Advances in experimental social psychology* (Vol. 8). New York: Academic.

Hanssen, R. O., & Fiedler, F. E. (1973). Perceived similarity, personality, and attraction to large organizations. *Journal of Applied Social Psychology, 55*, 196–201.

Hardy, R. C. (1971). Effect of leadership style on the performance of small classroom groups: A test of the contingency model. *Journal of Personality and Social Psychology, 19*, 367–374.

Hardy, R. C. (1975). A test of poor leader-member relations cells of the contingency model on elementary school children. *Child Development, 46*, 958–964.

Hardy, R. C., & Bohren, J. F. (1975). The effect of experience on teacher effectiveness: A test of the contingency model. *Journal of Psychology, 89*, 159–163.

Hardy, R. C., Sack, S., & Harpine, F. (1973). An experimental test of the Contingency Model on small classroom groups. *Journal of Psychology, 85*, 3–16.

Harvey, O., Hunt, D., & Schroeder, I. I. (1961). *Conceptual systems and personality and organization.* New York: Wiley.

Hasher, L., & Zacks, R. T. (1979). Automatic and effortful processes in memory. *Journal of Experimental Psychology: General, 108*, 356–388.

Heller, F. A. (1969). *Managerial decision making.* London: Tavistock Institute of Human Relations, Human Resources Center.

Hersey, P., & Blanchard, K. H. (1969). Life cycle theory of leadership. *Training and Development Journal, 23,* 26–34.

Hewitt, T. T., O'Brien, G. E., & Horwick, J. (1974). The effects of work, organizational, leadership style, and member compatibility upon productivity of small groups working on a manipulation task. *Organizational Behavior and Human Performance, 11,* 283–301.

Hill, W. (1969). The validation and extension of Fiedler's theory of leadership effectiveness. *Academy of Management Journal, 12,* 33–47.

Hollander, E. P. (1958). Conformity, status, and idiosyncrasy credit. *Psychological Review, 65,* 117–127.

Hollander, E. P. (1960). Competence and conformity in the acceptance of influence. *Journal of Abnormal Social Psychology, 61,* 365–369.

Hollander, E. P. (1978). *Leadership dynamics: A practical guide to effective relationships.* New York: Free Press.

Hollander, E. P., & Julian, J. W. (1970). Studies in leader legitimacy, influence, and innovation. In L. Berkowitz (Ed.), *Advances in experimental social psychology* (Vol. 5). New York: Academic.

Hollingsworth, A. T., Meglino, B. M., & Shaner, M. C. (1977). Predicting the effectiveness of emergent leaders: An extension of the contingency model. *Journal of Economics and Business, 30*(1), 68–72.

Holmes, T. H., & Rahe, R. H. (1967). The social readjustment rating scale. *Journal of Psychosomatic Research, 11,* 213–218.

Horn, J. L. (1968). Organization of abilities and the development of intelligence. *Psychological Review, 75,* 242–259.

Horn, J. L. (1977). Personality and ability theory. In R. B. Cattell & R. M. Dreger (Eds.), *Handbook of modern personality theory.* Washington, DC: Hemisphere.

Horn, J. L. (1978). Human ability systems. In P. B. Baltes (Ed.), *Life-span development and behavior* (Vol. 1). New York: Academic.

Horn, J. L. (1979). The rise and fall of human abilities. *Journal of Research and Development in Education, 12*(2), 59–78.

House, R. J. (1971). A path goal theory of leader effectiveness. *Administrative Science Quarterly, 16,* 321–338.

House, R. J. (1972). Some new applications and tests of the path goal theory of leadership. *Proceedings of the National Behavioral Organizational Conference.*

House, R. J. (1977). A 1976 theory of charismatic leadership. In J. G. Hunt & L. L. Larsen (Eds.), *Leadership: The cutting edge.* Carbondale: Southern Illinois University Press.

House, R. J., & Mitchel, T. R. (1974). Path–goal theory of leadership. *Journal of Contemporary Behavior, 3,* 81–97.

House, R. J., & Rizzo, J. R. (1972). Toward the measurement of organizational practices: Scale development and validation. *Journal of Applied Psychology, 56,* 388–396.

Hovey, D. E. (1974). The low-powered leader confronts a messy problem: A test of Fiedler's theory. *Academy of Management Journal, 17,* 358–362.

Hunt, J. G. (1967). Fiedler's contingency model: An empirical test of three organizations. *Organizational Behavior and Human Performance, 2,* 290–308.

Hunter, J. E., Schmidt, F. L., & Jackson, G. B. (1982). *Meta-analysis formulating research findings across studies.* Beverly Hills, CA: Sage.

Janis, I., & Mann, L. (1959). *Decision making.* New York: Free Press.

Kabanoff, B. (1981). The potential influence index as a measure of situation favorability in the contingency model of leadership. *Australian Journal of Psychology, 33,* 47–59.

Kahn, R. L., Wolfe, D. M., Quinn, R. P., Snock, J. D., & Rosenthal, R. A. (1964). *Organizational stress: Studies in role conflict and ambiguity*. New York: Wiley.

Kahneman, D. (1973). *Attention and effort*. Englewood Cliffs, NJ: Prentice-Hall.

Kaplan, A. (1964). *The conduct of inquiry*. San Francisco: Chandler.

Kennedy, J. K. (1982). Middle LPC leaders and the contingency model of leadership effectiveness. *Organizational Behavior and Human Performance, 30*, 1–14.

Kerr, S. (1984). Leadership and participation. In A. Brief (Ed.), *Research on productivity*. New York: Praeger.

Kerr, S., & Jermier, J. M. (1978). Substitutes for leadership: Their meaning and measurement. *Organizational Behavior and Human Performance, 12*, 62–82.

Kipnis, D., Schmidt, S. M., Swaffin-Smith, C., & Wilkinson, I. (1984). Patterns of managerial influence: Shotgun managers, tacticians, and bystanders. *Organizational Dynamics, 12*, 58–67.

Knowlton, W. A., Jr. (1979). *The effects of causal attributions on a supervisor's evaluation of subordinate performance*. Unpublished master's thesis, University of Washington, Seattle.

Konar-Goldband, E., Rice, R. W., & Monkarsh, W. (1979). Time-phased interrelationships of group atmosphere, group performance, and leader style. *Journal of Applied Psychology, 64*, 401–409.

Korman, A. K. (1966). "Consideration," "initiating structure," and organizational criteria. *Personnel Psychology, 18*, 349–360.

Korman, A. K. (1968). The prediction of managerial performance: A review. *Personnel Psychology, 21*, 295–322.

Korten, D. C. (1968). Situational determinants of leadership structure. In D. Cartwright & A. Zander (Eds.), *Group dynamics: Research and theory*. New York: Harper & Row.

Lamke, T. A., Nelson, M. J., & French, J. L. (1973). *The Henman–Nelson tests of mental ability*. Boston: Houghton Mifflin.

Landman, J., & Manis, M. (1983). Social cognition: Some historical and theoretical perspectives. In L. Berkowitz (Ed.), *Advances in experimental social psychology* (Vol. 16). New York: Academic.

Landy, F. J., & Lamiell-Landy, A. (1978). Dimensions of teacher behavior. *Journal of Applied Psychology, 63*, 522–526.

Larson, L. L., & Rowland, K. M. (1973). Leadership style, stress, and behavior in task performance. *Organizational Behavior and Human Performance, 9*, 407–420.

Lawrence, L. C., & Smith, P. C. (1955). Group decision and employee participation. *Journal of Applied Psychology, 39*, 334–337.

Lawrence, P. R., & Lorsch, J. W. (1967). Differentiation and integration in complex organizations. *Administrative Science Quarterly, 12*, 1–47.

Lazarus, R. S. (1966). *Psychological stress and the coping process*. New York: McGraw-Hill.

Lewin, K., Lippitt, R., & White, R. K. (1939). Patterns of aggressive behavior in experimentally created social climates. *Journal of Social Psychology, 10*, 271–301.

Likert, R. (1961). An emerging theory of organizations, leadership, and management. In L. Petrullo & B. M. Bass (Eds.), *Leadership and interpersonal behavior*. New York: Holt.

Likert, R. (1967). *The human organization*. New York: McGraw-Hill.

Lord, R. G. Binning, J. F., Rush, M. C., & Thomas, J. C. (1978). The effect of performance cues and leader behavior in questionnaire ratings of leadership behavior. *Organizational Behavior and Human Performance, 21*, 27–39.

Lord, R. G., & Smith, J. E. (1983). Theoretical, information processing, and situational factors affecting attribution theory models of organizational behavior. *Academy of Management Review, 8*, 50–60.

Mai-Dalton, R. R. (1975). *The influence of training and changes in position power in leader behavior.* Unpublished master's thesis, University of Washington, Seattle.

Maier, N. R. F. (1970). *Problem solving and creativity in individuals and groups.* Belmont, CA: Brooks/Cole.

Maier, N. R. F., & Hoffman, L. R. (1961). Organization and creative problem solving. *Journal of Applied Psychology, 45,* 277–280.

Mann, R. D. (1959). A review of the relationships between personality and performance in small groups. *Psychological Bulletin, 56,* 241–270.

Maslow, A. H. (1954). *Motivation and personality.* New York: Harper.

Mayo, E. L. (1933). *The human problems of an industrial civilization.* New York: McMillan.

McClelland, D. C. (1961). *The achieving society.* Princeton, NJ: Van Nostrand.

McClelland, D. C. (1975). *Power: The inner experience.* New York: Irvington.

McClelland, D. C. (1985). *Human motivation.* Glenview, IL: Scott, Foresman.

McGrath, J. E. (Ed.). (1970). *Social and psychological factors in stress.* New York: Holt, Rinehart & Winston.

McGrath, J. E. (1976). Stress and behavior in organizations. In M. D. Dunnette (Ed.), *Handbook of industrial and organizational psychology.* Chicago: Rand McNally.

McGrath, J. E., & Altman, I. (1966). *Small group research: A synthesis and critique.* New York: Holt, Rinehart & Winston.

McGregor, D. (1944). Conditions of effective leadership in the industrial organization. *Journal of Consulting Psychology, 8,* 55–63.

McGregor, D. (1960). *The human side of enterprise.* New York: McGraw-Hill.

McMahon, J. T. (1972). The contingency theory: Logical method revisited. *Personnel Psychology, 25,* 697–710.

McNamara, V. D. (1968). *Leadership, staff, and school effectiveness.* Unpublished doctoral dissertation, University of Alberta, Alberta, Canada.

Mehrens, W. A., & Lehman, I. J. (1969). *Standardized tests in education.* New York: Holt.

Meuwese, W. (1964). *The effect of leader's ability and interpersonal attitudes on group creativity under varying conditions of stress.* Unpublished doctoral dissertation, Municipal University of Amsterdam.

Meuwese, W. A. T., & Fiedler, F. E. (1965). *Leadership and group creativity under varying conditions of stress* (Tech. Rep.). Urbana: University of Illinois, Group Effectiveness Research Laboratory.

Michaelson, L. K. (1973). Leader orientation, leader behavior, group effectiveness, and situational favorability: An empirical extension of the contingency model. *Organizational Behavior and Human Performance, 9,* 226–245.

Miller, W. S. (1926). *Miller analogies test.* New York: The Psychological Corporation.

Miner, J. B. (1978). 20 years of research on role-motivation theory of managerial effectiveness. *Personnel Psychology, 31,* 739–760.

Misumi, J. (1985). *The behavioral science of leadership: An interdisciplinary Japanese research program.* Ann Arbor: University of Michigan Press.

Mitchell, T. R. (1970a). The construct validity of three dimensions of leadership research. *Journal of Social Psychology, 80,* 89–94.

Mitchell, T. R. (1970b). Leader complexity and leadership style. *Journal of Personality and Social Psychology, 16,* 166–174.

Mitchell, T. R., Biglan, A., Oncken, G. R., & Fiedler, F. E. (1970). The contingency model: Criticism and suggestions. *Academy of Management Journal, 13,* 253–267.

Morse, N. C., & Reimer, E. (1956). The experimental change of a major organizational variable. *Journal of Abnormal Social Psychology, 52,* 120–129.

Murray, H. A. (1943). *Manual of thematic apperception test*. Cambridge, MA: Harvard.

Nealey, S. M., & Blood, M. R. (1968). Leadership performance of nursing supervisors at two organizational levels. *Journal of Applied Psychology, 52*, 414–422.

Nealey, S. M., & Owen, T. W. (1970). A multitrait–multilevel method analysis of the predictors and criteria of nursing performance. *Organizational Behavior and Human Performance, 5*, 348–365.

Nebeker, D. M. (1975). Situational favorability and environmental uncertainty: An integrative study. *Administrative Science Quarterly, 20*, 281–294.

Nebeker, D. M., & Hansson, R. O. (1972). *Confidence in human nature and leader style* (Tech. Rep. No. 72-37). Seattle: University of Washington, Organizational Research Group.

Nisbett, R., & Ross, L. (1980). *Human inference: Strategies and shortcomings of social judgement*. Englewood Cliffs, NJ: Prentice-Hall.

O'Brien, G. E., Fiedler, F. E., Hewett, T. T. (1967). The effects of programmed culture training upon the performance of volunteer medical teams in Central America. *Human Relations, 24*, 209–231.

O'Brien, G. E. (1969). Group structure and measurement of potential leader influence. *Australian Journal of Psychology, 21*, 277–289.

Peters, L. H., Hartke, D. D., & Pohlmann, J. T. (1985). Fiedler's contingency theory of leadership: An application of the meta-analysis procedure of Schmidt and Hunter. *Psychological Bulletin, 97*, 274–285.

Pepler, R. D. (1958). Warmth and performance: An investigation in the tropics. *Ergonomics, 2*, 63–88.

Phillips, J. S., & Lord, R. G. (1981). Causal attributions and perceptions of leadership. *Organizational Behavior and Human Performance, 28*, 143–163.

Podsakoff, P. M., Todor, W. D., Grover, R. A., & Huber, U. L. (1984). Situation modifiers of leader reward and punishment behaviors: Fact or fiction. *Organizational Behavior and Human Performance, 34*, 21–63.

Podsakoff, P. M., Todor, W. D., & Schuler, R. S. (1983). Leader expertise as a moderator of the effects of instrumental and supportive leader behaviors. *Journal of Management, 9*, 173–185.

Posthuma, A. B. (1970). *Normative data on the least preferred coworker scale (LPC) and the group atmosphere questionnaire (GA)* (Organizational Research, Tech. Rep. No. 70-8). Seattle: University of Washington.

Potter, E. H., & Fiedler, F. E. (1981). The utilization of staff member intelligence and experience under high and low stress. *Academy of Management Journal, 24*(2), 361–376.

Prothero, J., & Fiedler, F. E. (1974). *The effect of situational change on individual behavior and performance: An extension of the contingency model* (Tech. Rep. No. 74-59). Seattle: University of Washington, Organizational Research Group.

Pugh, D. S., Hickson, D. J., Hinnings, C. R., & Turner, C. (1968). Dimensions of organization structure. *Administrative Science Quarterly, 13*, 65–105.

Rice, R. W. (1978a). Psychometric properties of the esteem for least preferred coworker (LPC scale). *Academy of Management Review, 3*, 106–118.

Rice, R. W. (1978b). Construct validity of the least preferred coworker. *Psychological Bulletin, 85*, 1199–1237.

Rice, R. W., Bender, L. R., & Vitters, A. G. (1982). Testing the validity of the contingency model for female and male leaders. *Basic and Applied Social Psychology, 3*, 231–247.

Rice, R. W., & Chemers, M. M. (1973). Personality and situational determinants of leader's behavior. *Journal of Applied Psychology, 60*, 20–27.

Rice, R. W., & Kastenbaum, D. R. (1983). The contingency model of leadership: Some current issues. *Basic and Applied Social Psychology, 4*(4), 373–392.

Rice, R. W., & Seaman, F. J. (1981). Internal analyses of the least preferred coworker (LPC) scale. *Educational and Psychological Measurement, 41*(1), 109–120.

Roberts, H. M. (1979). *Robert's rules of order: Revised/III.* New York: Morrow Quill.

Robinson, J. P., & Shaver, P. R. (1973). *Measures of social psychological attitudes.* Ann Arbor, MI: Institute for Social Research.

Rosenthal, R. (1978). Combining results of independent studies. *Psychological Bulletin, 85*(1), 185–193.

Rosenthal, R. (1984). *Meta-analytic procedures for social research.* Beverly Hills, CA: Sage.

Sample, J. A., & Wilson, T. R. (1965). Leader behavior, group productivity, and ratings of least preferred co-worker. *Journal of Personality and Social Psychology, 1,* 266–270.

Sanders, G. S. (1981). Driven by distraction: An integrative review of social facilitation theory and research. *Journal of Experimental Social Psychology, 17,* 227–251.

Sarason, I. G. (1975). Anxiety and self-preoccupation. In I. G. Sarason & C. D. Spielberger (Eds.), *Stress and anxiety.* New York: Wiley.

Sarason, I. G. (Ed.). (1980). *Test anxiety: Theory, research, and applications.* Hillsdale, NJ: Erlbaum.

Sarason, I. G. (1984). Stress, anxiety, and cognitive interference: Reactions to tests. *Journal of Personality and Social Psychology, 46,* 929–938.

Sasfy, J., & Okun, M. (1974). Form of evaluation and audience expertness as joint determinants of audience effects. *Journal of Experimental Social Psychology, 10,* 461–467.

Sashkin, M. (1972). Leadership style and group decision effectiveness: Correlational and behavioral tests of Fiedler's Contingency Model. *Organizational Behavior and Human Performance, 8,* 347–362.

Sashkin, M., Taylor, F. C., & Tripathi, R. C. (1974). An analysis of situation moderating effects on the relationships between least preferred co-worker and other psychological measures. *Journal of Applied Psychology, 59,* 731–740.

Sax, G. (1974). *Principles of education measurement and evaluation.* Belmont, CA: Wadsworth.

Schacter, S. (1964). The interaction of cognitive and physiological determinants of emotional state. In L. Berkowitz (Ed.), *Advances in experimental social psychology* (pp. 49–80). New York: Academic.

Schacter, S., & Singer, J. (1962). Cognitive, social and physiological determinants of emotional state. *Psychological Review, 69,* 379–399.

Schmidt, R. L., & Hunter, J. E. (1977). Development of a general solution to the problem of validity generalization. *Journal of Applied Psychology, 62,* 529–540.

Schneider, W., & Shiffrin, R. M. (1977). Controlled and automatic human information processing: I. Detection, search and attention. *Psychological Review, 84,* 1–66.

Schneier, C. E. (1978). The contingency model of leadership: An extension of emergent leadership and leader's sex. *Organizational Behavior and Human Performance, 21,* 220–239.

Schriesheim, C. A., & Kerr, S. (1977a). Theories and measures of leadership: A critical appraisal of present and future directions. In J. G. Hunt & L. L. Larson (Eds.), *Leadership: The cutting edge.* Carbondale: Southern Illinois University Press.

Schriesheim, C. A., & Kerr, S. (1977b). R.I.P. LPC: A response to Fiedler. In J. G. Hunt & L. L. Larson (Eds.), *Leadership: the cutting edge.* Carbondale, IL: Southern Illinois University Press.

Schuler, R. S. (1980). Definition and conceptualization of stress in organizations. *Organizational Behavior and Human Performance, 25,* 184–215.

Selznick, P. (1957). *Leadership in administration: A sociological interpretation.* Evanston, IL: Row, Peterson.

Seyle, H. (1956). *The stress of life.* New York: McGraw-Hill.

Seyle, H. (1979). The stress concept and some of its implications. In V. Hamilton & D. M. Warburton (Eds.), *Human stress and cognition.* New York: Wiley.

Shartle, C. L. (1961). Leadership and organizational behavior. In L. Petrullo & B. M. Bass (Eds.), *Leadership and interpersonal behavior.* New York: Holt, Rinehart & Winston.

Shaw, M. E. (1963). *Scaling group tasks: A method for dimensional analysis* (Tech. Rep. No. 1). Gainesville: University of Florida.

Shaw, M. E. (1973). Scaling group tasks: A method for dimensional analysis. *JSAS Catalog of Selected Documents in Psychology, 3,* 8.

Shaw, M. E., & Blum, J. M. (1966). Effects of leadership style upon group performance as a function of task structure. *Journal of Personality and Social Psychology, 3,* 238–242.

Shiffrin, R. M., & Schneider, W. (1977). Controlled and automatic human information processing: II. Perceptual learning, automatic attending, and a general theory. *Psychological Review, 84,* 127–190.

Shiflett, S. C. (1973). The contingency model of leadership effectiveness: Some implications of its statistical and methodological properties. *Behavioral Science, 18,* 429–440.

Shiflett, S. C., & Nealey, S. M. (1972). The effects of changing leader power: A test of situational engineering. *Organizational Behavior and Human Performance, 7,* 371–382.

Shima, H. (1968). The relationship between the leader's model of interpersonal cognition and the performance of the group. *Japanese Psychological Research, 10,* 13–30.

Shirakashi, S. (1980). The interaction effects for behavior of least preferred coworker (LPC) score and group-task situations: a reanalysis. *The Commercial Review of Seinan Gakuin University, 27*(2).

Siegel, J. M., & Loftus, E. F. (1978). Impact of anxiety and life stress upon eyewitness testimony. *Bulletin of the Psychonomic Society, 12,* 439–480.

Simon, H. A. (1947). *Administrative behavior: A study of decision-making process in administrative organizations.* New York: Macmillan.

Simpson, R. H. (1938). *A study of those who influence and of those who are influenced in discussion.* New York: Teachers College Contributions to Education.

Smith, E. R., & Lerner, M. (1986). Development of automatism of social judgements. *Journal of Social and Personality Psychology, 50,* 246–259.

Smith, S., & Haythorn, W. W. (1972). Effects of compatibility, crowding, group size, and leadership seniority on stress, anxiety, hostility and annoyance in isolated groups. *Journal of Personality and Social Psychology, 22,* 67.

Smock, C. D. (1955). The influence of stress on the perception of incongruity. *Journal of Abnormal and Social Psychology, 50,* 354–356.

Spielberger, C. D., & Katzenmeyer, W. G. (1959). Manifest anxiety, intelligence, and college grades. *Journal of Consulting Psychology, 22,* 278.

Staw, B. M., Sandelan, L. E., & Dutton, J. E. (1981). Threat-rigidity effects in organizational behavior—A multilevel analysis. *Administrative Science Quarterly, 26*(4), 501–524.

Steiner, I. D. (1972). *Group process and productivity.* New York: Academic Press.

Stephenson, W. (1953). *The study of behavior: Q-technique and its methodology.* Chicago: University of Chicago Press.

Sternberg, R. J. (1977). *Intelligence, information processing, and analogical reasoning: The componential analysis of human abilities.* Hillsdale, NJ: Erlbaum.

Stinson, J. E., & Tracy, L. (1974). Some disturbing characteristics of the LPC scale. *Personnel Psychology, 24,* 477–485.

Stogdill, R. M. (1948). Personal factors associated with leadership: A survey of the literature. *Journal of Psychology, 25*, 35–71.

Stogdill, R. M. (1963). *Manual for the Leader Behavior Description Questionnaire—Form XII: An experimental revision.* Columbus: Ohio State University Press.

Stogdill, R. M. (1974). *Handbook of leadership: A survey of theory and research.* New York: Free Press.

Stogdill, R. M., & Coons, A. E. (1957). *Leader behavior: Its description and measurement.* Columbus: Ohio State University, Bureau of Business Research.

Stokols, D. (1976). The experience of crowding in primary and secondary environments. *Environment and Behavior, 8*, 49–86.

Stokols, D., & Schumaker, S. A. (1982). The psychological context of residential mobility and well-being. *Journal of Social Issues, 38*, 149–171.

Streufert, S., Streufert, S. C., & Castore, C. H. (1968). Leadership in negotiations and the complexity of conceptual structure. *Journal of Applied Psychology, 52*, 218–223.

Streufert, S., & Swezey, R. W. (1986). *Organizations and complexity.* New York: Academic.

Strube, M. J., & Garcia, J. E. (1981). A meta-analytical investigation of Fiedler's Contingency Model of leadership effectness. *Psychological Bulletin, 90*, 307–321.

Tannenbaum, R., & Schmidt, W. H. (1958). How to choose a leadership pattern. *Harvard Business Review, 36*, 95–101.

Teichner, W. H., & Kobrick, J. L. (1955). Effects of prolonged exposure to low temperature on visual-motor performance. *Journal of Experimental Psychology, 49*, 122–126.

Terman, L. M. (1904). A preliminary study of the psychology and pedagogy of leadership. *Pedagogical Seminary, 11*, 413–451.

Thurstone, L. L. (1938). *Primary mental abilities.* Chicago: University of Chicago Press.

Triandis, H. C. (1979). Values, attitudes, and interpersonal behavior. In H. E. Howe (Ed.), *Nebraska symposium on motivation 1979: Beliefs, attitudes and values. Vol. 27.* Lincoln: University of Nebraska Press.

Turner, J. (1972). *The contingency theory of leadership: A behavioral investigation.* Paper presented at the meeting of the Eastern Academy of Management, Boston.

Tyron, G. S. (1980). The measurement and treatment of test anxiety. *Review of Educational Research, 50*, 343–372.

Uhlaner, J. E. (1972). Human performance effectiveness and the systems measurement bed. *Journal of Applied Psychology, 56*(3), 202–210.

Vroom, V. H. (1959). Some personality determinants of the effects of participation. *Journal of Abnormal Social Psychology, 59*, 322–327.

Vroom, V. H. (1960). *Some personality determinants of the effects of participation.* Englewood Cliffs, NJ: Prentice-Hall.

Vroom, V. H., & Yetton, P. W. (1973). *Leadership and decision-making.* Pittsburgh, PA: University of Pittsburgh Press.

Weber, M. (1946). The sociology of the charismatic authority. In H. H. Mills & C. W. Mills (Eds. and Trans.), *From Max Weber: Essays in sociology.* New York: Oxford University Press.

Weber, M. (1947). *The theory of social and economic organization.* New York: Oxford University Press.

Wexley, K. N., & Latham, F. P. (1981). *Developing and training human resources in organizations.* Glenview, IL: Scott, Foresman.

Wonderlic, E. F. (1977). *Wonderlic personnel test.* Northfield, IL: Wonderlic.

Woodward, J. (1958). *Management and technology.* London: Her Majesty's Stationery Office.

Woodward, J. (1965) *Industrial organization: Theory and practice.* Oxford: Oxford University Press.

Yukl, G. A. (1981). *Leadership in organizations.* Englewood Cliffs, NJ: Prentice-Hall.

Zais, M. M. (1979). *The impact on intelligence and experience on the performance of army line and staff officers.* Unpublished master's thesis, University of Washington, Seattle.

Zajonc, R. B. (1965). Social facilitation. *Science, 149*(3681), 269–274.

Zeleny, L. D. (1939). Characteristics of group leaders. *Sociology and Social Research, 24,* 140–149.

Author Index

Subject Index